PERSONALITY
AND
FAMILY DEVELOPMENT

An Intergenerational
Longitudinal Comparison

PERSONALITY AND FAMILY DEVELOPMENT

An Intergenerational Longitudinal Comparison

KLAUS A. SCHNEEWIND
STEFAN RUPPERT
Ludwig Maximilians University, Munich

Translated by
Jonathan Harrow

Psychology Press
Taylor & Francis Group
NEW YORK AND HOVE

First published 1998 by Lawrence Erlbaum Associates, Inc., Publishers

This edition published 2013 by Psychology Press

Psychology Press
Taylor & Francis
711 Third Avenue
New York, NY 10017

Psychology Press
Taylor & Francis
27 Church Road
Hove
East Sussex BN3 2FA

First issued in paperback 2014

*Psychology Press is an imprint of the Taylor and Francis Group,
an informa business*

Library of Congress Cataloging-in-Publication Data

Schneewind, Klaus A., 1939–
    Personality and family development : an intergenerational
longitudinal comparison / Klaus A. Schneewind, Stefan Ruppert.
        p.   cm.
    Includes bibliographical references and index.
    ISBN 0-8058-2512-6 (alk. paper).
    1. Family—Germany (West)—Longitudinal studies. 2. Social
surveys—Germany (West)—Longitudinal studies. 3. Parent and adult
child—Germany (West)—Longitudinal studies. 4. Intergenerational
relations—Germany (West)—Longitudinal studies. 5. Personality.
I. Ruppert, Stefan. II. Title.
HQ626.S375 1997
306.85′0943—dc21
                                                          97-1096
                                                          CIP

ISBN 13: 978-1-138-88287-4 (pbk)
ISBN 13: 978-0-8058-2512-1 (hbk)

CONTENTS

FOREWORD

The early 1970s—a time marked by, among other things, student unrest in Germany—was also a period of crisis and criticism for the model of the "bourgeois family." It came to be viewed as a stronghold of repression and a contributory factor in the stabilization of undesirable societal attitudes. However, most such claims were based more on subjective beliefs than on the findings of solid empirical research. In this respect, Klaus Schneewind's project on "Parent–Child Relations" represented an important scientific contribution to the discussion, particularly through its focus on the role of societal conditions in family life and their impact on individual development. The GfK Nuremberg (Association for Consumer and Market Research) was able to help make this project possible.

In line with the commitment to basic research laid down in our constitution, in 1991 we asked Klaus Schneewind whether he would be prepared to follow up this study. This seemed to be a good idea because we still had addresses for the 570 West German families surveyed in 1976. To our great delight, Dr. Schneewind and his colleague Stefan Ruppert accepted. We supported the project with funding, personnel, and translation costs, and we are pleased to see it culminate in this book.

We hope that the results of this study, which is probably the only research project of its kind in the world, will be positively received, not just in the scientific forum, but also among the general public.

Robert Radler
GfK Nuremberg
Association for Consumer and Market Research

PREFACE

This book presents a report on development over a 16-year period, from 1976 to 1992, in two generations linked together by being members of the same families. The book focuses on the personality development of the individual members of the family, the development of their relations within the family context, and their perceptions of biographical events and societal framing conditions, in each case using comparisons across time and generations.

The starting point was the "Parent–Child Relations" Project (PCR Project) carried out in the 1970s. This was financed by the German Research Association (DFG), initially as part of the Special Research Unit on "Socialization and Communication Research" at the University of Erlangen–Nuremberg, and later as individual projects at the Universities of Trier and Munich. In contrast to classic research on childrearing styles, this project was expressly concerned with viewing childrearing and childhood socialization within the broader context of the family and society.

At the beginning of this project, the GfK Nuremberg (Association for Consumer and Market Research) and, in particular, its director, Robert Radler, provided us with major support by carrying out empirical tests on our new assessment instruments. When, in 1991, the GfK Nuremberg approached us and asked whether we were interested in following up the sample of 570 families with children who had been studied in such detail during the mid-1970s when they were between the ages of 9 and 14, we were given the unique opportunity to revive the old PCR Project. With the generous financial and personnel support of the GfK Nuremberg, this plan was implemented in 1992. We were able to renew contacts with approximately

200 of the original 570 families 16 years after the original survey, and we persuaded them to work with us once more. After 16 years, most of their children had grown into young adults, and many of the parents already found themselves in the so-called "empty nest" phase.

In some ways, this book deviates from the normal style used in the presentation of psychological literature. First, we have tried to burden the text with as few technical details as possible. Occasional methodological details are mostly banished to the "end notes," in which interested readers can find additional information. Second, the text abandons the usual procedure of giving references to relevant research literature. This information is also given in the end notes for each chapter. Although we cannot (and would not want to) deny that our theoretical and methodological orientation is toward the canons of modern empirical psychology, we nonetheless hope that these measures have made the book more readable. For the hasty reader, whom we wish to welcome in only exceptional circumstances, we have sketched the main findings of our study at the end of each chapter under the heading "A Brief Summary of the Most Important Points."

As mentioned before, this book would not have been possible without the generous support of the GfK Nuremberg, which, incidentally, was extended to the English translation of the German version of this book. Therefore, our thanks first go to the director of the GfK Nuremberg for his invaluable support. We also have not forgotten and continue to appreciate that the DFG first laid the basis for this longitudinal study through the original funding during the 1970s. In addition, by financing a 6-month sabbatical for the first author in the summer of 1993, the DFG made it possible to complete the work on this project. We sincerely thank the DFG for this support.

We also wish to thank Hilde Maier-Krisch and Dietlind Schnebel, who never lost their patience while retyping several versions of the German manuscript, as well as Birgit Pooth for successfully tackling some difficult problems with the graphics. We are especially indebted to Jonathan Harrow who, in our perspective, did an excellent job translating the German manuscript into English. Last, but not least, we thank the older and younger members of the families surveyed for allowing us insight into their personal and family lives, despite the increased severity of the laws governing the protection of personal data.

Klaus A. Schneewind
Stefan Ruppert

1

FAMILIES IN CONTEXT

How's your memory? Can you still remember what was happening in the world in 1976? Here are a few selected events.

In 1976, a civil war broke out in Angola and there was a military putsch in Argentina. In Cambodia, Pol Pot seized power, and the Khmer Rouge set up a regime of terror that led to the deaths of about one million people. The founder of the People's Republic of China, Mao Tse-tung, died at the age of 82, triggering a fierce tug of war regarding his successor. At the same time, an earthquake in the northern city of Tangshan led to the deaths of more than 650,000 people—the greatest number of earthquake victims ever recorded. An environmental catastrophe was caused by human hand in the Northern Italian city of Seveso, when an explosion in a chemical plant released highly poisonous dioxin into the atmosphere and contaminated the environment for miles around. In the United States, Jimmy Carter was elected as the 39th president. In the Federal Republic of Germany (FRG), in contrast, Helmut Schmidt was still Federal Chancellor, whereas, in the German Democratic Republic (GDR), Erich Honnecker took over the office of Head of the National Council.

What were the major events of 1992? Here are also some examples:

In 1992, the war in El Salvador came to an end and South Africa abolished apartheid. Czechoslovakia split into the Czech and Slovak Republics. The people of the United States elected Bill Clinton as their 42nd president. During the same year—starting in Los Angeles—racial unrest spread across several U.S. states. Unified Germany was also afflicted with unrest: Violence toward foreigners escalated; Rostock and Mölln became symbolic for more than 2,000 attacks on foreigners throughout the year. Nonetheless, this racial hatred did not go unopposed. In Munich, for example, more than 400,000 people formed a 45-kilometer-long human light chain to protest against radical right-wing violence. The political parties reached a compromise on the refugee issue with a controversial third-country ruling. Otherwise, attempts were made to process the problems of German unification: An act was passed providing free access to East German secret police files, Erich Honnecker was put on trial alongside five other leading communist politicians, and the first judgments were pronounced in trials on shooting incidents along the East–West German border.[1]

During this time, we were also busy. In 1976, a comprehensive survey of 570 families with children between the ages of 9 and 14 years was carried out in six of the federal states of the old FRG.[2] In 1992, it was possible to trace approximately 200 of these families whose children were now grown up and survey them for a second time. This provides the rare opportunity to describe personal and familial courses of development over 16 years. Each chapter takes a step-by-step approach to each topic. First, this chapter provides a short overview of the basic approach of the study, its theoretical and methodological basis, and the central research questions.

PERSONALITY AND FAMILY: APPROACHES TO A DIFFICULT TOPIC

First of all, let us go back to 1976. In the preceding year, the Second Family Report commissioned by the federal government was debated in the German parliament.[3] One of the concerns of this report had been to define general goals for personality development in a modern industrial state. At the top of the list were characteristics such as self-assurance, conscientiousness, intellectual abilities, and achievement motivation, as well as the ability to express empathy and solidarity, and to cope with problems constructively. The report was concerned with the personal preconditions for successfully shaping one's individual life, as well as with the role of such personality dispositions in a social, economic, and working culture that should be able to assert itself and develop within an international context.

One central, although not exclusive, role in the development of such individually and socially desirable personality characteristics is that of the family—or, to put it more precisely, the quality of childrearing and sociali-zation within the context of the family. The general hypothesis is that the form and direction of children's personality development depends on the degree of stimulation and the experiences of social learning that children gain through contact with their parents and other family members.

Despite the initial plausibility of this hypothesis, it is rather difficult to confirm it empirically in general terms. It is not by chance that ideas regard-ing the type, extent, and impact of parental childrearing and socialization efforts have become increasingly more complex within those disciplines that are concerned with issues addressing the impact of parents or families on child development (e.g., ethology, psychology, sociology, and education). Although this is not the place for a detailed description and historical appraisal of these different theoretical approaches, a short sketch is presented of how work on this topic has grown into an increasingly more complex affair over the last 50 years. In simplified terms, one can differentiate among the following five phases.

1. Maternal Childrearing Behavior as a "One-Way Street." Roughly speaking, this early phase in the investigation of the impact of parental childrearing on childhood personality development can be traced back to two central assumptions. The first is an exclusive emphasis on the mother as the main source of influence on the process of childhood personality formation. This is reflected particularly in the basic principles of ethology and psychoanalysis. The second is a perspective that views children—nonetheless on the basis of their biophysical structure—as more or less passive receivers of maternal childrearing and socialization influences.[4] According to this perspective, infant personality develops above all during "sensitive phases," in which a behavioral imprinting occurs, or that the child goes through a sequence of "psychosexual stages," in which the type of parental behavior determines whether personality development will be healthy.

2. The Contribution of the Child. The next important step was a radical revision of ideas on the role of the child in his or her contacts with primary reference persons. Using precise observations and creative experiments, research in developmental psychology was able to confirm that children are already actively learning, social, and unique human beings from birth onward.[5] For example, in light of their thousands and thousands of contacts with their parents, children with a "difficult" temperament bring completely different preconditions into their relationships, compared with those who are described somewhat loosely as "easy to care for." Depending on how easy or difficult they make it for parents to carry out their everyday care and childrearing tasks, the more or less confident and patient the parents will also be in their dealings with their children, and this, in turn, has repercussions on the children's development. In a certain sense, this not only turns children into "producers of their development,"[6] but also means that, from birth onward, they play a decisive role in shaping the quality of the relationship that develops between themselves and their parents. This turning away from the "one-way street" model of development and childrearing was a decisive step toward viewing personality development—even in early infancy—as a process that is shaped by reciprocal influences in which the child plays a decisively active role.

3. Fathers, the Neglected Third Members of the Group. Despite the introduction of the child as an active shaper of his or her social relationships, the majority of relevant research in developmental and family psychology in the subsequent years continued to focus on the detailed study of mother–child relations. It was only in the 1970s that attention also slowly began to focus on the role of the father.[7] Parallel to the study of mother–child relations, a research tradition gradually became established that examined whether fathers could be just as good "mothers" as their wives, and whether fathers introduce another quality of relationships through their contacts with their children. However, it is important to recognize that—analogue to the study of mother–child relations—this research on fathers focused almost exclusively on the dyadic relationship between father and child.

4. The Family as System. The next decisive step was to view the family as a whole (i.e., as a unit of three or more interaction partners). One important finding that gave rise to this new perspective was the observation that fathers, but also mothers, behave differently toward their children when the other partner is present compared with when they are alone with their children.[8] Such observations made it necessary to review statements on childrearing effects whose validity had been based on viewing parent–child relations in dyadic terms. The conception of the family as a system of persons who reciprocally influence each other was also stimulated by, among others, the general considerations within systems theory that were increasingly shaping theoretical work in the field of technology or biology, but also in the human and behavioral sciences.

Although such a perspective brought research closer to the real phenomena of family life, it also led to an exponential increase in the complexity of the object of research. Depending on the size of the nuclear family, there were no longer just a few, but now a whole series of dyadic, triadic, and larger constellations of relationships within a single family. This led to a breaking down of the family system into a number of subsystems (e.g., the marriage subsystem, the children or sibling subsystem, the parent–child subsystem, or the gender subsystem), and a closer study of the relations within and among these subsystems.[9]

5. The Family Within Historical and Sociocultural Contexts. However, this systemic extension of the perspective on the family as a context of social relations for individual development still did not represent the highest stage of complexity. Families do not exist in a vacuum; they are themselves embedded in turn, not only within a historical framework, but also, and above all, within their direct social, economic, and ecological life space. These concrete life conditions—which include not only financial resources, housing, and work; the social network of friends, acquaintances, and members of the extended family; and the more or less restricted availability of experiences in the proximal environment—represent important framing conditions for the shaping of relationships within the family.[10]

Hence, the development of families and their members is not just linked to the context of the relations experienced within family, but is also code-termined by the ecological surroundings in which the family more or less self-constructively shapes its process of development as "a unit of interacting personalities."[11] Here as well, it is important to bear in mind that the family does not function as a passive receiver of influences from its ecological surroundings, but influences its environment through active selection and behavior. The way in which a family exploits the degree of stimulation in its life space—what sociologists would call "developmental opportunities"—depends on the more or less overt rules that determine its internal relations. The structure of these rules and interaction habits describes the family "style" or "climate."[12] The family's characteristic climate thus functions as an important mediator between the developmental needs of the individual family members and the exploitation of the experiences available in the family's ecological surroundings. For example, a family that cultivates social, cultural, and leisure-time contacts with the "outside world," in the sense of an "open system," taps its ecological surroundings in a completely different way than a largely "closed family system" that concentrates strongly on how relationships develop within the family.

This last theoretical step—the embeddedness of the family system within its ecological surroundings—attains a stage of complexity that goes far beyond that which, for example, psychology has traditionally defined as the perspective on parent–child relations (viz., the impact of parental childrearing styles on childhood personality development). What is more, this expanded perspective also places greater demands on the theoretical design of any research project wanting to implement such a "family-in-context" approach.

In 1976, we took on the challenges of such an integrative perspective in our conception of a comprehensive empirical field study. The following presents a brief design sketch of the field study carried out in 1976, and then explains the conception of the follow-up study carried out in 1992, 16 years later.

THE PARENT–CHILD RELATIONS PROJECT—1976

In 1976, funded by the German Research Association (*Deutsche Forschungsgemeinschaft*, DFG), we carried out a detailed survey of 570 family units consisting of father, mother, and one child under the heading "Parent–Child Relations" (PCR Project). The families came from six of the old Federal German states (Baden-Wuerttemberg, Bavaria, Hesse, North Rhine-Westphalia, Rhineland Palatinate, and Saarland). They were recruited on the basis of a fixed research design. From the outset, we decided to include the mother, father, and one child from intact families in the survey. We also considered the following aspects when compiling the sample. First, we wanted an equal number of boys and girls in the sample of children. Second, the children's ages should vary in three stages between 9–14 years. Third, socioeconomic status should be controlled by recruiting an equal number of families from the lower, middle, and upper classes. A fourth factor, which was not varied systematically in the design, ensured that the families were also divided roughly equally between urban and rural areas. In all, the plan was to recruit at least 30 families to fill each cell of the research design created through a combination of the three former sample criteria. Table 1.1 presents an overview of this design.

Because of these criteria, the sample was not representative, as shown by the almost equal distribution across social class. However, this field study was not designed to make representative statements about the situation of families with children ages 9–14 years. Instead, in line with the study's ecopsychological approach, we wanted to represent the widest possible range of family life conditions within one sufficiently large sample.

In line with the extended perspective of "families in context," the empirical assessments were designed to take account of the individual personality characteristics of the single family members and their relations to each other, as well as the ecological surroundings of these families. Family climate was included as an intervening variable between the structure of family relations and the family's external surroundings. This led to the research model that is presented in a simplified form in Fig. 1.1. To apply this research model empirically, it was necessary to collect data on the following different levels.

1. Individual Level. The concern here was to obtain the most differentiated statements possible on the personalities of the parents and children.

TABLE 1.1
Research Plan for the 1976 PCR Project

Socioeconomic status of the family	Child's age						Total
	9-10 years		11-12 years		13-14 years		
	Gender		Gender		Gender		
	Boys	Girls	Boys	Girls	Boys	Girls	
Lower class	30	30	30	30	30	30	180
Middle class	33	32	32	34	34	33	198
Upper class	34	31	32	32	30	33	192
Total	97	93	94	96	94	95	570

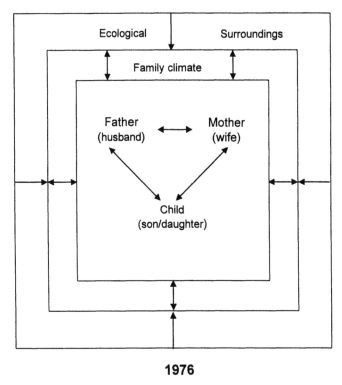

1976

FIG. 1.1.   Research model for the 1976 PCR Project.

On the one hand, we used standard instruments of multidimensional personality diagnosis. On the other hand, we used a system of personality rating scales to assess diverse aspects of self- and peer judgments in all the members of the families involved. For example, parents did not just have to give real and ideal ratings on themselves, but also corresponding ratings on their partners as well as the child involved in the study. In the children, personality data were supplemented with objective measures of intelligence, creativity, and achievement motivation.

2. *Relations Level.* This data set focused on information about behavior in relationships, as well as perceptions of relationships collected from two members of each family system. Because we were particularly interested in performing a differentiated assessment of parental childrearing style, we constructed a special set of instruments for the project. The concept of childrearing style was first broken down into three components—namely, childrearing goals (i.e., the parents' ideal demands on their children), childrearing attitudes (i.e., basic dispositions that parents perceive in their contacts with their children), and childrearing practices (i.e., concrete behaviors that the parents use to reward or punish their children). A series

of internal aspects were assessed within each of these components of parental childrearing style. Because we were particularly concerned with subjective perspectives, both parents and children were asked about diverse aspects of parental childrearing style.

A further important aspect of perceived relationships and relationship behavior in dyads refers to the quality of the partnership between the two parents. Here as well, we applied a specially constructed survey instrument that assessed several different aspects of the marriage relationship. As in the assessment of parental childrearing style, this included the perspectives of both persons involved (i.e., the wife and the husband).

3. Family Level. In contrast to the instruments designed to assess dyads on the relations level, this aspect of the survey focused on the family as a whole. Alongside the usual features of family structure (e.g., intactness and the persons making up the family), we were particularly interested in assessing the quality of the emotional climate, the family rules and interaction habits, as well as the family activities directed toward internal and external relationships. Here as well, the subjective perspectives of all members of the family taking part in the study were taken into account.

4. Ecological Level. This part of the assessment collected detailed information on the materials and social situations of sample families. In addition to sociodemographic data on their economic situation, educational background, and occupational status, we were particularly interested in information on the embeddedness of the family within its social network (i.e., the relations to the family of origin, as well as contacts with friends and acquaintances), on the concrete work situation (e.g., job quality and job demands), on the housing situation, and on the potential stimulation available in the proximal or distal residential environment.

All these different approaches to data collection should be viewed as operationalizations of the general research model presented earlier, in which individual family members and their relationships to each other are placed within the context of the entire family system and its socioecological life space. Because the most important findings of this study have been published elsewhere, they will not be repeated here.[13] Therefore, we turn to the families who were followed up in 1992. Some comments on the "reactivation" of the sample are presented first.

THE PROJECT "PARENT–CHILD RELATIONS/FOLLOW-UP" (PCR/FU)—1992

In 1991, we submitted a proposal to follow up the sample of 570 families investigated in 1976. With the financial support of the *Gesellschaft für Konsumforschung* (GFK, Consumer Research Association) at Nuremberg, it was possible to put this plan into operation in 1992, although not for all 570 families.

This broadens the theoretical perspective of the PCR Project of 1976, emphasizing the relation of the individual to his or her family context and conceiving of the family, in turn, as embedded within a larger ecological environment by adding a further dimension that is important for our understanding of family relations: the time dimension. The interval of 16 years covered by these two waves of measurement is a phase in which numerous events influencing development could occur for both the individual and the family as a whole.

In the 16 years between the two waves, the child generation has passed from late childhood through adolescence up to young adulthood, and some of them have even started their own families. If we look at this interval from the perspective of the concept of individual developmental tasks, some of the tasks confronted by the children are: separation from the parental home, establishing a working career, entering a partnership or marriage, and birth of their own children.[14]

In 1992, the members of the parent generation found themselves either in the phase of separation from their children or already in the phase of "postparental partnership," also known as the "empty-nest phase." Thus, they are also having to deal with phase-specific developmental tasks. These include separation of the children from the parental home, redefinition of the marriage relationship, or retirement from working life. Although these individual developmental tasks are reported separately for each generation, they are closely related to the family. Therefore, a more suitable concept for this approach is that of the familial developmental task, which focuses on the intergenerational relationships in the solution of these tasks.[15]

This study now makes it possible to describe at least some of these changes and developments by comparing the data from Wave 1 in 1976 with those of Wave 2 in 1992. However, we must not forget that we are not just interested in the observation of changes. It is just as intriguing to detect and describe what has remained stable in families and individuals. Thus, one of the main goals of this book is to describe the interplay and interweaving of change and stability in the development of family relations.

Recruitment of the Sample for the Follow-Up in 1992

The first step in the PCR/FU Project was to obtain the cooperation of the largest possible number of the families who participated in 1976. The conception of the study made it particularly interesting to follow up as many complete family units as possible (i.e., to obtain data from the father, mother, and child in each family). Several steps were involved in the recruitment of the sample for the Wave 2.

1. We started with the addresses of the 570 families recorded for the first wave. We ascertained which of these addresses were still correct and which

had changed. These efforts resulted in 400 current addresses; 170 of the families that participated in the 1976 study could no longer be traced.

2. We wrote to the 400 confirmed addresses asking the families to participate in the new survey. These letters also asked parents for the addresses of their children who participated in 1976. Because these children were ages 25–30 years in 1992, we had to assume that most of them would no longer be living with their parents. The only way to obtain these addresses was through their parents.

3. The next step was to write to the children whose addresses we had obtained from their parents and ask them to participate in the follow-up.

4. At the end of our efforts to recruit the sample, 214 fathers and 215 mothers agreed to participate. It is important to point out here that these were not always married partners. Sometimes either only the father or only the mother were willing to participate in the follow-up. However, even parents who were unwilling to participate themselves gave us the addresses of their children. As a result, we were finally able to survey 98 sons and 100 daughters.

This selection of subjects hardly ever agrees with the sample sizes referred to in the findings reported in the following chapters, for the following reasons. First, each person surveyed did not always complete all the questionnaires, although we always checked whether data were complete and returned questionnaires when necessary. Second, we also had incomplete family units that delivered data from two, rather than three, family members. Of course, we wanted to survey as many complete family units as possible. However, depending on the research question and the missing data from certain family members in the corresponding assessment instrument, the sample sizes for complete family units oscillate between 160 and 170. Nonetheless, several of the research questions in which we were interested could be examined through a separate analysis of data from fathers, mothers, or children. If we had limited ourselves only to persons from complete families when analyzing these issues, sample sizes would sometimes have been reduced by as many as 40 subjects for no compelling reason. This explains the different reports on sample sizes that appear in later chapters of this book.[16]

Data Collection

In 1976, the survey was carried out through direct contact with the family. Specially trained interviewers (mostly graduate psychology students) each spent 2–3 days carrying out the surveys with each family. Because interviewers were used, it was also possible to use measurement instruments that would have been hard or even completely impossible for subjects to work on by themselves (e.g., the intelligence, creativity, and achievement motivation tests on children). In the 1992 data collection, we also retained limited access to interviewers.[17] This made it possible to ensure that the more difficult questions were worked on under the correct instructions.

Data Collected in the PCR/FU Project

To save time and money, we had to make major cuts in the breadth of the survey compared with the first wave in 1976. This was mostly done in two ways: First, by applying methodological controls to the 1976 data, we were able to shorten a great number of the questionnaires.[18] Second, because some topics had to be included in any case for theoretical reasons, we had to discard some areas of questioning that had taken up a broad area in the 1976 wave. Areas that were studied less intensively in 1992 included the large set covering the socioecological surroundings of the family.

Apart from these cuts, the fact that we were dealing with a 16-year follow-up meant that some new aspects also had to be taken into account. The most important innovation was the assessment of critical life events in the interval between the two waves. This is reported in more detail later. Nonetheless, the structure was still given by the four levels of data collection used during the first wave.

1. Individual Level. This used the same instruments as those reported in the previous section for the first wave. In addition, questions were posed on physical health, as well as scales on "self-efficacy" and "social desirability." A reassessment of "intelligence," "creativity," and "achievement motivation" in the child generation was dropped.

2. Relations Level. There were several changes in the assessment of internal family relations in 1992. In 1976, the relations between parents and children could be described adequately through the reports on childrearing behavior. It was no longer possible to use this path in 1992. The relation between adult children and their parents and vice versa can hardly be assessed through the concept of childrearing alone. Because data collection also had to reflect that these relationships now function on an adult level, we constructed a new instrument in which parents and children judged their relationships to each other on the dimensions of "closeness–distance," "control–autonomy," "conflict," and "communication." This is reported in detail in chapter 5.

However, these data are no replacement for the important content area of childrearing style that continues to play a central role at the second wave. However, the type of questions had changed, and the age structure of our sample in 1992 suggested certain questions on the area of childrearing style. Because the children from 1976 were now young adults and some of them had their own children, it seemed a good idea to ask these young adults how they would or would not raise their own children. An additional question was how the parent generation would raise their child today, or how the parent generation rate the childrearing behavior of their own adult children. These and similar questions were presented to our sample in the second wave. The tripartite separation of the childrearing style concept into goals, attitudes, and practices was nonetheless retained.

Data on relations also included descriptions of their own partnerships by the older and younger generations collected with survey instruments already applied in 1976. In addition, a new, specially developed instrument was used, in which the children judged the relationship between their parents, and the parents also judged their children's relationships with partners.

3. Family Level. Information on the family as a whole was obtained with the family climate scales already used in 1976. Here as well, the instructions were modified: Both parents and children were asked to give retrospective ratings on the family climate in 1976. Parents were additionally asked to describe the current family climate in 1992. However, this task was dropped for the child generation because many of the now adult children no longer lived in their family of origin.

4. Ecological Level. This set of questions, which took up a large amount of space as a main focus of the study in 1976, was cut back to a great extent in the second wave to make room for the more elaborate assessment of relationships and the questions on the interval between the two waves. Essentially, data collection was restricted to the most important sociodemographic details on the participants in the survey.

A comparison of data from two waves separated by 16 years raises this question: What has happened to the participants in the intervening time? Which decisive experiences have they made during this interval? How do they perceive the general changes in the society in which they live? Sixteen years is a long time, not only for the individual persons with all the crises and challenges of their personal biographies, but also for the societal system in which the individual is embedded and that represents the individual's life context.

In the introduction to this chapter, a few selected political and social events were used to describe the years 1976 and 1992. The concern was to provide a few reference points for the historical framework of these two . waves. Examples were used to show how much has changed during this relatively long period—changes that have accompanied the lives of the families we have studied and had or continue to have a more or less strong impact on the shaping of each individual's life.

The information collected from our family members over this 16-year period is distributed correspondingly across these two classes of events.

On the one hand, there are events that affect persons directly on the individual level. In these terms, the previous 16 years can be described by the "critical life events" that each person has experienced. These include negative events, such as death or illness, as well as positive events, such as the birth of children and grandchildren or marriage. Our questions referred to whether a person has actually experienced these events, as well as how far they perceive them to be an enrichment or a strain, and how long they had to deal with such events or their consequences—in brief, questions on coping with these events.

A second class of events that is important for the 16-year period refers to the societal level. This concerns matters that, in principle, can be viewed objectively, but may, nonetheless, differ in the ways in which individuals evaluate them subjectively. Separated into sections on "general life conditions" (e.g., extent of egotism in society, work ethos, loneliness of individuals), "important areas of life" (e.g., family life, living with children, work, and career), "social institutions" (e.g., politics, economy, advertising), and "threats" (e.g., environmental disasters, poverty, incurable diseases), we asked whether the individual aspects of societal life had changed over the past 16 years, or whether they had remained the same.

Against this background, we can now extend the model used for the first wave in 1976 (Fig. 1.1). On the one hand, the extension consists of linking together the data assessed at both waves on the four content levels—the individual, relations, family, and ecological levels—and, on the other hand, of taking into account the changes over the last 16 years in individually and socially important events insofar as they are reflected in the experience of the individual. Figure 1.2 presents an impression of the extended research model that forms the conceptual basis for the 1992 study.

The research model presented in Fig. 1.2 is simultaneously an orientation guideline for the individual issues addressed in this book. Before giving a brief overview of these questions, some information on the characteristics of the families and their members who participated in the follow-up study in 1992 is presented.

THE SAMPLE OF PARENTS AND CHILDREN IN 1992

What sort of people agreed to take part in the follow-up study? How old are they? What is their socioeconomic class? Information on such sociodemographic features of a sample generally is reported at the beginning of any analysis of research in the social and behavioral sciences. It forms the essential background for interpreting the later findings on, for example, personality development or family relations. An overview of the sociodemographic features of the parent sample is presented first.

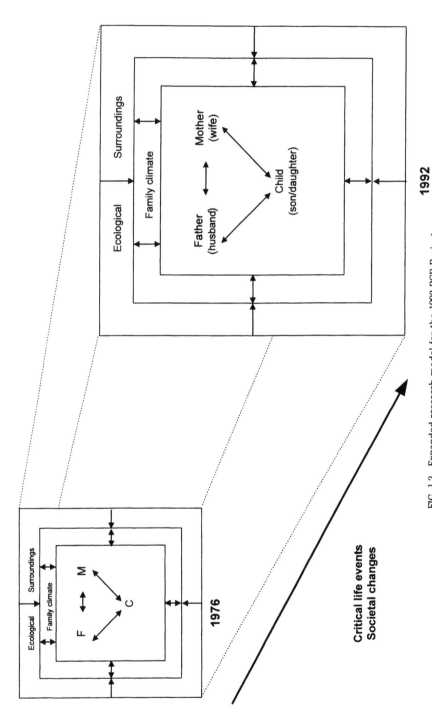

FIG. 1.2. Expanded research model for the 1992 PCR Project.

The Parent Sample

First, it is interesting to learn how many complete family units participated. In all, data were obtained from 225 families. In 172 cases, all family members participated. In 32 cases, data were obtained only from fathers and mothers; in 11 cases, only from mothers; and in a further 10 cases, only fathers. Some of the reasons that only one parent took part in the study can be seen in Table 1.2, which reports the family status of the fathers and mothers. As can be seen, some parents are already widows or widowers. The proportion of divorced parents is relatively low. This may also be an effect of sample recruitment. It is conceivable that we were unable to contact 170 families for our follow-up because their addresses may have changed because of divorce. The low number of divorced persons in our sample makes it impossible to take a separate look at families of divorce, however interesting this might be.[19]

The next feature is the age distribution of mothers and fathers. This is presented in Table 1.3. The mothers had a mean age of 50 years, with a range of 45–71 years. The fathers had a mean age of 58; the youngest father was 43 and the oldest was 76. Information on the mothers' and fathers' religion is reported in Table 1.4. The distribution is similar to that found in the general population. A further area that provides important information about the sample is the educational background and occupational status of the parent generation. Here as well, mothers and fathers both answered the same questions. Table 1.5 presents an overview of the parents' educational background.

Two facts are immediately apparent. First, the fathers' educational background is, on average, higher than that of the mothers. For example, there are far more men with college degrees than women. However, the general

TABLE 1.2
Family Status of Parents

Family status	Mothers	Fathers
Married	203	200
Remarried	1	1
Separated	1	2
Divorced	6	5
Widowed	4	6
Total	215	214

TABLE 1.3
Age Distribution of Parents

Age in	Mothers		Fathers	
years	n	%	n	%
Up to 50	36	16.7	14	6.5
51-55	96	44.7	57	26.6
56-60	47	21.9	73	34.1
61-65	30	14.0	53	24.8
66-70	5	2.3	12	5.6
Over 70	1	0.5	5	2.3
Total	215	100	214	100

level of education seems to be very high. Low-qualification school-leaving certificates and vocational trainings are reported comparatively rarely. This is a first indication that our sample has experienced a bias since the first wave. It is particularly the lower class families from the original sample who are no longer represented to the same degree as the middle- and upper class families.

TABLE 1.4
Parents' Confession

Confession	Mothers (%)	Fathers (%)
Catholic	44.7	39.6
Evangelical	40.4	40.4
Other	1.3	2.6
No religion	1.3	1.7
No information given	12.3	16.7
Total	100	100

TABLE 1.5
Parents' Educational Background

	Fathers		Mothers	
Qualifications	*n*	%	*n*	%
Basic secondary school with no school-leaving certificate	1	0.5	2	0.9
Basic secondary school with school-leaving certificate	37	17.2	7	3.3
Basic secondary school plus vocational training	52	24.2	59	27.6
Technical secondary school with no school-leaving certificate	14	6.5	6	2.8
Intermediate school-leaving certificate but no vocational training	25	11.6	3	1.4
Intermediate school-leaving certificate plus vocational training	23	10.7	22	10.3
Higher secondary school with school-leaving certificate	21	9.8	20	9.3
College entrance qualification	18	8.4	12	5.6
College but no degree	10	4.7	3	1.4
College with degree	14	6.5	80	37.4
Total	215	100	214	100

Similar conclusions are also suggested by the data on occupational groups and net income summarized in Tables 1.6 and 1.7. Again, the higher rated occupational groups and the higher income groups are represented much more strongly. The income table (Table 1.7) requires some explanation. The 199 mothers who reported that they had no personal income were housewives. The high number of mothers with incomes below 1,000 DM (about $600) per month is because 34% of the mothers worked only half days or part time. Only 11% of the mothers pursued full-time employment. In addition, the income levels reported here do not discriminate between working and retired

TABLE 1.6
Parents' Occupational Groups

Occupational status	Fathers		Mothers	
	n	%	*n*	%
Unskilled blue-collar worker	2	0.9	19	8.8
Semiskilled blue-collar worker	2	0.9	12	5.6
Skilled blue-collar worker	15	7.0	10	4.7
Foreman	5	2.3	0	0
Skilled industrial worker	2	0.9	0	0
Craftsman	5	2.3	5	2.3
Master craftsman	2	0.9	1	0.5
Farmer	5	2.3	7	3.3
Low-level white-collar worker	0	0	30	14.0
Intermediate-level white-collar worker	26	12.1	50	23.3
High-level white-collar worker	53	24.8	16	7.4
Low-ranking civil servant	2	0.9	1	0.5
Intermediate-ranking civil servant	23	10.7	8	3.7
High-ranking civil servant	46	21.5	2	0.9
Self-employed	13	6.1	8	3.7
Self-employed manager	13	6.1	10	4.7
Total	214	100	179	100

18

TABLE 1.7
Parents' Net Income

Monthly income in German Marks	Fathers	Mothers
Under 1000	1	40
1001-1500	0	17
1501-2000	12	15
2001-2500	14	9
2501-3000	12	2
3001-3500	18	4
3501-4000	16	1
4001-6000	73	7
Over 6000	63	1
No income	0	119
Total	209	215

parents. Among the fathers, 68% were still working, whereas 30% had already retired. Only four respondents were unemployed.

Housing conditions revealed an almost equal distribution of families across rural and urban areas (from village to large city with more than 500,000 residents). Eighty percent of the parents lived in their own houses, 3% lived in their own apartments, and only 17% lived in rented accommodations. On average, the family homes contained four to eight rooms and 100–150 square meters of accommodation. As could be expected, approximately 90% of the parents also reported that they were satisfied or even very satisfied with their housing, whereas only 5% expressed dissatisfaction. However, who generally lives in such comfortable housing conditions? Half of the parents lived alone. Thirty-nine percent reported that up to seven persons lived with them. Approximately 34% of parents reported that they still lived together with one or more of their children. Only nine families reported that the parents of the parents were still living with them.

Finally, a few comments on the composition of the families. First, Table 1.8 presents an overview of the number of children. Turning to the previous

TABLE 1.8
Distribution of Number of Children
in Parent Sample

Number of children	n	%
1	18	8.1
2	77	34.5
3	77	34.5
4	29	13.0
5	15	6.7
6	6	2.7
7	1	0.4
Total	223	100

generation (i.e., the parents of the parents), we wanted to know how many of these persons were still alive. For later research questions, this is particularly important when making observations across three generations. Table 1.9 provides an overview of the corresponding figures. The majority of the parent generation has already lost their parents. Only 7% of mothers and fathers still have both parents. In view of the high life expectancy for

TABLE 1.9
Surviving Members of Grandparent Generation

Grandparent generation	Fathers		Mothers	
	n	%	n	%
Both dead	135	63.7	113	54.3
Both alive	13	6.1	17	8.2
Father still alive	9	4.2	12	5.8
Mother still alive	55	25.9	66	31.7
Total	212	100	208	100

women in our society, it is not surprising that a much higher percentage of mothers of the parent generation are still alive, compared with fathers.

The Child Sample

This section presents the sample of children in the same way as the parent sample. However, sons and daughters are also treated separately on features that seem to warrant a gender comparison. The sample of the children's generation contained 198 persons made up of 98 sons and 100 daughters. These also included a few children who were the only persons representing their families in the follow-up.

First, the age variable is highlighted. Both sons and daughters had a mean age of 28 years, with a range of 25–30. Because the 1976 sample was graded systematically according to the children's age, the question is whether this pattern can still be found in 1992. Therefore, the members of the second wave were separated according to the same three relative age groups as in 1976. Table 1.10 presents the distribution for the entire sample and split according to sons and daughters. It is clear that there is a successive increase in the representation of the higher age groups. This increasing willingness to participate as a function of higher age probably relates to the fact that the older children—as the data show—were more often parents, and therefore more interested in a study of parent–child relations.

Information on the current partnership situation is presented in Table 1.11. Two aspects are particularly conspicuous. First, almost twice as many sons compared with daughters are living without a permanent partner. Second, daughters seem to be more willing to seal a relationship through marriage.

Turning to religious confession, children report no religion more frequently than their parents do, or they provide no answer to this question, which may possibly be interpreted as an indication of no religion. When looking at the age distribution, it was already mentioned that some of the

TABLE 1.10
Age Distribution in Children's Sample

Age group	Sons	Daughters	Total
Up to 26 years	27	22	49
27-28 years	30	37	67
29 years and older	41	41	82
Total	98	100	198

TABLE 1.11
Children's Partnerships

Partnership situation	Sons (%)	Daughters (%)	Total (%)
Married	34.7	50.0	42.4
Steady partnership	35.7	36.0	35.9
Single	29.6	14.0	21.7
Total	100	100	100

children are already parents themselves. Table 1.12 shows how many have their own children, first, in the entire sample and then split according to age group. The upper number in each cell reports the absolute frequency—the lower number, the column percentage. One quarter of the participants in the child generation are already parents. The concentration of children among the older respondents mentioned earlier is well illustrated in Table 1.12.

TABLE 1.12
Number of Own Children in Children's Sample as a Function of Age Group

Number of children	Up to 26 years	27-28 years	29 years and older	Total
0	45[1] 91.8 %[2]	52 77.6 %	50 61.0 %	147 74.2 %
1	4 8.2 %	9 13.4 %	19 23.2 %	32 16.2 %
2	/	5 7.5 %	9 11.0 %	14 7.1 %
3	/	1 1.5 %	3 3.7 %	4 2.0 %
4	/	/	1 1.2 %	1 0.5 %
All	49 100 %	67 100 %	82 100 %	198 100 %

Note. 1: Absolute numbers. 2: Percentage by column.

We now turn from the next generation after our children's sample to the previous generations (i.e., their parents and grandparents). We limit ourselves to reporting current numbers. First, regarding the grandparent generation, 40% of the children's generation already lost all four grandparents. Thirty-six percent still have one grandmother or grandfather; 18% still have two; 5% three; and 1% (i.e., two cases) still have all four grandparents alive. Thus, 60% of the child sample still has at least one grandparent. Turning to parents, the majority of the children's sample (188) still has both parents; seven have lost their mother, and three have lost their father. None of the sample has lost both parents, which is a logical consequence of the way in which the sample was recruited. It would have been hard to obtain children's addresses from parents who were already dead.

The next area of interest in this overview of the children's generation is their qualifications and jobs. Table 1.13 presents an overview of the highest level of qualification attained. Data are reported in percentages because with sample sizes of approximately 100—percentages of sons and daughters—are almost identical with absolute values. As the table shows, most of the sample have higher qualifications. Only 4% of respondents report that their highest qualification is a basic secondary school-leaving certificate (*Volksschulabschluß*) alone or in combination with subsequent vocational training. Sixty-five percent have college entrance qualifications (*Abitur*) or higher, and 40% have attended or are still attending college. More men than women have taken advantage of their opportunity to attend college.

The overview on occupational groups presented in Table 1.14 reveals that approximately 50% of the young adults are employed. The "blue-collar worker" or "craftsman" groups are hardly represented at all. However, the number of self-employed is notable at 9%, with daughters being represented overproportionately in this group. Table 1.15 also shows that almost 90% of the sample is currently gainfully employed, whereas only 0.5% report that they are not working. The rest are still at college. Finally, it is worth mentioning something that is not immediately apparent in Table 1.15—namely, that 17% of the daughters are housewives. Compared with the mothers, of whom more than 50% are housewives, this is a very low percentage. However, it has to be considered that only 31% of daughters already have their own children.

The income of the children's generation is presented in Table 1.15. Women are clearly overrepresented in the lower income groups, whereas men are the higher earners. A comparison with the occupational qualifications described earlier, in which no clear gender differences can be ascertained (see Table 1.13), provides a striking illustration of the problem of equality of opportunity for women in occupational life, despite sufficient occupational qualifications.

The housing conditions in the children's generation reveal a clear trend in favor of the cities. Only 24% live in a village, 30% in small towns, and 46%

TABLE 1.13
Children's Level of Education

Qualifications	Sons (%)	Daughters (%)	Both (%)
Basic secondary school with no school-leaving certificate	0	0	0
Basic secondary school with no school-leaving certificate	0	0	0
Basic secondary school plus vocational training	4.2	4.0	4.1
Technical school with no school-leaving certificate	2.1	1.0	1.5
Intermediate school-leaving certificate but no vocational training	0	1.0	0.5
Intermediate school-leaving certificate plus vocational training	13.5	23.2	18.5
Higher secondary school with school-leaving certificate	8.3	10.1	9.2
College entrance qualifications	25.0	24.2	24.6
College but no degree	6.3	7.1	6.7
College with degree	40.6	29.3	34.9
Total	100	100	100

in large cities. In line with this, 80% of the respondents live in rented accommodations, whereas 20% already own their own apartments or houses. In the majority of cases, the size of accommodation ranges between 40 and 100 square meters, mostly distributed across two to four rooms. Who do the respondents live with? Twenty-four (12%) adult sons and daughters still live at home with their parents and in the same apartment or house. Sixty percent of the children's generation live with a partner. If this figure is compared with the reports on partnership, it means that 20% of the children have a partner but do not live together, 23% live alone, and 6% report that they live with one or more persons with whom they are not related.

TABLE 1.14
Occupational Group Membership of Children

Occupational status	Sons %	Daughters %	Both %
Unskilled blue-collar worker	1.0	0	0.5
Semiskilled blue-collar worker	1.0	0	0.5
Skilled blue-collar worker	11.3	1.0	6.1
Foreman	1.0	0	0.5
Skilled industrial worker	0	0	0
Craftsman	3.1	1.0	2.0
Master craftsman	2.1	0	1.0
Farmer	1.0	1.0	1.0
Low-level white-collar worker	9.3	10.1	9.7
Intermediate-level white-collar worker	25.8	44.4	35.2
High-level white-collar worker	13.4	15.2	14.3
Low-ranking civil servant	1.0	1.0	1.0
Intermediate-level civil servant	2.1	3.0	2.6
High-ranking civil servant	3.1	5.1	4.1
Self-employed	5.2	13.1	9.2
Self-employed manager	5.2	1.0	3.1
Student	14.4	3.0	8.7
Not working	0	1.0	0.5
Total	100	100	100

TABLE 1.15
Children's Net Income

Monthly income in German Marks	Sons	Daughters	Both
Under 1000	12	14	26
1001-1500	8	15	23
1501-2000	8	19	27
2001-2500	10	12	22
2501-3000	16	26	42
3001-3500	11	5	16
3501-4000	11	3	14
4001-6000	12	2	14
Over 6000	1	0	1
Total	89	96	185

THE COMPARABILITY OF THE SAMPLES BETWEEN WAVES I AND 2

How far one can generalize the results of a study depends on the composition of the samples involved. In the ideal case, a sample is representative and statements can be generalized to the entire population. Although this was not even the case for the first wave, as reported earlier, the research plan nonetheless shows that attention was paid to the distributions of some important demographic variables, such as children's age, children's gender, and family socioeconomic class when compiling the sample. Controlling these features at the beginning of recruitment provides a broader foundation for interpreting the data.

The goal of any study like this—that draws on data from two waves—is to construct a comparison between the results of the first wave and those of the second wave. As the description of the procedure used to recruit the sample for the second wave reveals, a high mortality rate was accepted in the original sample of 570 complete families. Because any comparison of data across the two waves has to refer to the reduced sample, when looking at the results for 1976, one can only draw on the subsample that could be followed up at the second wave. However, this restriction may destroy the original balance in the sample composition, and thus make the data harder to interpret.

An example may clarify this problem. If one makes a statement on the intelligence of the children's generation on the basis of the total 1976 sample ($N = 570$), then the composition of this sample ensures that this statement refers to 285 boys and 285 girls, and thus controls for the gender variable. We had no control over the composition of the follow-up sample in 1992. Theoretically, we could have been faced with only 150 girls and no boys at all in the follow-up. If this were the case, any statement on the children's generation in 1992 would have to be interpreted against the background that it was drawn on a purely female and, in addition, strongly reduced sample, which would clearly limit the power of the results.

The description of the parent and child samples has already revealed that the reduced sample in 1992 tends to be composed of persons with higher educational backgrounds and higher incomes. It is now necessary to use statistics to test whether these shifts in the sample that are, at first, only apparent to the naked eye are also significant. The following procedure was chosen. Using the 1976 data, we formed two subsamples of "1992 participants" and "1992 nonparticipants." These were then compared in terms of the most important sociodemographic and psychological variables. Depending on the quality of the data, we tested either the means of the two samples or whether the distributions in the samples indicated that they originated from the same basic population.[20] In addition to the sociodemographic variables, we also focused on important psychological concepts such as personality variables and perceived family climate because these are also the main focus of the further analyses.

Sociodemographic Features

The first important aspect here is those variables that were used to grade the original sample in 1976. First, there have been no changes in the gender distribution of the children. The 98 sons and 100 daughters in the new sample give an equal distribution of the gender variable. The same applies to age. Although the children participating in the second wave are not distributed completely equally across the three age categories, none of the deviations was statistically significant. The same also applies to the age and gender of the parents participating in 1992. There are also no differences in the number of children in participant families compared with the group of nonparticipant families. The mean number of children in both groups lies between two and three.

A further area that has to be tested for possible sample bias is the school attendance of the children in 1976. What we want to know here is whether

the children participating in the follow-up in 1992 differ from the nonparticipants in terms of the "type of school they are attending" or their "academic
performance." In 1976, information was obtained on this from the children's
mothers. We compared the following variables in the two subsamples: type
of school attended, mean grades on the most important school subjects,
maternal rating of child's academic performance, and maternal reports on
how well children do their homework. There were no significant differences
in the distribution of any of these variables.

The example of type of school attended is used to show how this sample
comparison was performed (see Table 1.16). What is particularly interesting
here is the percentage scores in each cell. These report what percentage of
the sample under consideration attended which type of school. Clearly,
apart from slight variations, these percentages are almost equal across both
subsamples for each type of school considered. Statistical tests also revealed no significant differences between the two subsamples.

In summary, the 1992 children's sample has undergone no significant
shifts on the most important sociodemographic variables in comparison
with the total sample. However, this is not the case with the parent sample.
Although the distributions of age and religious confession have remained
the same, there have been clear, statistically significant shifts in highest
academic qualification, net family income, occupational group, and place of

TABLE 1.16
Comparison of Participant Versus Nonparticipant Samples
on Variable "Type of School" Attended

Type of school attended	1976 SAMPLE		
	Participants	Non-participants	Both
Elementary school	42 21.9 %	69 18.3 %	111 19.5 %
Lower level secondary school	14 7.3 %	37 9.8 %	51 8.9 %
Technical secondary school	35 18.2 %	82 21.7 %	117 20.5 %
Higher secondary school	101 52.6 %	190 50.3 %	291 51.1 %
Total	$n = 192$	$n = 378$	$n = 570$

residence. Compared with 1992 nonparticipants, the parents participating in the 1992 follow-up have higher occupational qualifications, higher net incomes, work in more highly rated occupational groups, and tend to live more in cities than in the country. Thus, the original systematic variation of socioeconomic status (SES) is no longer present in the new sample. Results show that we are now dealing predominantly with middle- and upper class families, whereas the families labeled as *lower class* in 1976 are clearly underrepresented in the follow-up.

Psychological Variables

The distinctive features of the sample mentioned earlier have to be taken into account in the interpretation of later findings. However, because the main concern is with psychological concepts and issues, the most important question is whether the changes in the sociodemographic features of the sample are also accompanied by shifts in the psychological variables. If this were true, the power of all the following analyses would be reduced.

To clarify this issue, data were tested on personality and family climate. It is not anticipated that the psychological variables will remain wholly unaffected by the sample bias. For example, it can be assumed that certain family climate scales that relate to SES will also be biased. However, if shifts in distribution are found, they should lie within acceptable bounds and their content should be interpretable. The parent generation is observed first.

At first glance, the comparisons made for the parent sample reveal no differences between the two subsamples on the majority of the psychological variables tested in either the fathers or the mothers. Although the exceptions reported later are statistically significant, the actual differences in means are anything but dramatically large.[21] These exceptions include the following variables. The fathers and mothers in 1992 report a stronger cultural orientation and more external contacts in their family climate. This seems to be completely plausible when it is considered that both higher academic qualifications and higher income go hand in hand with an increased use of cultural facilities (e.g., theaters, concerts, museums). The fathers additionally show a somewhat higher achievement orientation. The scales of a multidimensional personality test, which is reported in detail in chapter 2, also hardly differentiated between the two subsamples. Only the scales "Emotional stability" and "Abstractedness" showed slightly higher means for the parents in the new sample. In summary, the frequency and extent of differences ascertained on psychological variables in the parent sample remain within bounds that do not constrain the analysis of the issues that are important here.

The same applies to the children's sample. One important variable assessed here was the intelligence measured in 1976.[22] The new and old samples do not differ on either their total intelligence scores or their scores on the subtests "word recognition," "arithmetic," "numerical symbols," and "spatial concepts." Family climate reveals the same picture as in the parents. The only difference to be found is on the "cultural orientation" scale. To test for possible differences in childhood personality structure, a comprehensive personality inventory was used, in which several subscales are used to measure each of the following areas: motives, behavioral style, and self-image. Only the scale "Tendency toward upward evaluation of self" produced slightly higher scores in the new sample. Hence, for the children's generation as well, it seems to be confirmed that the 1992 sample exhibits no serious selection effects regarding psychological variables.

RESEARCH QUESTIONS

Now that the main theoretical and methodological background of this longitudinal study have been presented, this chapter is rounded off with a short overview of the topics that will be addressed in detail in the rest of this book. This overview follows the research model presented in Fig. 1.2, which differentiates between several interrelated levels of analysis—the individual, the relations, the family, and the ecological levels.

Chapters 2 and 3 are concerned with the individual level. Chapter 2 first focuses on the aspect of personality development. Using different personality assessment procedures, it investigates whether and how far personality characteristics such as openness toward others, self-confidence, or emotional stability have remained constant across time or have changed in the parent and children's generations. Chapter 2 also tackles the question of whether any developmental trends can be found in the age and generation comparison that indicate a specific—perhaps epochally determined—direction of personality change.

Chapter 3 is devoted to the concept of critical life events and coping. It addresses which decisive biographical events have occurred and their importance to the individual, and examines whether there are classes of events that are perceived as belonging together, and whether such classes reveal generational differences. It also investigates whether there is a relationship between certain classes of events and specific ways of coping with them. Finally, it considers the relationship between critical life events and physical health.

The next three chapters focus on the relations level. Chapter 4 analyzes age- and generation-specific changes in parental childrearing style—broken down into the components of childrearing goals, attitudes, and practices. The analysis is based on the general hypothesis that the internal features of parental childrearing style make a major contribution to the personality development of the following generation. The chapter is particularly interested in which direction changes in parental childrearing style have taken, and whether there are any signs that childrearing behavior is handed down from one generation to the next.

Chapter 5 turns its attention to the current relationship between parents and their adult children. This concerns central aspects of relationships such as commitment and autonomy from the perspective of each partner. Here as well, differences between generations is a central topic. However, the chapter also pays attention to whether the quality of the current parent–child relation can be predicted from features of the childrearing style previously practiced by the parents.

The quality of marriages or partnerships is the topic of chapter 6. First, it shows how the marriage relationship has developed over the prior 16 years. Then it explores if we can find any indications for whether, and under which circumstances, the marital relationship between the parents has influenced the shaping of the partnerships of the young adults. In each case, the chapter looks at the different perceptual perspectives of the two generations, so that reciprocal processes of influence between young and old also can be uncovered.

Chapter 7 moves on to the next level of the research model—namely, the family level. The focus is on the perceived family climate and the ways in which it differs from family to family as revealed by such features as solidarity, joint activities, or reciprocal control. Once more, the analysis focuses on changes across time, as well as differences between the parent and the children's generations. In addition, it concentrates on the question of how far discrepancies between the current assessment of family climate in 1976 and the retrospective assessment in 1992 contribute to an explanation of the quality of current parent–child relations.

Chapter 8 focuses on the ecological level. From the perspective of 1992, it addresses the perception of processes of social change, drawn on the previous 16 years. It works out similarities and differences between the parent and children's generations for the domains "life conditions," "life areas," "societal institutions," and "threatening factors." In addition, it investigates whether different ways of perceiving social change are handed down from one generation to the next. Finally, it inspects some variables that may provide explanations for why judgments on the extent of social change differ from individual to individual.

Chapter 9 takes another look at the findings from the previous chapters. It is necessary to examine whether the multitude of findings can be pieced together to form a picture that complies with the central goal of the study—namely, to gain an insight into the long-term processes of personality and family development in two generations that are linked together by being members of the same family.

A BRIEF SUMMARY OF THE MOST IMPORTANT POINTS

• In 1992, we were able to follow up approximately 200 of an original sample of 570 families who had participated in our study in 1976 when their children were ages 9–14. Therefore, this is a longitudinal study covering an interval of 16 years.

• At the time of the second wave, in 1992, the mothers had a mean age of 55 years, and the fathers had a mean age of 58. The members of the children's generation—half young women and half young men—had a mean age of 28 years.

• The study is based on an approach that views personality and family development in context. This assigns a major role to the relationships between parents and children, between (marriage) partners, and among the members of the entire family. The study also covers important biographical events, as well as how respondents perceive changes in their social framing conditions.

• The families that participated in both the original 1976 study and the 1992 follow-up ("participants") revealed a higher educational background and a superior occupational status, compared with the families that took part only in 1976 ("nonparticipants"). However, no important differences between participants and nonparticipants could be found for the psychological aspects of personality and relationships addressed in this study.

• The particular quality of the present study is that it examines the longitudinal development of two generations that are linked together through their family relationship. This makes it possible to present both time- and generation-determined developmental effects.

• The rest of the book summarizes the most important findings on the following topics, taking these time- and generation-determined effects into account in each case: (a) personality development, (b) biographical events and coping with stress, (c) change in parental childrearing style, (d) current relationships between parents and their adult sons and daughters, (e) marriage (partner) relationships in the parent and children's generation, (f) changes in family climate, and (g) perceived changes in social framing conditions.

END NOTES

1. This synopsis of data and events for the years 1976 and 1992 is taken from the book *Harenberg Schlüsseldaten 20. Jahrhundert* (Harenberg, 1993, pp. 652–653, 789–790) published by Harenberg Verlag.

2. A detailed documentation of the DFG-funded Parents–Child Relations Project and its findings can be found in the final report to the DFG (Schneewind et al., 1981) and in the book *Eltern und Kinder* (Parents and children; Schneewind, Beckmann, & Engfer, 1983).

3. See Bundesminister für Jugend, Familie, und Gesundheit (1975).
4. See, for example, the work of Mahler, Pine, and Bergmann (1975), as well as Bowlby (1969).
5. See, in particular, Thomas and Chess (1977) with their internationally renowned New York study on the development of differences in temperament.
6. Taken from the title of Lerner and Busch-Rossnagel's (1981) book, in which persons are viewed as individuals who play an active part in their process of development.
7. One of the most important promoters of psychological research on fathers in the United States is Lamb (1976).
8. Clarke-Stewart (1978) presented a pioneering study on this topic.
9. Family therapy has played a decisive role in promoting a systemic perspective on families since the beginning of the 1950s. A good example is Minuchin's structural family therapy (see Minuchin, 1974; Minuchin & Fishman, 1981) .
10. Bronfenbrenner (1979, 1986) can be viewed as the internationally most well-known proponent of an ecopsychological approach.
11. Taken from the title of an article written as long ago as 1926 by the American sociologist Burgess.
12. Compare the approaches for conceptualizing and assessing social climates in Moos (1979). In the present context, particular attention is drawn to the Family Environment Scale developed by Moos and Moos (1986). The German-language adaptation is described in detail in chapter 7.
13. Compare Note 2.
14. The importance of individual developmental tasks for the developmental course of individual persons has been pointed out particularly by Havighurst (1953) and Oerter (1986).
15. The concept of "family developmental task" has been particularly promoted by Duvall (1977) and Aldous (1978) in the field of sociological family research. In recent times, the usefulness of the concept has also been recognized in family therapy (see Carter & McGoldrick, 1988).
16. For each research question, we have included all subjects who provided appropriate data in order to provide a maximum exploitation of information.
17. The interviews were carried out by a selected staff of interviewers from the Association for Consumer and Market Research, at Nuremberg (Gesellschaft für Konsumforschung E.V. Nürnberg; GfK) who were specially trained for the study. More information on this can be found in the unpublished manual documenting this study (see Schneewind & Ruppert, 1992).
18. The major concern was to reduce each of the long versions of psychological scales through an appropriate selection of items. Technically, this was done by taking items of intermediate difficulty and high discrimination indices to obtain the highest possible consistency coefficients in the sense of Cronbach's (1951) alpha. In addition, the validity of the scales was tested with factor analysis.
19. An average divorce rate of 15% has to be anticipated for the marital cohorts on which our study is based (see Bretz et al., 1990, p. 129). The much lower divorce rate of 1.5% in our reactivated sample indicates a selection bias toward "intact" families.
20. Depending on the quality of each scale, we used either the chi-square test, the Kolmogorov-Smirnov Test, or the t test (Siegel, 1956).
21. To test the effect sizes of differences between names, Hays (1963) developed his so-called Omega-Square Method. This reports what percentage of the total variance of a feature can be explained by the grouping variable—in this case, "participants versus nonparticipants."
22. The children's intelligence was measured with the German adaptation (Hardesty & Priester, 1966) of the Wechsler Intelligence Scale for Children (WISC; Wechsler, 1949).

2

PERSONALITY DEVELOPMENT ACROSS THE GENERATIONS

"Personality is like love: Everybody knows that it exists, but nobody knows what it is."[1] It is certainly true that it is difficult to put human personality, which Goethe called "the greatest happiness for children of this earth," into scientific terms.[2] In fact, there are almost as many approaches to personality as there are scientists who have tackled this issue.

We do not want to get involved in an academic discussion on which theoretical basic principles, methodological approaches, and content-related aspects can be used to discriminate between human beings in terms of the type and quality of their behavior or perceptions. We prefer to take a pragmatic position and, on the one hand, assume that there is a larger or smaller number of content-related aspects of personality description. On the other hand, we consider that functional assessment instruments are available that provide a sufficiently reliable and valid depiction of individual differences in terms of distinctive personality characteristics.[3] We have drawn on two assessment methods that are frequently used in empirical personality research—namely, the questionnaire method and the method of judging personality with rating scales. For our personality questionnaire, we chose the nationally and internationally well-known Sixteen Personality Factor Questionnaire (16 PF), which, as its name indicates, assesses 16 different personality characteristics, and thus covers a comparatively broad spectrum of personality traits.[4]

The following section discusses the contents of the 16 PF in more detail. The single point that has to be made at present is that the 16 PF can only be used on adults. For this reason, we gave it to the parents alone in the families studied in 1976. We assessed the children in the first wave with a

34

personality inventory designed for their age range—the *Persönlichkeitsfrage-bogen für Kinder zwischen 9–14 Jahren* (Personality questionnaire for 9- to 14-year-old children; PFK 9–14). The PFK 9–14 is also a procedure covering a wide range of content that provides a comprehensive assessment of childhood personality. It is described in detail herein.[5] In 1992, the 16 PF was used to assess the parents for a second time and, because the children had now grown up, they were also given the 16 PF instead of the PFK 9–14.

This means that, for the parents, we can use one and the same instrument to say something about whether, and in which domains, their personality has changed over the course of the 16 years between the two waves. Things are not so easy with the children because, as mentioned earlier, we had to work with different personality questionnaires at each wave. Nonetheless, as is shown here, relationships between child and adult personality can be studied in terms of their content.

The situation was more straightforward for the personality rating scales, which were specially constructed for the Parent–Child Relations Project on the basis of a series of pilot studies. This instrument contains 12 bipolar rating scales that can be classified into four, clearly differentiable factors of personality judgment. These are also described in more detail later. This inventory of personality rating scales was given to both parents and children at each wave, so that comparable information on the stability or change in personality ratings is available for both generations. We asked our respondents to perform self-ratings as well as ratings on the other members of the family participating in the study following the same judgment criteria. Thus, parents, for example, had to give a real and an ideal rating of themselves, as well as corresponding ratings on both their partner and their child. This provides a multitude of rating perspectives for our analyses. One advantage of this is that self-reports on personality, as well as how other close members of the family see this personality, can be compared both with each other and over the course of time.

Using these two methodological approaches—the questionnaire method and the rating method—changes in personality in the parent generation are first studied. Then the same approach is applied to study personality changes in the children's generation (i.e., their personality development from childhood to young adulthood). Finally, this chapter considers whether and in which areas differences in personality development between the generations can be confirmed.

PERSONALITY DEVELOPMENT: THE PARENT GENERATION

In the parent generation, we surveyed mothers and fathers from the same families. In 1976, the fathers had a mean age of 42 years, and the mothers had a mean age of 39. In 1992, the mean age of the fathers was correspondingly 58 years, and the mothers, 55. Thus, the period under study covers most of the middle years of adulthood—a time during which most families have become firmly established in occupational, economic, and social terms. Because of the far-reaching consolidation of living conditions, in most cases, we can also anticipate that there will be hardly any turbulent changes in the domain of personality either. We assume that the personality structure in most of our respondents will have become so consolidated that we can hypothesize more stability than change in personality development in this group of adults.

However, before detecting any changes in individual aspects of personality, the assessment instruments have to fulfill two methodological preconditions. First, it must be ensured that individual differences have been assessed with sufficient reliability at both waves. Second, it must be clarified that no great structural changes in personality organization have occurred over the course of time (i.e., that the way individual personality characteristics relate to each other has not changed). Both methodological preconditions—reliability of the assessment instrument and structural stability of personality organization—were tested and found satisfactory, providing a sound basis for making statements on questions of stability and change in individual personality dispositions.[6]

Questionnaire Findings on Personality Development in the Parent Generation

This section first deals with findings obtained with the 16 PF questionnaire. To make it easier to understand which internal aspects of personality are assessed with the 16 PF, Table 2.1 presents the labels of each bipolar personality dimension, as well as a description of their content. It should be noted that the "Reasoning" scale (a short intelligence test integrated into the 16 PF) was used only for the first wave in 1976, so that no measure of change can be determined here. As a result, the following findings refer to 15 instead of 16 personality traits.[7] In the sense of a hierarchical model of personality, the primary scales can be summarized into higher level, second-order factors. Individually, these are: (a) extraversion, (b) anxiety, (c) tough-mindedness, (d) independence, and (e) self-control.[8]

A preliminary answer to the question of whether adult personality has tended to remain stable or has changed across time can be obtained by ascertaining the relative position of the respondents at the first and second waves in comparison with the mean score for the total sample. In other words, does a mother, who exhibited above-average warmth in 1976, reveal the same score in 1992? Vice versa, one can also ask whether a mother characterized by a high degree of distance (low warmth) in 1976 continues to exhibit an above-average distance in 1992. Generalized across the sample of all mothers,

TABLE 2.1
Overview of the 16 PF Scales

FACTOR		Meaning of the left side pole	Meaning of the right side pole
A	Warmth	Reserved, Impersonal, Distant	Warm, Outgoing, Attentive to Others
C	Emotional Stability	Reactive, Emotionally Changeable	Emotionally Stable, Adaptive, Mature
E	Dominance	Deferential, Cooperative, Avoids Conflicts	Dominant, Forceful, Assertive
F	Liveliness	Serious, Restrained, Careful	Lively, Animated, Spontaneous
G	Rule-Consciousness	Expedient, Nonconforming	Rule-Conscious, Dutiful
H	Social Boldness	Shy, Threat-Sensitive, Timid	Socially Bold, Venturesome, Thick-Skinned
I	Sensitivity	Utilitarian, Objective, Unsentimental	Sensitive, Aesthetic, Sentimental
L	Vigilance	Trusting, Unsuspecting, Accepting	Vigilant, Suspicious, Skeptical, Wary
M	Abstractedness	Grounded, Practical, Solution-Oriented	Abstracted, Imaginative, Idea-Oriented
N	Privateness	Forthright, Genuine, Artless	Private, Discreet, Non-Disclosing
O	Apprenhension	Self-Assured, Unworried, Complacent	Apprehensive, Self-Doubting, Worried
Q1	Openness to Change	Traditional, Attached to Familiar	Open to Change, Experimenting
Q2	Self-Reliance	Group-Oriented, Affiliative	Self-Reliant, Solitary, Individualistic
Q3	Perfectionism	Tolerates Disorder, Unexacting, Flexible	Perfectionist, Organized, Self-Disciplined
Q4	Tension	Relaxed, Placid, Patient	Tense, High Energy, Impatient, Driven

this means: Can the individual differences found on the personality dimension of warmth in 1976 still be presented in approximately the same way in 1992? If this is the case, we can talk about a high relative or differential stability in this personality characteristic across the 16-year interval.[9]

This type of answer to the stability issue can be found for mothers as well as fathers, or—independent of gender—the total sample of parents. In addition, it can be ascertained for all 15 personality dimensions in the 16 PF. The correlation coefficient varying between the values $r = -1.00$ and $r = +1.00$ provides a quantitative measure of the strength of the stability hypothesis. A positive correlation coefficient of $r = +1.00$ would indicate a maximum differential stability in the personality characteristic studied. In contrast, a correlation of $r = -1.00$ would provide an inverse relation for the personality characteristic in question. In concrete terms, this would mean that all those who had exhibited, for example, a warm and outgoing attitude in 1976 had in some way performed a complete about-face by 1992, and now were rather reserved and distant. Finally, a correlation of $r = 0.00$ would indicate that there was no relation between the personality differences obtained in 1976 and 1992. These last two cases would be examples of differential instability in the personality characteristic in question.

Table 2.2 presents the empirically ascertained stability coefficients for the personality dimensions of the 16 PF both for the total sample of all parents and split for mothers and fathers. A first glance at the table reveals that the personality traits assessed with the 16 PF have remained remarkably stable across the 16-year period. The total sample has a mean stability coefficient of $r = .59$, confirming that most adults have retained their relative position on the individual personality dimensions from 1976 to 1992. It should also be pointed out that this method for determining stability is a conservative procedure (i.e., it tends to underestimate it).[10]

A detailed study of Table 2.2 leaves the impression that some traits seem to exhibit a greater stability across time than others. For example, the emotional stability component, which refers to the degree to which one becomes upset or remains calm in the face of disappointments, has re-

TABLE 2.2
Relative Stabilities of the 16 PF Scales From 1976 to 1992

16 PF scales	Father $n = 209$	Mother $n = 213$	Both $n = 422$
Warmth	.60	.60	.61
Emotional Stability	.52	.44	.47
Dominance	.44	.45	.50
Liveliness	.62	.60	.62
Rule-Consciousness	.59	.71	.66
Social Boldness	.70	.62	.69
Sensitivity	.73	.61	.76
Vigilance	.47	.51	.50
Abstractedness	.63	.55	.56
Privateness	.42	.57	.49
Apprehension	.56	.57	.62
Openness to Change	.54	.52	.53
Self-Reliance	.67	.44	.57
Perfectionism	.50	.50	.52
Tension	.62	.47	.58

Note. All coefficients: $p < .001$

mained less stable than the personality trait that discriminates people according to whether they take a more utilitarian and objective or a more sensitive and aesthetic attitude. Nonetheless, these differences between the stability coefficients are not statistically significant, so it is not possible to interpret their content.

The same applies for the comparison between the mother and father samples. Although the mean stability in women is somewhat lower than in men ($r = .52$ vs. $r = .58$), this difference is low enough to neglect. There are also no statistically interpretable differences between the genders in the 16-year stabilities on the level of individual personality traits. In summary, one can assume a rather high relative stability of personality in adulthood for both men and women, as well as for the individual personality traits. This also replicates the findings of other longitudinal studies.[11]

The aspect of stability in personality clarified so far is not incorrectly labeled *relative* or *differential stability* because it only tells something about whether the differences between the individual persons within a group have been maintained to a greater or lesser extent across time. Even if this were the case to the greatest possible extent, this would not necessarily mean that no personality change has occurred. For example, it would be highly conceivable that, although the members of a group have maintained their relative position over the course of time on, for example, the warmth dimension, the group as a whole may have shifted from a reserved to a warm attitude. If such an effect of change cannot be found, one can confirm the existence of differential stability, as well as an absolute stability of the personality characteristic in question.

This section thus turns to the question of whether and to what extent personality changes have occurred for our parent generation during 1976–1992 that can be used to counter the hypothesis of absolute stability. The relevant findings are presented in Table 2.3. First of all, the appropriate statistical procedures confirm that as many as 8 of the 15 personality traits have changed over the 16-year interval.[12] Although these results are all highly significant statistically because of the relatively large sample size, generally speaking, the change effects remain modest. This is revealed by the differences between means that lie between 0.4 and 0.9 on a scale extending from 0 to 12 units. The relatively low change effect can be seen even more clearly in the last column in Table 2.3. These values reveal something about what percentage of the entire variation in a personality characteristic can be traced back to a change effect tied to the 16-year interval.[13] For example, the warmth dimension reveals a mean increase toward a stronger social orientation. However, in relation to the total extent of individual differences that exist between the respondents, this effect explains only 6% of the variance. To put it the other way round, 94% of individual differences can be traced back to factors that have nothing to do

TABLE 2.3
Personality Changes in the 16 PF Scales for Total Sample of Parents From
1976 to 1992

16 PF scales	1976 Means and standard deviations	1992 Means and standard deviations	Difference between means	Significance	ω^2
Warmth	6.43 3.68	7.12 3.23	+ 0.69	.000	.062
Rule-Consciousness	7.97 3.14	8.39 2.82	+ 0.42	.001	.024
Social Boldness	6.31 3.87	6.94 3.56	+ 0.63	.000	.038
Sensitivity	5.81 3.67	6.33 3.39	+ 0.52	.000	.045
Vigilance	6.32 2.69	5.95 2.09	- 0.37	.008	.016
Abstractedness	3.69 2.90	4.61 2.55	+ 0.92	.000	.131
Openness to Change	6.54 2.94	6.12 2.45	- 0.42	.002	.022
Self-Reliance	4.09 2.80	4.45 2.54	+ 0.36	.003	.021

Note. Upper value = mean. Lower value = standard deviation.

with the 16-year interval. Besides measurement errors, these could be genetic aspects, gender differences, or specific biographical experiences that had already led to a consolidation of individual differences before 1976.

Time-dependent change effects are less strong for a number of other personality traits. For example, this applies to the increase in rule-consciousness or the decrease in vigilance, for which the change effects amount to only 2%. The dimension "Abstractedness" represents an exception because, at 13%, it shows the strongest change toward more imagination and idea-orientation. Despite these generally rather low dynamics of change, an overall view of the various personality characteristics nonetheless reveals a pattern of change that can be recognized in the following three aspects:

1. Consolidation of Personal Identity. Over the course of time, the parent generation has become more self-confident, more independent, and more unconventional. This indicates that the period of mid- to late adulthood brings about a stabilization of self-awareness and self-reflection that allows individuals to behave more freely and confidently, and to be less guided by external constraints. In some ways, individuals stand up for their own identity and live accordingly.

2. Social Opening. A series of indicators of change point toward an increase in a socially oriented attitude. The extent of this orientation toward contacts with others (i.e., warmth and openness toward them) has increased just as much as the willingness to respond to them with empathy. At the same time, reservations and skepticism about other persons has decreased. All this confirms that the "middle-aged generation" has become more open and approachable in socioemotional terms.

3. Emphasis on Tradition. Over the course of the 16 years, the adult generation shows a tendency to orient itself more toward the proven, to take fewer risks, and to place more value on orderly living conditions. In some ways, life is running in set grooves. There is no interest in great visions for the future and experiments. The concern is far more with consolidating that which has been achieved, and thus preserving the base of internal values for an increasingly consolidated personal and social identity.

These changes do not represent any dramatic shifts in the architecture of adult personality. Nonetheless, in an overall view, they provide a highly consistent picture of a pattern of change characterized by an increase in ego strength, social openness, and conservatism in the sense of an orientation toward tried and tested life principles.

Up to now, the total sample of parents has been considered (i.e., we have not discriminated between fathers and mothers). Therefore, we now investigate whether there have been different courses of personality development for men and women in the 16-year comparison. The findings reveal that this—with two exceptions—is not the case. In other words, on average, men and women have gone through the same shift of change in their personality development, although the genders also had thoroughly different weightings on a few personality characteristics at Wave 1. The latter applies for the four personality traits whose change is illustrated in Fig. 2.1, which depicts the developmental course separately for men and women.

On the one hand, the results in Fig. 2.1 reveal that the personality development of mothers and fathers has actually run parallel on these four traits from 1976 to 1992. On the other hand, it also becomes clear that the personality differences between the genders are, in part, much larger than the differences attributable to the time effect. This applies particularly to the traits "Social boldness" and "Sensitivity." Men portray themselves as much more active and challenging than women. In addition, they are comparatively more reality-oriented and less emotional. Although it would seem as if these differences reflect gender stereotypes, these gender-typical personality dispositions acquired during the process of socialization may be highly relevant for behavior. However, even in adulthood, they still seem to be

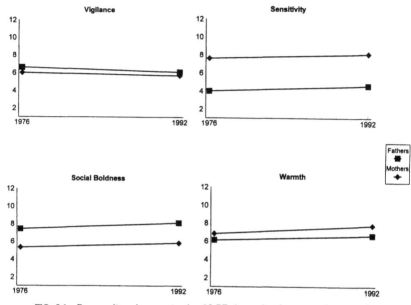

FIG. 2.1. Personality changes in the 16 PF that take the same direction for men and women.

subject to a process of change—although slight—that, interestingly, takes the same direction in both genders.

Finally, as already mentioned, this section considers the two exceptions for which a gender-typical, different course of personality development can be confirmed. These are the two dimensions of personality "Emotional stability" and "Abstractedness." Findings split according to gender are presented in Fig. 2.2. The figure shows that mothers and fathers had the same level of emotional stability in 1976. However, they then both developed in different directions. Fathers have become somewhat more balanced over time, whereas mothers have become more emotionally irritable during the same period. This should certainly also be viewed against the background that women generally respond far more strongly to negative emotions than men.[14] In addition, the divergent development of women and men provides an explanation for why a test of the time-change effect produced no difference. Namely, if one averages the values of women and men for 1992, the resulting score is almost identical to the initial score in 1976.

This is not the case for the personality trait "Abstractedness." It was shown earlier that a shift toward more imagination and idea-orientation can be seen in the total group of parents. This is recognizable in Fig. 2.2. However, it can also be seen that the slope is steeper for women than for men. Therefore, it seems as if the female gender has liberated itself somewhat more from pragmatic constraints compared with the male. However, it has

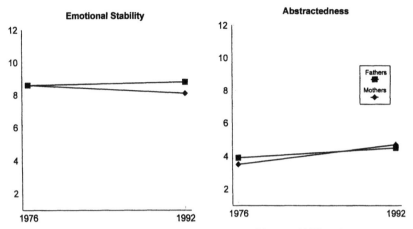

FIG. 2.2. Interaction effects "gender × wave" for two 16 PF scales.

to be noted that the differential change effects remain within modest limits for both these personality dimensions with gender-typical developmental courses, so that one should not assign too much meaning to them.

Before leaving the domain of adult personality development as assessed in questionnaires, we must exploit that this sample presents two special groups of adults—namely, adults who are married to each other. In view of our interest in personality changes across time, we can ask whether and, if so, on which personality dimensions the two partners in the parent genera- tion have drawn closer together (or further apart). For example, it could be assumed that spouses become more similar over time because of the great extent to which they share their lives. If this is true, then correlations between spouses should have increased over the course of 16 years on at least some personality characteristics. To illustrate this with an example, we have ascertained that the parent generation—and the mothers just as much as the fathers—have developed a stronger social orientation. Does this also mean that they have become more similar to each other on this trait? Has the temporal change effect also been accompanied by a process of becoming more alike through marriage? The correlations reported in Table 2.4 reveal whether this idea can be confirmed.

The results are clear. The mean correlation between spouses across all 15 personality traits is $r = .12$ in 1976 and $r = .13$ in 1992. In other words, no effect of increasing similarity can be confirmed. This also applies when the more differentiated perspective on the level of individual personality dimen- sions is taken. Although changes in the size of the correlations can some- times be seen, none of them attain statistical significance.[15]

A few further findings depicted in Table 2.4 deserve more attention. First, of the 18 correlations indicating any sort of relation between the partners on

TABLE 2.4
Paired Correlations for the 16 PF Scales for 1976 and 1992

16 PF scales	1976	1992
Warmth	.26 **	.18 *
Emotional Stability	.25 **	.34 **
Dominance	-.07	.01
Liveliness	-.02	.04
Rule-Consciousness	.18 *	.17 *
Social Boldness	.00	.16 *
Sensitivity	.12 *	.08
Vigilance	.27 **	.10
Abstractedness	.38 **	.33 **
Privateness	-.15 *	.14 *
Apprehension	-.07	-.03
Openness to Change	.35 **	.29 **
Self-Reliance	.12 *	.16 *
Perfectionism	-.05	-.08
Tension	-.12 *	.01
Mean correlation	.12	.13

$* p < .05. ** p < .01.$

the levels of individual personality characteristics, only 1 is negative. This suggests that spouses—at least in terms of the personality features assessed here—clearly mate according to the principle of "birds of a feather flock together," and not, for example, according to the motto "opposites attract." Second, although our findings cannot confirm this directly, there are numerous indications that the similarities between spouses can already be ascertained at the beginning of their marriage, which points toward a process of "assortative mating." Third, and this can certainly be confirmed with our data, the effect of selective partner choice, which probably becomes more stable over the course of the marriage, also remains broadly unchanged over the period of 16 years studied here. This particularly applies to those personality characteristics that already revealed a relatively high correlation between spouses in 1976. Above all, increases or decreases in emotional stability, abstractedness, and openness to change show moderately similar levels in both partners and maintain these levels across time. Thus, in addition to the much higher individual stabilities, which were reported at the beginning of this chapter, the stability hypothesis in terms of the similarity of personality on the level of married couples can also be confirmed.

Self- and Other Ratings on Personality Development in the Parent Generation

Our second source of information for assessing personality differences and their change over time was an inventory containing 12 bipolar personality rating scales. The respondents' task was to rate themselves, their partner, and the child participating in the study in terms of their real and ideal self-images on a 7-point scale. Each pole was marked by trait-descriptive adjectives that can be viewed as the extremes of a judgment continuum. Using this format, respondents had to report the strength of the aspect of personality in question. Methodologically sound pilot studies revealed that each of these scales could be assigned to one of four more general personality dimensions. Table 2.5 summarizes the 12 personality rating scales alongside the four more general personality dimensions.[16]

The following text concentrates on these four general personality dimensions. Each person's score on these personality dimensions is computed from his or her mean scores on the three personality rating scales categorized to it. We are also interested in what degree of relative stability the self- and other rating scales reveal over the period of 16 years. Table 2.6

TABLE 2.5
Overview of the Personality Rating Scales

Weak Willpower vs. Strong Willpower

no self-assertion vs. strong self-assertion
easy to discourage vs. persistent, tough
unambitious, weak-willed vs. ambitious, strong-willed

Introversion vs. Extraversion

dull, lethargic vs. lively
serious, dejected vs. cheerful, carefree
inward looking vs. open to others

Sober Egocentrism vs. Emotional Empathy

robust, hard vs. empathic, soft
sober, objective, cool vs. emotional, warm-hearted
stubborn vs. pliable, willing

Instability vs. Emotional Balance

nervous, easily aroused vs. relaxed, calm
superficial, imprecise vs. conscientious, thorough
moody, temperamental vs. balanced, steady

TABLE 2.6
Relative Stabilities for Self- and Other Ratings of Real Self-Image

Personality rating scales	Mothers (n = 205)		Fathers (n = 204)		Mean correlations
	Self-rating	Other rating by husband	Self-rating	Other rating by wife	
Weak Willpower vs. Strong Willpower	.56	.52	.50	.53	.52
Introversion vs. Extraversion	.57	.54	.59	.60	.58
Sober Egocentrism vs. Emotional Empathy	.48	.53	.45	.42	.47
Instability vs. Emotional Balance	.58	.64	.58	.62	.61
Mean correlations	.55	.56	.53	.55	.55

All correlations: $p < .001$.

provides information on this, based on the real self-ratings of the mothers and fathers and the real other ratings by their respective spouses.

In general, fluctuations in the relative stabilities of the four personality dimensions remain within a range that is also typical for personality data from questionnaires. Results confirm a notable stability over the 16-year period, with only slightly lower values on the dimension "Sober egocentricity versus emotional empathy." It is also notable that there is no gender difference (i.e., men and women have both retained their personality differences to the same extent over time). It is even more notable that this holds for both self-ratings and ratings by spouses. In other words, perceived differences in personality are broadly retained across time, regardless of whether ratings come from the persons or from their partners.

This raises the question of whether any relation at all can be found between self- and other ratings of one's own personality. For example, it is conceivable that the differences in personality that husbands perceive in their wives remain stable across time, whereas wives perceive themselves completely differently from the way in which they are perceived by their husbands. From the wives' perspective, the husbands in this case would, to some extent, maintain their "error" over how they see their wives across the years. Therefore, we tested, separately for both men and women, whether there was a relationship between the perceived differences in personality from the self-perspective and from the perspective of the spouse. We also extended the scope of the research question to include the comparison between the two waves. This allowed us to ascertain whether there was any relationship at all between self- and other ratings of own personality, and to test whether such relationships—if they exist—have increased or decreased over time. Answers to these questions can be read off the correlations reported in Table 2.7.

Results reveal that there is generally a statistically significant relationship between self- and other ratings of own personality. With a mean correlation coefficient of $r = 40$, this relationship is notably lower than the average of $r = .55$ for the 16-year stabilities in self- and other ratings, as shown in Table 2.6. However, each of the 16-year stabilities concerns the statements of only one single person, regardless of whether these are self- or other ratings. In both cases, rating is based on the same reference framework or subjective field of meaning that links the person to be rated with the given rating scale. Things are different for the relationship between self-rating and rating by the spouse. In this case, two different persons are rating one and the same personality. As a result, it can be assumed that the two subjective areas of meaning have only a partial overlap on the given trait scales. An example may clarify this. To some extent, a wife may associate other situations with the trait pair "Weak willpower versus strong willpower," compared with her husband. If this is generally true, it is bound to lead to a reduction of the interrater agreement between spouses. Looked at in this way, the correla-

TABLE 2.7
Correlations Between Real Self-Ratings and Ratings by Partner for 1976 and 1992

Personality rating scales	1976		1992		Mean correlations
	Real SR husband OR wife (n = 204)	Real SR wife OR husband (n = 205)	Real SR husband OR wife (n = 204)	Real SR wife OR husband (n = 205)	
Weak Willpower vs. Strong Willpower	.40	.38	.40	.31	.37
Introversion vs. Extraversion	.43	.41	.52	.47	.46
Sober Egocentrism vs. Emotional Empathy	.32	.35	.32	.39	.35
Instability vs. Emotional Balance	.34	.45	.45	.32	.39
Mean correlations	.37	.40	.40	.36	.40

Note. All correlations: $p < .001$. SR = Self-rating; OR = Other rating.

tions reported in Table 2.7 indicate a moderate, but nonetheless considerable, relationship between self- and other ratings by different raters on fixed personality rating scales.

It has to be emphasized here that women and men are equally capable of predicting the self-ratings of their spouses. There are also no interpretable differences between the individual personality dimensions. Above all, no changes across time can be confirmed. In other words, reciprocal personality ratings have not drawn closer together between 1976 and 1992, although this could have been anticipated on the basis of the long period of marital familiarity. Thus, in all, these findings indicate a moderately strong agreement between self- and other ratings of adult personality, as well as a stability of this relationship across time.

However, what do the average stabilities look like for the individual personality dimensions? We answered this question by comparing the means on the four rating dimensions for 1976 and 1992, split according to gender. The results are presented graphically in Fig. 2.3. The profiles for 1976 and 1992 show that, roughly speaking, there have been hardly any changes in mean self-ratings. Statistical tests reveal that both genders have become somewhat more introverted over time (i.e., they report that they are less lively and merry). However, men and women both perceive themselves as being emotionally more stable in the sense of being balanced and relaxed. For both genders, this developmental effect takes the same direction. However, it is only weak in comparison with the total variation in self-ratings of personality.

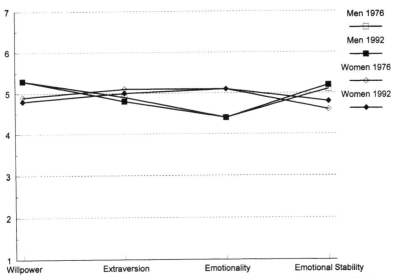

FIG. 2.3. Personality profile (real image ratings) of women and men for 1976 and 1992.

In all, the changes over the course of time account for almost 1% (introversion) or 3% (emotional balance) of the difference in self-ratings. What is much more striking—as a glance at Table 2.3 soon reveals—is the differences between genders that have also been maintained over the course of time. Compared with their husbands, wives particularly perceive themselves as being less self-assertive, more lively, emotionally less stable, and, above all, more emotional. These gender-typical differences account for between 4% (extraversion) and 28% (emotionality) of the total variation in personality ratings.

We now take a look at the perception of the personality from the perspective of each spouse. Two questions arise here. First, do the mean self-rating of personality and the mean rating carried out by the spouse agree? Second, does the description of the spouse's real personality change over time? The mean scores on the corresponding personality ratings reported in Table 2.8 provide information on both these questions.

An initial comparison of mean self-ratings with mean other ratings reveals that women, like men, generally get very close to the self-ratings of their spouses. The greatest discrepancies are found for the dimension "Weak willpower versus strong willpower." Here, both men and women assign more self-assertion, persistence, and ambition to their spouses than they claim for themselves. In addition, husbands tend to rate their wives as being more lively and open than the wives see themselves. However, the wives perceive themselves as being more emotional than their husbands perceive them.

The time comparison also produces a fairly stable picture of the perception of partner personality (i.e., the attribution of personality characteristics hardly changes). Two exceptions are worth mentioning. First, the husbands' willpower decreases in the eyes of their wives and simultaneously comes

TABLE 2.8
Mean Scores for Real Ratings by Partner for 1976 and 1992

Personality rating scales	Husband rates wife 1976 ($n = 204$)	Husband rates wife 1992 ($n = 204$)	Wife rates husband 1976 ($n = 205$)	Wife rates husband 1992 ($n = 205$)
Weak Willpower vs. Strong Willpower	5.1 (4.9)	5.1 (4.8)	5.7 (5.3)	5.4 (5.3)
Introversion vs. Extraversion	5.3 (5.1)	5.3 (5.0)	5.0 (4.9)	4.8 (4.8)
Sober Egocentrism vs. Emotional Empathy	4.9 (5.1)	4.9 (5.1)	4.3 (4.4)	4.4 (4.4)
Instability vs. Emotional Balance	4.6 (4.6)	5.0 (4.8)	5.3 (5.1)	5.2 (5.2)

Note. Scores in parentheses are the mean self-ratings of the persons being judged.

closer to the husbands' own self-reports. Second, husbands attribute more emotional stability to their wives as they get older, and, in doing this, slightly overestimate the wives' self-perceptions of this personality attribute.

Both findings suggest that, over the course of time, wives' ratings of their husbands come much closer to the self-ratings of their husbands than the husbands' ratings of their wives. This assumption has been tested by adding together the discrepancies between self-ratings and ratings by spouse across the four personality dimensions separately for husbands and wives and comparing these figures for 1976 and 1992. The result is displayed in Fig. 2.4.

There actually is a clear gender-specific change effect. In 1976, men and women made an equal number of "errors" in rating their spouses' personalities, whereas the discrepancy between the personality attributes that husbands assigned to their wives and their wives' self-ratings increased. In contrast, the corresponding discrepancy score for the wives dropped to almost zero. This suggests that, over the course of time—obviously better than their husbands—wives have learned to rate their husbands more precisely in line with the way that their husbands see themselves. However, the present findings cannot tell whether this can be traced back to the greater interpersonal sensitivity of the wives that also becomes evident in our data and is possibly stronger in later adulthood, or to specific life events that have given the wives a greater motivation to tackle their husbands' personalities more exactly.

However, it would be wrong to overrate the gender-specific "scissors effect" on the precision of the agreement between self-ratings and spouse-related other ratings. On the one hand, this effect is limited in quantitative terms. On the other hand, it should be recalled that there were no gender-typical differences in the differential agreement between self- and other ratings, as the correlations reported in Table 2.4 show. If both findings are added together, wives seem to adjust their ratings on their husbands better

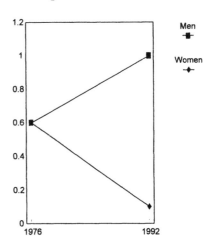

FIG. 2.4. Discrepancies between self- and other ratings for 1976 and 1992 (total score).

to the level of their husbands' self-ratings over time, whereas men seem to show a trend in the opposite direction. Regarding the precision of the perception of personality differences, if one takes the self-ratings of the spouse being rated as the benchmark in each case, no gender-typical advantages or deficits in competence can be ascertained.

Another question that can be posed analogue to the analyses on the questionnaire level is whether there has been a change in the self-ratings of the spouse over time (e.g., in the sense of an alignment effect). Here as well, this question can be specified more precisely by asking whether such an alignment effect can be confirmed as an increasing similarity between wives and husbands in terms of their mean ratings on their real self-images, or whether the scores on the individual personality dimensions have drawn closer together between spouses over time.

Neither supposition can be confirmed. Returning to Fig. 2.3, which depicts the self-rating profiles of husbands and wives for 1976 and 1992, it can be seen immediately that no changes in discrepancy have occurred in the mean self-ratings of both genders. Numerically, the sum of the discrepancies has remained exactly the same at both waves with a value of 1.8. The intrapair correlations, which state something about the degree of similarity in the self-ratings of personality by spouses, are unequivocal. With mean of $r = .04$ for 1976 and $r = .02$ for 1992, it is clear that there are no communalities between the partners on the level of their self-rated personality characteristics, and that no reciprocal drawing together has occurred in this regard over the years. Thus, the empirical findings again indicate that, to a great extent, personality development in adulthood is characterized by stability.

PERSONALITY DEVELOPMENT: THE CHILDREN'S GENERATION

This section discusses the personality development in the children's generation in detail. We are interested in how far the boys and girls who were an average of 12 years old in 1976 and 28 years old in 1992 have changed in terms of their personality during this 16-year period, or whether their individual characters have remained basically stable. Most of them must have passed through a relatively stormy development over the past 16 years. Events such as puberty, school graduation, separation from the family of origin, starting work, entering partnerships, and, in some cases, even founding their own families represent significant challenges for one's own life plans. Therefore, we can already anticipate a greater change in personality differences than that found—as revealed in the previous section—in the middle years. As in the parent generation, we first study personality development in the younger generation on the level of questionnaire data before turning to self- and other ratings of personality.

Questionnaire Findings on Personality Development in the Children's Generation

The beginning of this chapter pointed out that, for both objective and psychological reasons, we were unable to draw on the same personality inventory for the filial generation in childhood that we had used in adulthood. Thus, we are also unable to carry out direct comparisons of matched personality traits in childhood and adulthood, as was the case with the parent generation. Instead, we had to use a child-appropriate personality assessment that covers the widest possible spectrum of personality traits in childhood in a similar way to the 16 PF. In the German-speaking world, the *Persönlichkeitsfragebogen für Kinder zwischen 9 und 14 Jahren* (Personality questionnaire for 9- to 14-year-olds; PFK 9–14) is available. The PFK 9–14 assesses 15 personality characteristics that combine into three groups: (a) motives—desires and needs of children and their attitudes toward their environment (e.g., the motive for more or less aggressive ego assertion); (b) behavior styles—specific, externally observable behaviors of children (e.g., that they are easily upset by stress); and (c) self-image aspects—children's statements about themselves (e.g., their self-perceptions that they tend to react anxiously in many situations).[17]

For each personality characteristic, the children were given a series of statements that had been selected according to specific psychometric criteria. They had to mark whether these statements were either "true" or "not true" (examples for such statements for the motive of ego assertion are "Sometimes I've thrown things at somebody who annoyed me" and "Sometimes I don't give up until I've got what I want"). To give an impression of the breadth of the PFK 9–14's content, Table 2.9 presents short descriptions of the 15 personality traits assessed in the questionnaire, arranged according to motives, behavior styles, and self-image aspects.

A glance at the table reveals the variety of personality aspects that can be assessed with this personality questionnaire for children, and that some of these personality characteristics are similar in content to the descriptions in the 16 PF (see Table 2.1). For example, strong scores on the motive scale "Masculinity" in the PFK 9–14 correspond roughly to low sensitivity on the 16 PF. Nonetheless, the two personality questionnaires are not equivalent assessment instruments in terms of their psychological meaning. Therefore, the research reported here is not directed toward testing personality change on the basis of identical assessment methods, but toward asking whether measurable differences in personality in childhood reveal any relation at all to differences in personality in adulthood. We are also interested in the content-related question regarding whether such relations can be interpreted meaningfully in psychological terms.

We first present an overview of the relations between personality characteristics that were assessed in both childhood and young adulthood. We

TABLE 2.9
Overview of the PFK 9–14 Scales

Motives

Self-Assertion

Wishes to assert own wishes in preference to and in contrast to others; likes to annoy others and enjoys their mishaps; reacts aggressively when thwarted; likes to oppose

Self-Sufficiency

Likes being alone; prefers to work and play alone rather than with others; can spend time alone; needs few friends; does not feel unhappy when alone; is happy to be left in peace by others

Academic Ambition

Wants to be one of the best in the class and to receive recognition at school; likes examinations and enjoys school work; is keen to cooperate in class; is frequently praised and assigned tasks by teachers

Social Commitment

Shows emotional involvement in the experiences of others; is willing to help and considerate; enjoys working with others

Dependence on Adults

Follows parents' instructions and obeys immediately without protest; feels linked to parents and exhibits trust in them; considers that one should be quiet when spoken to by adults

Masculinity

Prefers rough-and-ready experiences to sensitive-aesthetic ones; prefers active-dynamic behaviors to controlled, mediating, caring ones; tends to react robustly and aggressively to situations rather than sensitively and cooperatively

Behavior styles

Emotional Arousal

Is irritable; is easily confused by uncomfortable conditions and emotional stress; is easily frustrated by resistance

Lack of Self-Control

Has difficulties in suppressing own needs and complying with the instructions and demands of teachers; readily infringes social rules of play; does not like to admit own weaknesses and likes to use excuses; only obeys rules when supervised; easily loses control over own behavior

(continued)

TABLE 2.9
(Continued)

Extraversion

Exhibits spontaneous activity and social initiative; enjoys mastering difficult situations; is cheerful

Social Shyness

Is reticent about social contacts, avoids social confrontation; dislikes approaching others; feels inhibited in the presence of others; is quiet and timid

Aspects of self-image

General Anxiety

Worries about hurting him or herself or becoming ill; is afraid of the dark, being alone, new things, and uncertainty; has trouble falling asleep because of fears and is frightened and has nightmares during the night; is frightened and nervous when threatened

Self-Confidence

Is confident in forming opinions and making decisions; believes that own opinions are recognized by others; is decisive in planning own goals; believes in the success of own efforts and the attainment of own goals; believes in own abilities--even when tackling difficult problems; is convinced of being loved by most people

Impulsiveness

Strong mobility drive; tends to be neglectful; is less tidy and does not keep possessions very neat; finds it hard to be patient and to accept advantages for others; is not very persistent in solving tasks; has to rest repeatedly; allows others to help him or her and gives up quickly

Self-Enhancement

Wants to receive attention and seeks attention through own behavior; considers that he or she is more, possesses more, has experienced more than others; has a better opinion of self than of others; likes to show off own strengths

Inferiority

Views others more positively than self; considers that he or she achieves less than others; admires others because they can do something better than he or she can; wants to be like others found that some of these relations showed strong qualitative and quantitative gender differences. For this reason, the findings reported in Table 2.10 are split according to gender. The table only reports correlations that are statistically significant on at least the 5% level. Furthermore, stepwise multiple correlations were computed that used each personality scale assessed with the PFK 9–14 during childhood to predict the 16 PF scales measured 16 years later.[18] In cases in which more than one aspect of childhood personality contributed to predicting a feature of personality in early adulthood, Table 2.10 also gives the multiple correlation coefficient as a measure for the interaction of several aspects of child personality in predicting adult personality.[19]

A first glance at Table 2.10 shows that one aspect of adult personality—rule-consciousness—cannot be predicted on the basis of child personality in either the male or female samples. One possible explanation for this is that the conception of the PFK 9–14 does not pay any attention to this feature. However, it is also conceivable that this facet of adult personality, which is a major indicator for the extent of norm commitment and adjustment, does not yet have a strong counterpart in childhood and early adolescent personality profiles.

A second conspicuous aspect in the table is the differences in the predictability of adult personality in women and men on the basis of their childhood personality. Apart from the 16 PF scale "Rule-consciousness," which is not predictable for either gender, no personality correlates in early childhood can be found for four further aspects of adult personality in young women, compared with only one personality characteristic in young men. For adult female personality, these are the 16 PF scales "Vigilance," "Abstractedness," "Privateness," and "Tension," whereas in men the scale "Dominance" cannot be predicted from characteristics of child personality.

Those aspects of adult personality that cannot be predicted in women relate particularly to a careful and distanced self-presentation that takes the consequences of one's own behavior into account. Possibly, these facets of personality development only become relevant at a later stage during the female biography, so that it is not yet possible to find correspondences in childhood personality. This interpretation is supported by the finding that there seem to be no precursors for individual differences in the extent of inner tension and nervousness in the personality of young girls, whereas this is one of the most highly predictable personality characteristics in boys (cf. the scores on the 16 PF dimension "Tension"). Therefore, it would seem as if girls are initially less inhibited in expressing their behavior, and perhaps they "censor" it less. This can also be derived from the fact that the self-confident aspect of their child personality is also a better predictor of adulthood than in boys (cf. the findings on the 16 PF scale "Social boldness"). However, because the differences that young women exhibit in the earlier mentioned

TABLE 2.10
Relations Between PFK 9-14 (1976) and 16 PF (1992)

16 PF scales	Sons (n = 98)		Daughters (n = 99)	
Warmth	*Impulsiveness*	.25**	*Academic Ambition*	.28**
	Inferiority	.20	Extraversion	.23**
	Extraversion	.19	Self-Enhancement	.21*
			Dependence on Adults	.21*
Emotional Stability	*Self-Assertion*	-.20*	*Dependence on Adults*	.22*
	Social Commitment	.19*		
Dominance			*Self-Enhancement*	.32**
			Academic Ambition	.29**
			Self-Confidence	.23
			Self-Assertion	.20*
			Lack of Self-Control	.17*
Liveliness	*Impulsiveness*	.27**	*Extraversion*	.37**
	Inferiority	.21	*Social Shyness*	-.33**
			Academic Ambition	.33**
			Social Commitment	.23*
			Self-Confidence	.18*
Rule-consciousness				$R = .41$**

(table continues)

TABLE 2.10
(Continued)

16 PF scales	Sons (n = 98)		Daughters (n = 99)	
Social Boldness	Social Commitment	.25**	Extraversion	.46**
	Extraversion	.19*	Academic Ambition	.40**
	Masculinity	.17*	Social Shyness	-.38**
			Dependence on Adults	.34**
			Social Commitment	.30**
			Lack of Self-Control	-.15
				R = .51**
Sensitivity	Academic Ambition	.26**	Masculinity	-.22**
			Self-Assertion	-.20*
			Lack of Self-Control	-.17*
Vigilance	Masculinity	.25**		
	Lack of Self-Control	.17**		
Abstractedness	Social Shyness	.21*		
	Self-Sufficiency	.19*		
	Extraversion	.18*		
	Masculinity	-.17*		
		R = .36**		

(table continues)

58

16 PF scales	Sons (n = 98)		Daughters (n = 99)	
Privateness	Extraversion	-.22**	Dependence on Adults	-.24**
	General Anxiety	.21	Social Shyness	.21*
	Dependence on Adults	-.21*	Extraversion	-.20*
	Self-Assertion	.19	Inferiority	.20*
	Social Shyness	-.15	Impulsiveness	.17*
		R = .35**	General Anxiety	.15*
				R = .32**
Apprehension	Emotional Arousability	.23**		
	Academic Ambition	.19*		
	General Anxiety	.18*		
	Social Commitment	-.17*		
		R = .33**		
Openness to Change	Extraversion	.28**	Lack of Self-Control	.17*
	Self-Enhancement	.23**		
	Self-Confidence	.20*		
Self-Reliance	Self-Sufficiency	.25**	Social Shyness	.29**
			Dependence on Adults	-.20*
			Inferiority	.19*

(table continues)

59

TABLE 2.10
(Continued)

16 PF scales		Sons (n = 98)		Daughters (n = 99)	
Perfectionism	Self-Sufficiency	-.22**	Impulsiveness	-.29**	
	General Anxiety	-.22	Lack of Self-Control	-.22*	
	Impulsiveness	-.22	Emotional Arousability	-.17*	
	Self-Assertion	-.22			
	Social Shyness	-.22			
Tension	Masculinity	.27**			
	General Anxiety	.22*			
	Emotional Arousability	.21			
	Self-Assertion	.20*			
	Impulsiveness	.20*			
	Self-Confidence	-.19*			
	Lack of Self-Control	.18*			
	Social Commitment	-.18*			
	Extraversion	-.15			
		R = .42**			

* p < .05. ** p < .01.

60

personality characteristics can nonetheless be assessed with a high reliability, there is some indication that they have gone through a stronger change in personality during youth and early adulthood that is less predictable on the basis of childhood personality than is the case in young men.

The differences in personality predictions for both genders can also be seen when each best predicted trait in adult personality is compared separately according to gender. For the sample of young men, three of the four most predictable personality characteristics have absolutely no correspondence in the women's child personality. These are, in the sequence of high predictability, the 16 PF scales "Tension" ($r = .42$), "Abstractedness" ($r = .36$), and "Privateness" ($r = .35$). The dimension "Apprehension" ($r = .33$) can be predicted almost equally strongly from the child personality data for both men and women. A closer look at the aspects of child personality that predict individual personality characteristics produces the following picture in men:

1. *Tension.* The more that young men had already focused on a masculine role understanding as children—while simultaneously exhibiting a stronger degree of anxiety, emotional arousal, and a lack of self-control, coupled with a low social orientation—the more they present themselves as easily aroused, nervous, and less relaxed in adulthood as well. What is particularly surprising is the lack of control of affective impulses linked to the male gender role stereotype that probably expresses itself in childhood as an anxiety-motivated acting out of affective conflicts, whereas in adulthood it is internalized as a high level of inner tension. These are the young men who tend to easily "fly off the handle" and have great difficulty in bringing their pent-up emotions under control.

2. *Abstractedness.* Men who tend to deviate from the norm and look for new paths without being held back by set constraints and the opinions of others reveal an interesting personality constellation during childhood. On the one hand, they tend to work out their problems by themselves and avoid social contacts with others. On the other hand, they exhibit an attitude that suggests initiative and optimism in coping with problems. A further feature of these boys is that they tend not to orient themselves toward a male gender role stereotype, but are more sensitive and thus have a more feminine attitude. These may marginalize them in the male peer group, and thus further strengthen their nonconformism.

3. *Privateness.* The more that young adult men exhibit a deliberate, foresighted attitude and can adapt themselves skillfully to social situations, the more likely it is that they belonged to those children who exhibited less spontaneous activity without being socially inhibited. In addition, as children, they were less anxious, but also less interested in imposing their ideas aggressively on others. They also tended not to orient their behavior toward the demands and models of adult authority persons. In all, even in childhood,

this reveals the picture of a social style of internal distancing and careful deliberation. In adulthood, this social style is reflected in diplomatic calculations and social refinement—at times, even with a dash of strategically applied cunning—in order to master difficult situations without disclosing too much of themselves.

4. Apprehension. Although this personality characteristic is equally predictable in both men and women on the basis of childhood personality, there are some major gender differences in the childhood characteristics that are relevant for this prediction. For men, a high level of guilt-proneness has its roots in a strong emotional irritability and general anxiety in childhood, accompanied by high academic achievement motivation and greater social distance to others. Therefore, a pattern of relations can be seen whose internal dynamics consist of high self-appointed achievement goals and accompanying fears of failure, which create a higher internal arousal that is stabilized or even strengthened by a lack of social commitment. These may be those men who suffer from the strongest self-doubts, particularly in achievement situations or in the challenges confronting them in their careers.

Turning to the women, it is clear that, as mentioned earlier, the aspects that predict adult personality on the basis of childhood personality differ for women in comparison to men. The four most striking findings, ranked according to the closeness of the relationship between childhood and adult personality, refer to the 16 PF scales "Social boldness" ($r = .51$), "Liveliness" ($r = .41$), "Dominance" ($r = .32$), and "Apprehension" ($r = .32$). These are addressed in more detail later, where we also contrast the findings on the female sample with the corresponding findings on the male sample.

1. Social Boldness. The precursors in childhood personality for self-assurance among women are, above all, extraverted temperament, low social shyness or high social commitment, and high pride in academic achievement, coupled with an orientation toward the norms specified by adult reference persons. Two aspects are conspicuous: a strong willingness to be active in the socioemotional domain, and an attitude conforming to adult norms that probably allows their active and extraverted temperament to unfold without conflict. Both aspects are highly interpretable as integral components of a behavior pattern in girls that may be able to command a high level of social acceptance. In some ways, this behavior pattern reflects the aspect of female autonomy that conforms to gender norms, and finally expresses itself as a specific female kind of self-assurance in adulthood.

Social commitment and extraversion are—as in the women—also childhood precursors of self-assurance in young men. Interestingly, the adult-oriented aspects are lacking. Instead, a masculine gender role orientation associates with the childhood personality pattern that later expresses itself as self-assurance. However, it should not be ignored that the relationship between childhood and adult personality is generally much less close than in women. Nonetheless, the latter finding indicates that, in men as well, the extent of self-assurance is linked to earlier behavior that conforms to gender roles.

2. Liveliness. Interestingly, this dimension of adult personality reveals a similar pattern of female childhood personality to that described earlier for the scale "Social boldness." Once more, an active-extraverted temperament, low social shyness, and a high level of social commitment, coupled with a strong academic achievement motivation, are the most marked signs of childhood personality that result in a later capacity for spontaneity and enthusiasm. However, the adult-dependent components are lacking. They are replaced by the element of personal belief in one's own abilities. In all, however, female self-assurance and enthusiasm mostly grow from similar roots in childhood personality.

The men reveal a pattern of childhood personality that can be discriminated clearly from that of the women, although it does not reveal such a clear pattern. The precursors of capacity for liveliness in men are, above all, a high degree of impulsiveness and volatility that is accompanied, although to a lesser extent, by higher perceived inferiority. Thus, the childhood preconditions for capacity for spontaneity and enthusiasm in men seem to have much more negative connotations than in women. Girls use their active temperament to strengthen their autonomy within the context of their social relations, and thus stabilize the core of their personality—without losing their positive joy of expression—whereas the expression of spontaneity in men seems to be based more on an unbridled temperament and a more insecure self-esteem.

3. Dominance. Unlike young men, in whom absolutely no relations with childhood personality can be confirmed for this characteristic of adult personality, women exhibit the clear contours of a corresponding personality picture in childhood. Women who are very self-assured as young adults show a strong childhood tendency to put themselves in the limelight and draw the attention of others. This general need for attention from others is also expressed in the school context through an active demonstration of ambition and a search for recognition within the class. In addition, these girls believe very strongly in themselves and the correctness of their opinions, and they tend to assert their needs with a degree of aggressiveness.

Accordingly dominance in young adult women has to be prepared with comparatively strong ingredients in childhood that result in an active, if not aggressive, self-display. Interestingly, there is no comparable pattern of childhood personality in boys. One conceivable explanation for this is that the socialization of boys is, in any case, directed more strongly toward dominance. As a result, they do not have to fight so much for attention as girls, who have to break out of their stereotyped gender roles.

4. Apprehension. Earlier in this chapter, we reported that apprehension in boys feeds on the self-doubts in achievement situations that can be ascertained in childhood. Girls reveal a different picture. A greater distance to adults, but also a greater social shyness or lack of social openness in general, provide the best prediction that they will worry more and take criticism more to heart when they are young women. Another aspect is that, even as children, they show weak self-esteem. Thus, it seems as if girls, in contrast to boys, particularly develop signs of emotional instability when they are not integrated sufficiently into a secure and supportive social context. This again shows—as we have reported for other aspects of female personality development—the particularly important function of social relations in determining development.

The findings on the relationship between childhood and adult personality on the questionnaire level are summarized later. Findings on the filial generation obtained from an analysis of self- and other ratings of personality in the 16-year comparison are presented first.

Personality Development in the Children's Generation in Terms of Self- and Other Ratings

In contrast to the assessment of child and adult personality with personality questionnaires, the medium of personality ratings permits a direct comparison between 1976 and 1992 for the filial generation as well. Here, we used the same inventory of rating scales already presented in the section on the results for the parent generation. The content of the scales was described in Table 2.5. As in the parent generation, the following results refer to the four global personality dimensions that crystallized out of the 12 rating scales: (a) "Weak versus strong willpower," (b) "Introversion versus extraversion," (c) "Sober egocentrism versus emotional empathy," and (d) "Instability versus emotional balance."[20]

First of all, we consider the differential stabilities of the personality ratings (i.e., whether, and to what extent, the filial generation has retained its individual scores on real self-image from childhood to adulthood). Because the two parents rated the personality of their children in both 1976 and 1992, we can also include the differential stabilities of mothers' and fathers' ratings of their children's real self-image. These findings are reported in Table 2.11.

It is conspicuous that the mean stability coefficients for sons and daughters are only moderately high. Compared with the parent generation, in which the corresponding values are, on average, about $r = .50$, the children's mean of $r = .25$ indicates a much weaker relation across time. This is an initial indication that clear changes have occurred in the scores on various personality dimensions during youth and early adulthood. This trend places

TABLE 2.11
Relative Stabilities of Real Self- and Other Ratings of Child Personality

Personality rating scales	Sons (n = 84)			Daughters (n = 84)		
	Self	Mother	Father	Self	Mother	Father
Weak Willpower vs. Strong Willpower	.23*	.29*	.20*	.28*	.38**	.37**
Introversion vs. Extraversion	.09	.34**	.27*	.30*	.25*	.36**
Sober Egocentrism vs. Emotional Empathy	.26*	.26*	.00	.14	.46**	.42**
Instability vs. Emotional Balance	.36**	.42**	.12	.30*	.34**	.27**
Mean correlations	.24*	.33**	.15	.26*	.36**	.36**

* $p < .05$. ** $p < .01$.

major limitations on any prediction of adult personality on the basis of childhood self-ratings.

In predictive terms, the parents' ratings of their children are somewhat more favorable, with one exception. Across the 16-year comparison, they have generally retained a more stable picture of their children than the children have done of themselves. The exception is that fathers perceive a notably lower stability of personality in their sons compared with their daughters. Fathers also differ clearly from mothers here, who report much more stable personality ratings for both their sons and daughters. It is hard to say what has caused this loss of stability in the fathers' personality ratings of their sons. One conceivable explanation is that fathers perceive the sons as having changed more strongly in general than their daughters on the individual personality dimensions. This can also be confirmed by comparing the fathers' mean personality ratings of their sons for 1976 and 1992. This stronger change in the personality of sons compared with daughters from the fathers' perspectives generally takes a positive direction. On average, fathers assign their adult sons much more willpower and emotional stability than they did when they were still children.

Another question is whether and how far children and their parents agree in their ratings of real childhood self-image. This concerns the level of agreement between self- and other ratings in terms of perceived differences in childhood personality. Table 2.12 reports these findings, as well as how far the parents agree among themselves in their ratings of their children's personalities. The general pattern of correlations in Table 2.12 provides a clear picture that can be summarized as follows.

1. The mean agreement between the children's self-ratings and their parents' other ratings is $r = .34$. These correlations tend to be lower for sons (S) compared with daughters (D; $r_S = .31$ vs. $r_D = .36$). In addition, parent–child agreement tended to be somewhat lower in 1976 than in 1992 ($r_{1976} = .31$; $r_{1992} = .37$). In general, these findings indicate that there is a moderate relationship between children's self-ratings and the parent ratings of their children at different ages that is higher than the level of the differential stability coefficients.

2. With a mean correlation of $r = .53$, interparent agreement on the personality ratings of their children is markedly higher than the agreement between parents and children ($r = .34$). Variations due to the children's gender or the time of the survey had no significant impact on this. Thus, parents have a comparatively well-coordinated picture of the personality differences in their children that clearly is retained across time.

One possible explanation for the higher level of agreement in the parents' ratings is that the parents have clearer and more fixed ideas on the meaning of the individual personality scales than their children. Children first have to acquire the meaning of the abstractly formulated personality rating scales

TABLE 2.12
Agreements Between Real Self- and Other Ratings of Child Personality in 1976 and 1992

Personality rating scales		Sons (n = 84)			Daughters (n = 84)		
		S/M	S/F	M/F	D/M	D/F	M/F
Weak Willpower vs. Strong Willpower	1976	.22*	.28*	.59**	.41**	.38**	.56**
	1992	.26*	.36**	.56**	.46**	.49**	.61**
Introversion vs. Extraversion	1976	.29*	.33**	.66**	.34**	.39**	.45**
	1992	.26*	.36**	.54**	.54**	.48**	.49**
Sober Egocentrism vs. Emotional Empathy	1976	.28*	.22*	.51**	.26*	.18	.54**
	1992	.19*	.20*	.44**	.26*	.27*	.35**
Instability vs. Emotional Balance	1976	.33**	.31*	.45**	.28*	.35**	.54**
	1992	.40**	.52**	.57**	.43**	.38**	.56**
Mean correlations	1976	.28*	.29*	.55**	.32**	.33**	.52**
	1992	.31*	.36**	.53**	.39**	.41**	.50**

Note. S/M = Son/Mother; S/V = Son/Father; M/F = Mother/Father; D/M = Daughter/Mother; D/V = Daughter/Father; * $p < .05$. ** $p < .01$.

during the course of their further development. The fact that there is a certain degree of increasing similarity in agreements between parents and children over time provides some support for this interpretation. In addition, parents have probably exchanged information about the particularities of their children's personalities more frequently among themselves than with their children. This, in turn, may represent the basis for a stronger consensus in the parents' impressions of their children.

It should also be considered that the agreement between parents is based on two other ratings, whereas the parent–child agreements are based on a comparison between self- and other ratings. Research has shown that it is generally easier to make dispositional judgments about other persons than about oneself because one's own behavior is viewed as being much more situation-dependent than that of others.[21] Therefore, it can be anticipated that correlations between self- and other ratings of personality will be lower than correlations based exclusively on ratings by others.

So far, we have dealt only with the differential stabilities or self- and other rating agreements in the judgment of personality differences in the children's generation. We now turn to the constancy or change in individual personality dimensions among the children's generation. We do this by comparing the mean scores in 1976 and 1992 on the real self-image ratings of the four personality dimensions combined into profiles. Because some of these changes were found to be sensitive to gender, Fig. 2.5 reports separate personality profiles for sons and daughters.

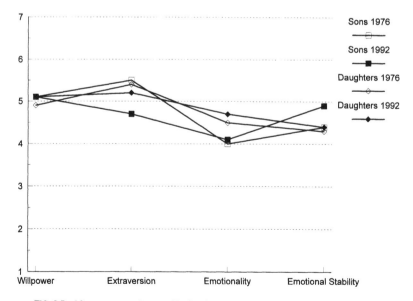

FIG. 2.5. Mean personality profile (real image ratings) of the children for 1976 and 1992.

The first conspicuous finding in the figure is that mean personality changes in sons are stronger than in daughters. This applies particularly to the dimensions "Introversion versus extraversion" and "Instability versus emotional balance" (in both cases, $p < .001$). First, the sons view themselves as being much less extraverted in 1992 (i.e., less cheerful, lively, and open), which also indicates that they have distanced themselves from their own ideal self-image. However, at the same time, they have developed more emotional balance, and thus reduced the discrepancy with their ideal self.

Changes across time on two personality dimensions can also be ascertained in the daughters, but in both cases these are only marginally significant ($p < .05$). Individually, daughters have developed stronger willpower over the course of time (i.e., in adulthood, they perceive themselves as being more able to assert themselves, as having more stamina, and as being more ambitious than they were in childhood). At the same time, this has also brought them closer to their ideal selves. The same applies to the slight increase in emotionality that expresses itself in self-ratings such as sensitive, emotional, and adaptable. This dimension also shows a strong difference between the genders that is retained across time. This provides a clear picture of the characteristic gender role stereotype for this aspect of personality, according to which women are more sensitive and emotional and men more robust and sober.

In all, the changes in personality in the children's generation revealed in ratings of their real self-image are much stronger than those for the parent generation, and it is particularly sons who contribute to these changes. We consider it a matter of some concern that sons perceive a clear loss of their original liveliness and social openness over the course of time, and this contradicts their ideal personality. In youth and young adulthood, the effects of male socialization seem to have a more negative impact on this aspect of personality development. A search for the specific reasons for this will require a more detailed examination that should also include such aspects as the occupational and social biography of the men.

PERSONALITY DEVELOPMENT IN THE PARENT AND CHILDREN'S GENERATIONS: A COMPARISON

After investigating the question of constancy and change in personality for the parent and the children's generations, we finally present findings on some comparisons between the generations.

Comparisons on the Questionnaire Level

First of all, we consider the intergenerational comparisons that can be made on the basis of personality questionnaires. Table 2.12 reports mean scores on the 16 PF scales for the parent and children's generations. We can perform generation comparisons for 1992 only because no comparable personality data are available for the children's generation in 1976. Nonetheless, we have also entered the parent generation's mean scores in the first wave in the table because this allows us to ascertain whether a developmental trend that can be confirmed in the parent generation also continues in the children's generation or takes the opposite direction. Therefore, we have first—for the parent generation—computed the difference between the means for 1976 and 1992 on each 16 PF scale. This is called the *age effect* of the parent generation. We have also computed a second difference between the mean scores of the parent and children's generations in 1992, and thus defined a measure for the generation effect. These values are also reported in Table 2.13, along with information on the statistical significance of the differences between means.

We first look at the differences between means on the 16 PF scales for the parent and children's generations in 1992. These are presented in the last column of Table 2.13. Significant generation effects can be confirmed for 11 of the 15 scales. If these differences are classified according to the five second-order personality dimensions that can be formed from the primary scales of

TABLE 2.13
Age and Generation Effects for the 16 PF Scales

16 PF scales	Parents (n = 422)		Children (n = 192)	Age effect parents	Generation effect
	1976	1992	1992		
Warmth	6.43	7.12	7.46	+ 0.69*	+ 0.34
Emotional Stability	8.57	8.46	8.66	- 0.11	+ 0.20
Dominance	4.59	4.63	5.79	+ 0.04	+ 1.16*
Liveliness	5.26	5.23	6.87	- 0.03	+ 1.64*
Rule-Consciousness	7.97	8.39	5.76	+ 0.42*	- 2.63*
Social Boldness	6.31	6.94	7.65	+ 0.63*	- 0.74*
Sensitivity	5.81	6.33	6.42	+ 0.52*	+ 0.09
Vigilance	6.32	5.95	6.56	- 0.37*	+ 0.61*
Abstractedness	3.69	4.61	5.43	+ 0.92*	+ 0.82*
Privateness	5.97	6.09	3.54	- 0.12	- 2.55*
Apprehension	4.33	4.37	3.98	+ 0.04	- 0.39
Openness to Change	6.54	6.12	8.31	- 0.42*	+ 2.19*
Self-Reliance	4.09	4.45	3.47	+ 0.36*	- 0.98*
Perfectionism	8.25	8.05	6.97	- 0.20	- 1.08*
Tension	7.15	6.96	7.71	- 0.19	+ 0.75*

*$p < .05$.

the 16 PF, it becomes clear that differences on the primary scale level particularly load on two of these second-factor personality dimensions—namely, "Self-control" and "Independence." The younger generation shows a much lower measure of norm commitment, which means that sons and daughters are less dutiful than their parents, but more open to change, unconventional, uninhibited, and spontaneous. Two of these personality characteristics—namely, "Rule-consciousness" and "Openness to change"—reveal a statistically significant change in the parent generation between 1976–1992. The extent of dutifulness has increased, whereas an experimenting attitude has decreased. This heightens the differences between the generations because the children's generation in 1992 reveal a much lower dutifulness and a higher orientation to change in comparison with the parents in 1992 and 1976. In both cases, the age effect seems to run contrary to the epochal trend that reveals a general shift toward more flexibility and openness. However, in some cases, the difference between the generations is not so apparent because, between 1976 and 1992, development in the parent generation has taken a direction that brings it closer to the level of the children's generation in 1992. This is the case, for example, for the personality characteristic "Abstractedness," which is also an indicator for norm commitment. The parent generation has become less conventional over the 16 years, and thus has come closer to the mean score of its children, although the difference remains significant. In this case, it is assumed that the age effect takes the same direction as the trend in the epochal change characterized by a generally higher level of unconventionality and less pragmatism.

Alongside a much lower norm commitment in the younger generation, there is also a clear generation difference for the second-order personality dimension "Independence." In detail, this means that the children's generation shows higher levels of self-assertion, self-confidence, skepticism, and enthusiasm than the parents. Interestingly, the parents' age effect for skepticism runs counter to the generation difference. In other words, parents have become more open to trust over time, whereas their children exhibit a level of reserve toward others that is even higher than their parents' level in 1976. We have to ask ourselves whether this finding should be interpreted as a reaction to a social system in which being careful, on one's mettle, and mistrusting have a high adaptation level in order to survive. However, the findings also indicate that there has been a general trend toward more dominance. Even the parent generation reveals a slight increase in self-assertion between 1976 and 1992 that is then overtaken by the children's generation. It looks as if this age effect in the parent generation proceeds hand in hand with an epochal change. Hence, this aspect also contributes to the total picture of a development in personality that is characterized by more independence.

A Digression on Estimating Epochal Effects of Personality Development

The previous section frequently spoke about epochal effects of personality development. However, the data do not provide any direct empirical access to a quantitative determination of such effects. What can be directly derived from the data is age effects for the parent generation. These can be found by determining the extent of personality change in the parents—who were, on average, 42 years old in 1976 and about 58 years old in 1992—as the difference in each personality characteristic between the two waves. Second, generation effects can be assessed for the year 1992 in the individual personality characteristics by ascertaining the difference on the corresponding personality scores between, on average, the 58-year-old parents and 28-year-old children in 1992. To ascertain an epochal or time-change effect for the 28-year-olds on an empirical basis, it would have been necessary to give the 16 PF to a sample of 28-year-olds in 1976 and then repeat this study 16 years later, when the members of this sample were an average of 44 years old.[22] The difference between the personality scores of this hypothetical sample of 28-year-olds in 1976 and the sample of 28-year-olds actually studied in 1992 would have generated a value that would reflect an epochal effect.

Unfortunately, we do not possess such data, and therefore we are unable to make direct, empirically based statements on this question. However, by making certain assumptions, we can attempt to estimate the epochal effect for the individual personality scales of the 16 PF. A relatively simple estimation can be based on two assumptions. First, it can be assumed that the generation difference between the 56-year-old parent and the 28-year-old children's generation measured in 1992 is distributed in equal amounts per year across the age difference between the two generations. This would mean that the age group of 44-year-olds in 1992 (i.e., those who are 12 years younger than the parent generation) would be assigned a proportion of 12/28 or 3/7 of the generation difference between the parent and children's generations. This gives us the value that the hypothetical sample of 28-year-olds in 1976 would have produced 16 years later.

A second assumption is that the age effect for the years 1976–1992 takes the same course regardless of the age of the samples in 1976. In other words, the age effect ascertained for the parent generation, which refers to the age of the roughly 40- to 56-year-olds, is the same as that for the hypothetical sample of 28-year-olds in 1976, who would have been 44 in 1992.

If both assumptions are valid, each mean personality score for the 28-year-olds can be determined for 1976 by starting with the generation difference of the 28- and 44-year-olds in 1992 and computing backward to the age effect for the 28-year-olds in 1976. The difference between the personality score of the 28-year-olds in 1976 and 1992 is then the estimated epochal effect for the personality characteristic in question.

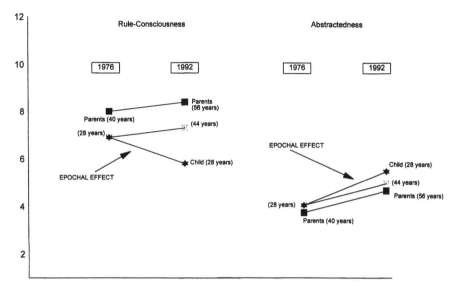

FIG. 2.6. Illustration of the estimated epochal effect for two 16 PF scales.

This line of thought is illustrated in Fig. 2.6. We have selected two primary scales of the 16 PF that represent the second-order factor personality dimension "Self-control." The one scale—"Rule-consciousness"—reveals a trend for the age effect that runs counter to the suspected epochal effect, whereas in the other scale—"Abstractedness"—both the suspected epochal effect and the age effect take the same direction.

The first thing to note about Fig. 2.6 is that the two scales' positive poles each carry high "loadings." The empirical scores are marked with solid squares (parent generation) or stars (children's generation). The scores for the hypothetical sample based on the two previously mentioned assumptions are marked by crosses. The difference between the 28-year-olds in 1976 and the corresponding age group in 1992 (i.e., the children's generation) marked by an arrow illustrates the estimated epochal effect.

Estimated epochal effects for all 16 PF scales were computed in the way described earlier. These are presented in Table 2.14. For comparative purposes, the table also displays once more the values for the corresponding age and generation effects. Under the assumption of approximately homogeneous variances in the samples used in the comparison (which is particularly important for the hypothetical sample), an estimated epochal effect that is larger than +0.5 can claim statistical significance. A glance at the table reveals that the estimated epochal effects increase or decrease depending on whether they take the same or opposite direction to the age effects. However, in all, the highest epochal effects are particularly found for per-

TABLE 2.14
Age, Generation, and Estimated Epochal Effects for the 16 PF Scales

16 PF scales	Age effect	Generation effect	Estimated epochal effect
Warmth	0.7	0.4	0.9
Emotional Stability	-0.1	0.2	0.0
Dominance	0.0	0.8	0.5
Liveliness	-0.1	1.7	0.9
Rule-Consciousness	0.4	-2.6	-1.1
Social Boldness	0.6	0.8	1.1
Sensitivity	0.5	0.1	0.6
Vigilance	-0.3	0.6	0.0
Abstractedness	0.9	0.8	1.4
Privateness	-0.1	-2.5	-1.5
Apprehension	0.1	-0.4	-0.1
Openness to Change	-0.4	2.1	0.9
Self-Reliance	0.4	-1.0	-0.2
Perfectionism	-0.2	-1.1	-0.8
Tension	-0.2	0.7	0.2

sonality characteristics that represent the second-order personality dimension "Self-control," in line with the generation effects reported previously.

To gain a more systematic picture of the impact of the estimated epochal effects on individual personality characteristics, the primary scales of the 16 PF have been categorized into their five second-order personality dimensions, and the corresponding scores for the epochal effects have been given.[23] Minus scores represent a lower "loading" on the second-order personality dimension or the first-mentioned aspect of the bipolar primary scale.

The values in Table 2.15 confirm that, in general, epochal effects take the direction of less self-control and higher independence, but also lower tough-mindedness. In other words, the children's generation (i.e., the generation of 28-year-olds in 1992) differ clearly from 28-year-olds in 1976 on these three personality dimensions. However, it is also interesting to see which domains of personality do not reveal significant effects. In general, these are those personality characteristics that represent the degree of anxiety and extraversion. According to our computational procedure, these do not discriminate between the group of 28-year-olds in 1976 and those in 1992.

TABLE 2.15
Estimated Epochal Effects for the 16 PF Second-Order Dimensions

16 PF second-order factors	Estimated epochal effect
Self-Control	
Rule-Consciousness	-1.1
Openness to Change (-)	-0.9
Abstractedness (-)	-1.4
Privateness	-1.5
Perfectionism	-0.8
Mean	-1.14
Anxiety	
Apprehension (-)	-0.1
Perfectionism	-0.8
Emotional Stability	0.0
Vigilance	0.0
Tension	-0.2
Social Boldness	1.1
Mean	0.00
Independence	
Dominance	0.5
Social Boldness	1.1
Vigilance	0.0
Liveliness	0.9
Mean	0.63
Tough-Mindedness	
Sensitivity (-)	-0.6
Warmth (-)	-0.9
Abstractedness (-)	-1.4
Social Boldness (-)	-1.1
Mean	-1.00
Extraversion	
Self-Reliance (-)	0.2
Liveliness	0.9
Warmth	0.9
Abstractedness (-)	-1.4
Perfectionism (-)	0.8
Dominance (-)	-0.5
Mean	0.15

Note. Negatively poled scales are marked with a minus sign.

This digression is rounded off by pointing out once more that the computation of the estimated epochal effects is based on an artificial measure that is used—on the basis of two assumptions—to derive an indirect value for each personality characteristic from the age and generation effects. Therefore, these are estimates that do not refer to a direct empirical base. Consequently, it is recommended that the aspect of epochal effects should also be taken into account when planning future studies of this kind.

Comparisons on the Level of Personality Ratings

After this digression, we return to the age and generation effects in the personality development of parents and children. This section started with the corresponding changes on the basis of questionnaire data, and now turns to a generation comparison of self- and other ratings of personality. This section concentrates on the real self-image of the parent and children's generations. In this case, such information is available for both generations at both waves. Table 2.16 reports the mean scores for the four dimensions of personality self-ratings without any separation for gender.

First, the table repeats the finding, already described separately for both parent and children's generations, that the children's generation has changed more strongly over the course of time than the parent generation. In these aggregated figures for both genders, the parent generation shows only a slight change across the 16 years in the direction of being more easygoing and relaxed on the dimension "Instability versus emotional balance." Otherwise, no statistically confirmed changes can be found.

Things are different in the children's generation, where one finds a general trend toward more introversion—an effect that, nonetheless, as presented in more detail earlier, can be traced back particularly to the male members of the children's generation. There is also an increase in emotional balance that, in this case, can be confirmed to the same extent in both genders.

However, it is interesting to see that an assimilation effect is found between the generations on both personality dimensions. In the case of extraversion, the children's generation shows a clear decline across time in liveliness and social openness toward the level of the parent generation, whereas in terms of emotional balance, the children's generation still remains notably below the mean score of their parents, despite a marked increase across time. This finding does not agree with the results obtained in the 16 PF for the second-order personality feature "Anxiety," whose

TABLE 2.16
Mean Real Image Rating in Generation and 16-Year Comparisons

Real image ratings	Generation	1976	1992
Weak Willpower vs. Strong Willpower	Parents Children	5.1 5.0	5.0 5.1
Introversion vs. Extraversion	Parents Children	5.0 5.4	4.9 4.9
Sober Egocentrism vs. Emotional Empathy	Parents Children	4.7 4.3	4.7 4.4
Instability vs. Emotional Balance	Parents Children	4.8 4.3	5.0 4.7

Note. Parents: $n = 409$; children: $n = 192$.

psychological content corresponds roughly to the self-rating dimension "Instability versus emotional balance." The relevant 16 PF scales generally show no marked age and generation effects. One reason for the difference in the self-ratings may be that this dimension reacts particularly sensitively to self-ratings. In addition, the fact that the children's generation had to compensate a deficit in this area attributed to them by their parents—recognizable in the high discrepancy between real and ideal ratings of their children—may have played a role.

A further interesting finding is the existence of a stable difference between the generations on the dimension "Sober egocentrism versus emotional empathy," revealed through the parent generation generally exhibiting a higher level of emotionality. Although there continue to be gender differences in this personality domain, as was seen earlier, in general the young generation (i.e., female members as well) seems to be more robust, more sober, and more committed to a personal point of view. Perhaps this generation difference reflects an attitude in line with the spirit of the times, which makes it necessary—from the perspective of the young generation—to present oneself as "cool," objective, and sovereign.

Finally, it has to be emphasized that, despite the confirmed age and generation differences found in the personality self-ratings, effects are generally not as strong as those in the diverse scales of the 16 PF. The findings based on questionnaire data provide a much more detailed picture of age- and generation-related influences on personality development than personality ratings. Nonetheless, the changes in self-ratings also reveal informative trends in terms of different identity constructions across the two generations that mirror the characteristic understanding of the self and the world for each generation.

A BRIEF SUMMARY OF THE MOST IMPORTANT POINTS

- On the questionnaire level, individual differences in adult personality remain remarkably stable over a 16-year period. In concrete terms, this means that persons in the older generation who exhibited a high level of warmth, emotional stability, or low inner tension in 1976 show a similarly high level on these personality characteristics in 1992. Vice versa, those who were particularly reserved, emotionally changeable, or internally tense in 1976 also tend to show a similar pattern of behavior in 1992.

- Against the background of the comparatively high, although in no way complete, relative stability of individual personality differences in personality, we nonetheless find a consistent pattern of change in the parent generation. This expresses itself generally in a consolidation of personal identity, a greater willingness to social openness, and a stronger emphasis on traditionalism.

• There is no indication that mothers' and fathers' personality structures draw closer together over the years. This means that, although both partners share many experiences over 16 years, they retain their individual differences.

• On the level of self- and other ratings of personality, there is also a remarkable stability in the parent generation—for both individual differences and mean scores. Compared with the first wave, the adult generation tends to become less lively and cheerful as it gets older, but it presents itself as being more relaxed and balanced.

• Spouses are able to rate the other partner's individual scores on personality characteristics relatively precisely. Over the course of time, wives can do this better than husbands.

• Personality development in the young generation, which extends from childhood to young adulthood, is highly predictable for a number of personality characteristics. Sometimes clear gender differences appear. For young women, close relations to child personality are found particularly in the socioemotional domain (liveliness and social boldness); in young men, it is predominantly aspects of socioemotional control (pragmatism, privateness) that can be predicated from individual differences in childhood.

• In self-ratings of personality in the children's generation, changes are stronger in young men than in young women. Here as well, this focuses on the aspect of socioemotional control in the young men. Over the course of time, they depict themselves as being less lively, happy, and open, but more balanced emotionally. Among the young women, a slight increase in assertiveness, ambition, and emotionality can be ascertained.

• The relative stability of individual differences in the personality ratings is lower for the children's generation than for the parent generation. However, parents are able to rate individual differences in their children rather precisely, during both childhood and young adulthood.

• Using the available personality data, we estimated epochal effects on personality development. These effects reveal that parents and children have both developed during the 16-year interval—although from a different starting level—toward greater independence, as well as lower self-control and tough-mindedness.

END NOTES

1. This bon mot comes from an interview with the American personality psychologist Raymond B. Cattell in *Psychology Today* (1973, p. 41).

2. Suleika says this to Hatem in Goethe's (1970) *West-östliche Diwan* (see Vol. 2 of G. Spierköt-ter's 10-volume edition of the works of Johann Wolfgang von Goethe, p. 70).
3. Among the many textbooks and edited volumes on personality theories and research, the reader is referred to: Buss and Cantor (1989), Hall and Lindzey (1978), McAdams (1994), McMartin (1995), Pervin (1990), and Phares (1994).
4. The Sixteen Personality Factor Questionnaire (16 PF) was developed by Raymond B. Cattell (Cattell, Eber, & Tatsuoka, 1970). Its first edition dates back to 1949. Since then, the 16 PF has been revised several times. The German adaptation of the 16 PF, on which the findings of this chapter are based, refers to the fourth English edition and was first published in Germany in 1983 (Schneewind, Schröder, & Cattell, 1986, 2nd ed.). In the meantime, the 16 PF Fifth Edition has been published (Russell & Karol, 1994; Conn & Rieke, 1994). A German adaptation of the latest English edition is in preparation.
5. Compare Seitz and Rausche (1992).
6. The results of these efforts are taken from previously unpublished analyses. The item compilation of the 16 PF for the present study based on these analyses is published in the documentation of the study (see Schneewind & Ruppert, 1992).
7. Although the labels of the 16 PF scales are somewhat different in the German adaptation of the 16 PF, we have retained the primary factor scale descriptors as used in the most recent administrator's manual of the 16 PF Fifth Edition (Russell & Karol, 1994, pp. 18–19).
8. Again, the second-order or global factor scales are labeled differently in the German adaptation of the 16 PF. Although some of the primary factor scales show a somewhat different loading pattern on the five global factors, we have decided to leave the original English terminology unchanged. For a fuller description of the five global 16 PF scales, the reader is referred to the administrator's and the technical manual of the 16 PF Fifth Edition (Russell & Karol, 1994; Conn & Rieke, 1994).
9. An excellent description of various aspects of the stability of data in differential and personality psychology can be found in Caspi and Bem (1990).
10. One of the reasons that the stability coefficients reported in Table 2.2 are rather conservative estimates is because we used 6-item instead of 12-item scales for each 16 PF primary factor scale. Had we used the common 12-item scales, we would have obtained much higher stability coefficients based on Spearman–Brown's correction of test length (cf. Guilford, 1965). Thus, for example, the mean stability coefficient of $r = .59$ across all 15 primary scales would have been raised to $r = .74$.
11. See, for example, the work of Heatherton and Weinberger (1994), McCrae and Costa (1990), and Moss and Susman (1980).
12. To test differences between means in interval-scaled data, we used—as in all other similarly designed questions—t tests for dependent and independent samples, as well as multi- and univariate analyses of variance (see Guilford, 1965).
13. These computations are based on the omega-square measure developed by Hays (1963).
14. Compare R. B. Cattell (1989, p. 223).
15. See the method for comparing correlation coefficients proposed by Steiger (1980), which can also be applied to all similar questions in the other chapters of this book.
16. See Schneewind (1992, Vol. 1, pp. 31–32) for a discussion of the problem of linking together personality attributes that refer to the personality rating scales used in this study.
17. See the test manual for the PFK 9–14 (Seitz & Rausche, 1992, pp. 49–52), on which the short descriptions of the 15 personality scales reported in Table 2.9 are based.
18. Not all significant correlations listed in Table 2.10 turned out to have significant beta weights in the corresponding regression analyses. Those with significant beta weights are printed in italics.
19. Here, as in many of the following sections of this book dealing with similar research questions, we have used bivariate and multiple correlation methods or regression analysis. These can be found in any good textbook on psychological statistics (e.g., Guilford, 1965).

Special treatment of these methods can be found in Cohen and Cohen (1983) and Berry and Feldman (1985).

20. See Note 15.

21. Jones and Nisbett (1971) were the first to describe this "actor–observer bias" and investigate it empirically.

22. On the methods of longitudinal research, particularly on research designs using sequence analysis, see Baltes, Reese, and Nesselroade (1977) and Schaie (1965).

23. On the second-order factors of the 16 PF, see Note 8.

3

CRITICAL LIFE EVENTS AND COPING WITH STRESS

The data in our study are based on two waves of measurement separated by 16 years. In 1976 and 1992, the parents and children in our survey provided us with an insight into their personal and family lives. Initial findings on changes and stabilities, based on comparing these two waves on the level of personality, were reported in chapter 2. However, in view of the long time span between the two data collections, we can also ask what has been happening in the lives of the individual families and their members. Such information is particularly important if one wants to go beyond a descriptive comparison of the results from the two waves to study how possible changes or stabilities can be explained.

The ideal case in scientific terms would be if we had been able to follow up our families several times at short intervals between 1976 and 1992. Such data, obtained across the greatest number of waves possible, would have allowed us to find differentiated approaches to explaining what has happened between 1976 and 1992, and plot family developmental courses in detail. However, because we did not use such a longitudinal design, we had to select another approach that would fill this 16-year gap. The concept of "critical life events" seemed to be a good solution.

THE CONCEPT OF "CRITICAL LIFE EVENTS"

When talking about development, one generally has in mind the idea of a more or less continuous change over the course of time. For a long time, developmental psychology viewed the interval between birth and adulthood as the only period of human development. Only in recent years has space been given to the idea that development is not completed with adulthood, but is far more a process that continues throughout adulthood and into old age. This led to the idea of life-span developmental psychology.[1] When looking at developmental processes, this study focuses on precisely those sections of life that scientists have tended to neglect in the past.

The generally accepted idea of development as a continuous process is nonetheless confronted with an experience that any of us can easily understand on the basis of our own lives. During the life course, every person is confronted with striking events that may have a significant impact on their further lives (e.g., the death of an important reference person or the birth of a child). The psychological concept of "critical life events" has been developed to enable us to study the significance and impact of such events for those involved.[2] The most important psychological properties of such a life event are best illustrated with an example.

One well-known example can be found in the story of Christ's apostles. One of the most embittered enemies of budding Christianity was Saul. He persecuted all followers of the new faith. The pursuit of his enemies led him through the desert on his way to Damascus. There, the God whose followers he was oppressing appeared before him. After the shock of this event, he was blinded for 3 days, ate and drank nothing, and finally changed his name from Saul to Paul and became one of the most enthusiastic preachers of the new faith.

Although the critical life events studied in psychological research are generally less spectacular (and do not require any divine interventions), this example nonetheless illustrates the most important features of a critical life event. First, as the term *event* already implies, it concerns something that stands out from the usual stream of everyday life in terms of both time (it is of limited duration) and content (it has the status of something unusual and not everyday). Each critical life event forces the person involved to tackle the event and its consequences. Psychological coping work has to be performed. Depending on the type of event and the personality of the person involved, this can be more or less strenuous and stressful.

The example from the Bible reveals an important characteristic of critical life events: They can (but do not have to) lead to changes in future life. In the biblical example, the change brought about is so obvious that it is even reflected in a change of name: Saul becomes Paul; an opponent of Christianity becomes a supporter. The experience of critical life events hardly ever leads to such drastic change, but this example shows the potential for change, and thus also for growth, that such events may possess.

Indeed, the example illustrates one further important aspect: A critical life event does not necessarily have to be something negative or have negative consequences. The quality of Saul's experience in the desert may perhaps still be open to discussion, whereas the result—the transformation of a violent man into a preacher of love—is a consequence that clearly can be interpreted positively. Adding the term *critical* to life event should not lead one to think that it means only negative experiences with negative consequences. Indeed, a frequently observed phenomenon is that the occurrence of such an event is followed initially by a more negatively toned phase of processing that then ends up in a positive outcome after longer processing. The conversion of Saul also occurred after a rather unpleasant 3 days of blindness and fasting. One of the most important goals of psychological research on life events is to find ways in which one can arrive at positive—or, at least, no longer developmentally impairing—outcomes by applying successful psychological coping strategies after negative events such as the death of a loved one.

This example clarifies that it is not just that an event occurs that is crucial. One also has to consider how the person involved perceives the event, how great the stress is, and which coping strategies are available. These aspects of the perception of a critical life event depend, in part, on the type of event. For example, a death is generally perceived as being negative. However, these aspects also depend, in part, on the attitudes of the person involved. For example, the birth of a child may be perceived as a positive event by one parent, whereas the negative and stressful aspects of the event and its consequences may dominate the perceptions of the other parent.

Therefore, if we want to fill the *tabula rasa* of the 16 years between the two surveys with information on critical life events, it is not enough to just ask what events our respondents have experienced during this time. We also need information on the significance they assigned to these events at the time, or may even still assign to them in the present day.

ASSESSMENT OF CRITICAL LIFE EVENTS

The range of methods for assessing critical life events is as broad as the criticisms raised against them.[3] Our procedure is based on the most frequently used method. We gave our respondents a list of events. For each event on the list, they had to report whether they had experienced it over the last 16 years, and, if yes, how long ago this was. The list reported in Table 3.1 differs for the members of the parent and children's generations because it has to take account of each generation's life situation.

The previously mentioned separations into the perception of events, the stress they bring, and the means of coping with them are covered by the following seven questions that had to be answered for each event that the respondent had experienced:

TABLE 3.1
List of critical Life Events in the study

Death (in family, among relatives, or in circle of friends or acquaintances)	
Serious illness or injury (including chronic diseases)	
Material or economic difficulties	
Particular personal problems (e.g., alcoholism, addiction, strong internal conflicts)	
Job problems (e.g., unemployment, completion of training, new job, problems at work)	for all
Problems in circle of friends (e.g., jjealousy, sexual difficulties, infidelity, separation)	respondents
Problems in partner relationship (e.g., jealousy, sexual difficulties, infidelity)	
Problems in earlier partnerships	
Separation or divorce from (marriage) partner	
Moving home	
Birth of one´s own child	
Particular problems in one´s own family of origin	
Particular problems in one´s spouses´ family of origin	
Special vacation or special journey	
Birth of a grandchild	
Departure of a child from family home	
Departure of last child from family home	for parent
School enrollment of a child	generation
Retirement	only
Marriage of a child	
Separation or divorce of parents	
Birth of a sibling	for children´s
Leaving the family home	generation
Marriage or entering a permanent partnership	only
Starting work	

84

1. Predictability. How predictable was the event even before it occurred?

2. Ability to cope. At the time, how well did you think you would be able to cope with the problems arising through the occurrence of the event?

3. Duration. How long did you have to deal with this event at the time?

4. Former stress. How strong was the stress that you perceived as a result of the event at that time?

5. Current stress. How strong is the stress that you still experience today as a result of the event?

6. Former gain. How far did you believe at that time that coping with this event would help you to improve your life?

7. Current gain. How much do you believe today that dealing with this event has helped you to improve your life?

Each of these questions was answered on a 4-point scale. Thus, scores varied from 1 to 4.[4]

CRITICAL LIFE EVENTS:
TWO ANALYSIS STRATEGIES

There seem to be two basic strategies for analyzing the information gathered on critical life events:

1. Person-Centered Analysis. The units of analysis focused on here are the individual persons or groups of persons who are compared with each other. The number of events that have occurred and the reports on how they are perceived and evaluated are viewed here as "properties" of the persons, regardless of which concrete events a person has experienced. Various groups of persons (generally parents vs. children or men vs. women) are compared in terms of these properties.

2. Event-Centered Analysis. This strategy focuses on the events and their properties. It is possible to compare individual events in terms of their properties, such as frequency of occurrence, stressful impact, and so forth. In addition, we investigate whether these properties can be used to categorize the events presented to our respondents into groups of similar events.

However, when analyzing the data according to one of these two principles, we always have to remember that we are dealing with simplifications. For example, an individual's score on the stress variables is influenced by both their own personality structure and the type of event experienced. Nonetheless, we have chosen to present these results separately here to make them easier to follow.

Person-Centered Analysis

The first steps in a person-centered analysis should, in the sense of the question raised earlier, provide information on what has happened in the lives of our respondents over the last 16 years. The next stages provide a more detailed analysis of how these events are perceived and evaluated.

What Has Happened During the Last 16 Years? If one recalls the features and effects of critical life events described previously, it seems conceivable that a person who has experienced a great number of such events may be overtaxed. However, it is possible that somebody who has experienced no or only a few critical life events may lead a stress-free life, but one that is more one-dimensional and does less to promote development. From this perspective, even information on the mere number of critical life events experienced may provide preliminary insights into the period under study. Figure 3.1 displays the distribution of the number of experienced events for the total sample of parents and children.

On average, seven critical life events per person are reported for the last 16 years. Seventy-five percent of respondents report that they have experienced between 5–10 events. Persons who report either very few or very many events are clearly in the minority. They each make up approximately 12% of the sample. However, these numbers still do not distinguish between the parent generation and the children's generation. One can now ask which of the two generations—the children in the life phase between 9–30 years or the parents in the transition from early to late adult life—has experienced more critical life events. Figure 3.2 compares the distributions for parents and children.

Even a cursory glance reveals that there are no strong differences between parents and children here: The two distributions are identical to a

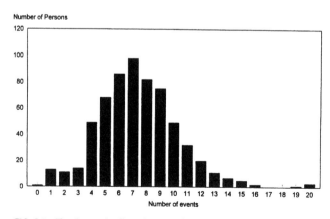

FIG. 3.1. Total sample: Distribution of number of experienced events.

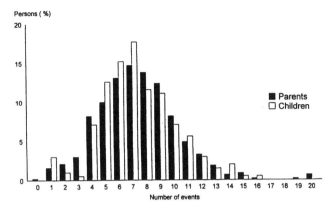

FIG. 3.2. Total Sample: Distribution of number of experienced events split for parents and children.

large extent. Apparently for both generations, their specific section of the entire life span offers approximately equal amounts of challenge or stress in the form of critical life events.

Beyond the mere number of experienced events, the next question is what kinds of event are involved. Table 3.2 ranks the six most frequently experienced events separately for parents and children. The percentages report the portion of the respective sample that has experienced the specific event.

Apart from the events "death" and "vacation or journey," which are experienced frequently in both subsamples, it is conspicuous that the other frequently named events are specific to the personal life situation of each generation. The most frequent critical life events are in line with the normative developmental tasks typical for the specific age group. Although this is not particularly surprising, it nonetheless provides empirical confirmation of existing theories on family development or family developmental tasks.[5]

However, how do things look for events whose occurrence is not linked to specific stages in the family developmental cycle? Table 3.3 compares the percentage frequencies for parents and children. This reveals clear differences in the frequencies with which parents and children experience specific events. It is easy to understand why the percentage of serious illnesses among parents is twice as high as among children. There is sufficient empirical confirmation that the risk of chronic illnesses increases with advancing age. More conspicuous and also more alarming than the difference between parents and children is the finding that 27% of the children (i.e., more than one quarter of them) have already experienced several serious illnesses between the ages of 25–30 years.

The other events reported in the table show an inverse picture. In all, the percentage of children who have experienced the event concerned is much higher than that of parents. Because this always concerns more nega-

TABLE 3.2
Ranking of the Six Most Frequent Events in Parent and Children

Parent Generation (n = 412)	
Departure of a child from family home	90 %
Death	87 %
Marriage of a child	67 %
Departure of last child from family home	56 %
Birth of a grandchild	53 %
Special vacation or special journey	53 %
Children´s Generation (n = 194)	
Leaving the family home	80 %
Starting work	78 %
Marriage or entering a permanent partnership	76 %
Death	75 %
Moving home	73 %
Special vacation or special journey	62 %

TABLE 3.3
Frequencies of Occurrence on Non-Normative Events

EVENT	PARENTS(%) (n = 410)	CHILDREN (%) (n = 194)
Particular personal problems	10	20
Problems in circle of friends	18	33
Job problems	13	36
Problems in partner relationship	17	26
Separation or divorce	6	23
Serious illness or injury	44	24

tive events, one could infer that life in the children's generation is much more difficult and fraught with problems in the personal domain in comparison with their parents. However, an analysis of information on how these events are perceived and evaluated reveals that this interpretation is inadequate. Even at this stage, some alternative explanations for these findings can already be found:

- Because we asked respondents to give retrospective reports over the last 16 years, it is possible that the children's recall is better than that of their parents.
- The children's generation may be more sensitive to such problems and more willing to tackle them, whereas their parents may tend not to perceive them or even to suppress them.
- Even if the children actually experience more problems, a more intensive processing of them may finally mean that the resulting personal gain is greater than the perceived stress.

This again clarifies that the mere fact that a certain event occurs is not sufficient to provide an understanding of the life situation associated with it. Therefore, it seems to be worth turning to the further information available on the subjective aspects of these events.

How Are the Events Perceived? Previously we dealt with how many and which events the parents and children in our sample have experienced. We now want to see how they have assessed the experienced events in terms of stress, duration of coping, and personal gain. The basis of our observations is the answers to the seven questions reported earlier. This information allows us to gain a more precise impression on how the respondents perceive the events of the last 16 years. These data can be analyzed for certain individual events or in aggregate for all the events a person has experienced. We tackle the latter approach first. Thus, each person produces a score for each of the seven questions that reports, for example, how much the person concerned has been stressed in general by all the events that he or she has experienced. We are particularly interested here in the comparison between the parent and children's generations, or, more precisely, in the differences among fathers, mothers, sons, and daughters.

It was noted earlier that the children report far more personal problems and problems with partnerships. So far, several possible hypotheses have been proposed to explain these findings. The following data permit a more unequivocal interpretation of this and other findings. After first presenting a short explanation of what we wanted to find out with each of these questions, we turn to the results of group comparisons.

1. Predictability. A glance at the events list given to our respondents reveals that the question on predictability is redundant for some events, because it is in their nature to be predictable (e.g., the birth of a child). However, other events can occur more or less without any advance warning. Regardless of which type of event is involved, one general theoretical assumption is that the more predictable an event is the less stressful it is.[6] As could be expected, the four groups do not differ regarding predictability. As reported earlier, the most frequently experienced events in both generations are transitions in the cycle of family life, and thus are generally highly predictable.

2. Ability to Cope. Predictability is a property of the specific event on which various persons also agree, whereas whether an event can be coped with depends to a far greater extent on the person judging it. Whether one considers that an event can be coped with well or badly depends on, among others, which competencies and abilities one assigns to oneself. The total mean ability to cope is 3.1. In a range from 1.0 to 4.0, this suggests that the respondents consider the events over the last 16 years to have been generally fairly easy to cope with. Group comparisons reveal interesting differences. It is not, as one might have expected, the difference between parents and children that is statistically significant, but the relation between men (fathers and sons) and women (mothers and daughters). The men report a higher ability to cope of 3.2, compared with the women's score of 2.9. Thus, men seem to be more confident than women when it comes to coping with critical life events.

3. Duration of Confrontation With the Event. The length of time that one needs to deal with a life event can also provide information on the importance of this event in one's life. Basically, it can be anticipated that a longer coping phase is accompanied by a more fundamental and comprehensive processing of the stress factors, and leads to a better integration of the developmental potentials of critical life events. The group comparisons clearly show significant differences in the duration of coping. On average, the parent generation spends less time dealing with the events that occur than the children's generation. The gender comparison shows even clearer differences. Women clearly spend more time dealing with life events than men. Nonetheless, the mean scores underlying these statistically significant differences oscillate between only 2.3 (men) and 2.6 (women). When it is recalled that the response format only permitted scores between 1.0–4.0, it can be seen that respondents generally rate the duration of coping as neither too short nor too long, despite all group differences.

4. Stress at the Time. One of the most important indicators in life-event research is the stress associated with an event and, in particular, the stress that is experienced in direct temporal connection with the event's occurrence. An accumulation of stressful life events can lead to permanent life stress, with all its accompanying negative consequences—in particular, mental and psychosomatic illness.[7] The mean of 2.3 in the total sample shows that most of the events that have occurred generate an intermediate level of stress. Comparisons of various subsamples reveal no differences between the parent and children's generations, but between men and women. Men experience less stress than women. This gender difference is strongest when fathers (2.2) are compared with daughters (2.5).

5. *Current Stress.* Although critical life events and their accompanying stress are more or less restricted in time, it is possible for a certain degree of stress to persist a long time after the event has occurred. On the one hand, this can be because an event is particularly traumatic (e.g., death of spouse). On the other hand, because of a lack of confrontation and coping at the time when the event occurred, the stress can, in some way, be "dragged along" for years. Therefore, it seems meaningful to test the level of current stress that our respondents assign to the critical life events of the past 16 years. The mean for all persons is 1.6. As can be anticipated, the current stress value is lower than that for the time when the event occurred. However, it can also be maintained that a certain remainder of stress persists from previous years. The group comparison shows only minimal trends here, indicating that residual stress is slightly higher in women than in men.

6. *Personal Gain at the Time.* When presenting the concept of critical life events, we emphasized that every intrinsically negative critical life event can also have a positive side. Coping successfully with the problems and difficulties arising through an event frequently results in a feeling of higher personal competence and self-efficacy. Emotional growth in the sense of more varied and mature possibilities of dealing with later life events can also be the consequence of initially very stressful experiences. All this is summarized in the question on the personal gain from dealing with the event at the time—that is, shortly after its occurrence.[8] The mean of 2.2 for the total group indicates that, although a personal gain was present at the time, it was nonetheless rather slight. However, a comparison of subgroups reveals that this total mean does not reveal the most important information on this issue. Starting with the fathers (1.8), across the mothers (2.1) and sons (2.7), up to the daughters (2.9), there is a continuous increase in the reported personal gain. It should be pointed out that parents' scores lie in a domain in which the gain is described as rather small, whereas the scores of the children suggest that they have profited from the occurrence of critical life events. This reveals a clear generation effect. There is also a clear gender difference: Women report more personal gain than men.

7. *Personal Gain Today.* The comparison between the stress at the time and the stress today reveals that, although this stress does not completely disappear over time, it declines significantly—a thoroughly desirable development from the perspective of those involved. With regard to personal

gain, it would be a positive finding if we could ascertain that this increases or at least remains stable over time. The comparison of the total means of former (2.2) and current gain (2.3) shows that personal gain is generally stable. Thus, it seems to be at least possible to conserve the positive outcomes of coping work over time. An inspection of subgroups also supports this trend. Small increases in means can even be found for all four subgroups. However, they are all extremely slight. The sequence of increasingly higher means across fathers (1.9), mothers (2.2), sons (2.8), and daughters (3.0) found in personal gain at the time is also retained. Mean differences in the rating of former and current gain also retains this ranking. In other words, the group that reports the highest former gain also has the highest growth in gain up to the present day and vice versa. However, these differences are so small that they can be viewed, at best, as a weak trend.

Figure 3.3 presents an overview of the comparisons between the four groups and the total group for the seven questions on event perception. Once more, this makes it particularly clear that most group differences reported, even when they are statistically significant, tend to be small. A clear discrimination between the groups only appears for the two questions on personal gain. These results answer the question raised earlier on whether children have a more stressful life than their parents because they report problematic events more frequently. The children's much higher scores on personal gain compared with the parents suggest that these

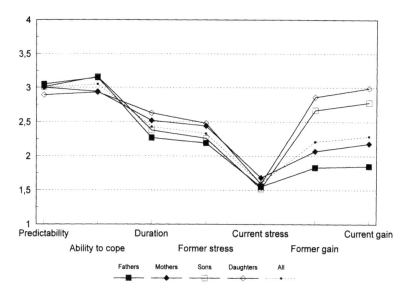

FIG. 3.3. Comparison of fathers, mothers, sons, and daughters for seven evaluation aspects of experienced events.

events can lead to positive change for the children, despite their higher frequency of occurrence.

Event-Centered Analysis

Up to now, this chapter has focused on describing and contrasting the persons involved and specific subgroups of persons. It now focuses attention on the events.

Death and Birth: A Contrast of Two Events. First, we examine whether particular individual events can be assigned typical properties, and then we look at this independently from the group of persons who have experienced these events. For this purpose, we compare the parent and children's generations in terms of their perceptions and evaluations of two events that are as different as possible—namely, "a death" and "birth of one's own child." If an event can be assigned specific properties as event-specific qualities, then different groups of persons should evaluate this event in a similar way. At least, it could be anticipated that a comparison of two different events would reveal that differences between the events are stronger than the differences between the groups of persons who evaluate the same event. Figures 3.4 and 3.5 support this hypothesis.

Figure 3.4 displays the means for the seven questions on the perception and evaluation of the event "a death." It can be seen that there are only minor differences between the estimations of children and parents. According to this

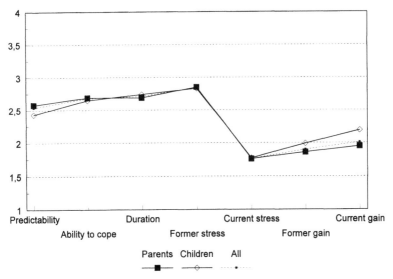

FIG. 3.4. Perception of the event "a death" in parents and children.

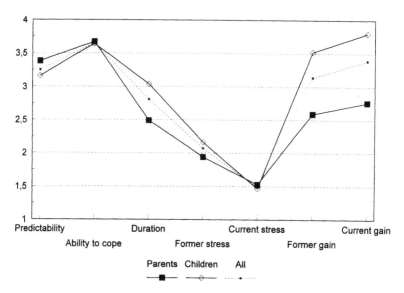

FIG. 3.5. Perception of the event "birth of own child" in parents and children.

profile, the event "a death" can be described as follows. A death tends to be hard to predict and is just as hard to cope with. It requires an intermediate period of time to deal with it, and the amount of stress at the time is also in the intermediate domain. Current stress is rated as low, and the same applies to the gains at the time, although this increases slightly over time.

Figure 3.5 shows the same scores for the event "birth of one's own child." It is clear that this profile results in a completely different description. The birth of a child is highly predictable and also can be coped with well. It is followed by a rather longer period of coping with a low level of stress at the time, which drops further over the course of time. Finally, both at the time and today, the birth of a child is viewed as a high personal gain.

A comparison of the two figures reveals that the courses of the two event profiles differ clearly. The differences between the parent and children's groups in the evaluation of the same event are, in contrast, less severe. For all seven questions, they tend toward zero for the case of a death, whereas they are slightly higher for the birth of one's own child. However, it is not difficult to understand that the significance of birth of a child in the children's generation, which frequently means the birth of the first child, is on a completely different level compared with the parent generation, who generally possess far more life experience in dealing with the birth of one's own child.

Grouping the Events. The previous section confirmed that the characteristics of each life event are, to some extent, independent from the person who experiences them. To demonstrate this, two qualitatively different events were consciously chosen. One could now continue this event-centered approach by making comparisons between all possible pairs of events. This would be time-consuming and rather overwhelming. Therefore, for a further description of the given events, we chose another path. We asked ourselves whether it would be possible to classify the given events into groups of similar events on the basis of the answers given to the seven questions. The goal is to form event groups that differ from each other as clearly as possible, whereas the events that are summarized into one group should be as similar as possible in terms of the seven descriptive aspects. These group formations were carried out separately for parents and children because we had used different event lists in each generation. We do not give a detailed description of the computational procedures used in this group formation, but proceed directly to the results.[9]

1. Group Content. For both parents and children, a division of the given events into three subgroups proved to be the most favorable solution. Table 3.4 reports which events are summarized into the three groups for both generations.

Group I. In both children and parents, Group I particularly contains events that are clearly negative or unpleasant. These include "death," "illness," or "economic difficulties." One could anticipate that reports on the degree of stress of these events would be higher, whereas the personal gain would be lower. The following description of group properties deals with this hypothesis in more detail.

Group II. Here as well one can find events for both parents and children that have a clearly problematic character. These particularly include personal and partner- or family-related difficulties. Therefore, one can ask why these should form a separate group. However, in contrast to Group I, these events tend to represent problems on a psychological level, or on the level of important social relationships. In addition, the occurrence of an event in Group II is much more under the control of the person involved than is the case for the events in Group I. For example, personal responsibility for the occurrence of partnership problems is generally much higher than for the occurrence of serious illnesses.

One could suspect that coping with these events also calls for a greater degree of "work on oneself" than the events in Group I. On the one hand, it could be anticipated that this would mean that they require more time to be dealt with, but that, on the other hand, successful coping will bring a greater degree of personal gain that will also persist over longer periods of time. It should also be pointed out that the contents of Groups I and II reveal interesting differences between parents and children. Problems in earlier partnerships, in one's own family of origin, and at work are placed in Group I for parents and Group II for children. If our charac-

TABLE 3.4
Distribution of Events Across Three Event Groups for Parents
and Children

	PARENTS	CHILDREN
GROUP I	Death 1 Death 2 Illness 1 Illness 2 Material difficulties Problems in circle of friends Problems in partner´s family of origin Problems in one´s own family of origin Problems in earlier partnerships Job problems	Death 1 Death 2 Illness 1 Illness 2 Material difficulties Problems in circle of friends Problems in partner´s family of origin Separation or divorce of parents
GROUP II	Personal problems Partner problems Separation or divorce	Personal problems Partner problems Separation or divorce Problems in one´s own family of origin Problems in earlier partnerships Job problems
GROUP III	Moving home Birth of own child Vacation, journey Birth of a grandchild Departure child 1 Departure child 2 Departure child 3 Departure of last child Child at school 1 Child at school 2 Retirement Marriage of child	Moving home Birth of own child Vacation, journey Birth of a sibling Leaving home Starting work Marriage or permanent partnership

terization of the groups is appropriate, this would mean that parents view these events as being less closely linked to their own personality or less strongly anchored in the domain of personal responsibility.

Group III. Whereas the discrimination between Groups I and II required a differentiated perspective, there is a clear demarcation for Group III. For the children, Group III contains events such as "birth of a child," "moving home," or "vacation," which seem to be thoroughly positive and, in addition, can be viewed as stages of personal development. For parents as well, there are also positive, probably less stressful events (e.g., moving home, vacation), together with events that represent certain transitions in the cycle of family life (e.g., birth of a grandchild, retirement). For this group, we can anticipate high predictability, a good ability to cope, and simultaneously low stress and high personal gain.

2. Properties of the Groups. The groups are formed on the basis of answers to the seven questions on the perception and evaluation of the events. The following figures show the profile of the three groups for these seven evaluation criteria separately for parents (Fig. 3.6) and children (Fig. 3.7). A first comparison of the profiles of the groups in parents and children reveals a high level of agreement. Only one exception is conspicuous. In Group III (i.e., the positive events), the events are characterized by a high degree of personal gain both at the time and today in children, whereas scores on these variables are almost exactly the same as those for Group I in parents, and tend to show low gain. The following gives a brief characterization of the three event groups using the mean weights of the seven evaluation criteria.

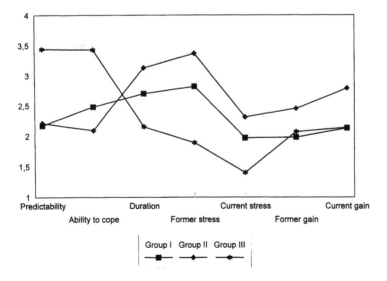

FIG. 3.6. Parents: Means for three groups of critical life events.

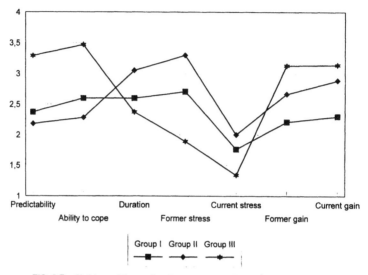

FIG. 3.7. Children: Means for three groups of critical life events.

Group I. The events in this group are, in comparison with those in the other groups, characterized by intermediate scores on predictability, ability to cope, duration, and stress at the time. The current stress, as well as the personal gain at the time and today, are lower than in all other event groups. These seem to be events that, although unpleasant, do not contain a high level of stress that would require long-term coping. In addition, it also seems that little is to be gained from dealing with these events. One could say that they are events that one has to accept or tolerate passively as more or less strong "strokes of fate." Put succinctly, one waits until everything is over and then returns to the status quo.

Group II. The situation is different in this group, although it also contains only negative events. The stronger personal involvement has already been discussed, and is confirmed by the profile course. Although the profile has a similar curve to that in Group I, there are important differences that support the hypothesis of stronger personal involvement. First, the estimation of ability to cope is much lower. Hence, one sees oneself as being confronted with greater problems. Second, the curve for the evaluation aspect is generally on a much lower level than in Group I, which could be the reason for the much higher duration of time spent on dealing with the events as well. Nonetheless this additional expenditure on emotional coping seems to be rewarded through much more personal gain at the time, as well as a continued increase up until the present day.

Group III. The course of the group of positive events or developmental tasks is a mirror image of the courses in Groups I and II. The high predictability lies in the nature of the events (e.g., birth, leaving the parental home). The high score on ability to cope can also be explained through the positive nature of the events in this group. What is perhaps somewhat surprising is the low score for the duration of coping. It would seem likely that one would have to spend long periods of time dealing with sections of life such as "leaving the parental home" or the "birth of a child," even when these are positive events. Perhaps it is precisely the fact that these are predictable, normative steps in the life course that is decisive for no longer perceiving any particularly long "period of coping and processing" when recalling these events. Coping with them is, so to speak, wrapped up in normal life, and is not viewed as a particularly decisive life event in retrospective.

What is conspicuous in Group III—as mentioned already—is the clear difference between parents and children in terms of personal gain. Among the children, the positive experiences gained from these events are much higher than in the other two event groups. Apparently the completed stages of development are booked very consciously as successes. The situation is different for the parents. In contradiction to current theoretical ideas that developmental tasks in mid- and late adulthood (e.g., "children leave the parental home," "end of working life") should also be resolved in the sense of personal growth, and thus anchor development as a life-long process, the parents in our sample exhibit only a low degree of personal gain, particularly in comparison with the children's generation.

There are two possible explanations for these findings. First, it is conceivable that most parents have not really mastered these developmental tasks. A mother whose last child has left home and who has not come to terms, or has difficulties in coming to terms with, this unavoidable fact will understandably not say that she has profited in any way from this event. However, this potential explanation is contradicted by the low score for the stress that is still perceived today. Second—and this is the more probable hypothesis—one can assume that the parents have successfully tackled their phase-specific developmental tasks and, after some time, perceive only slight stress from events in the past. However, at the same time, they are not able, in comparison with the younger generation, to perceive the positive sides and the potentials of such events as "retirement" or "the last child leaving home." This would then have less to do with a greater inability to cope with critical events, but more with an inability to see their positive aspects.

Coping With Stress

So far, this chapter has talked about stress and the coping work that it calls for. However, it has not said anything about the various possibilities that are available for coping with stressful life situations, nor how our respondents apply these coping strategies. This is the topic of the present section.

Psychological research on stress has investigated the direct consequences of perceived stress and, in particular, the emotional strain that it causes, and increasingly also addresses how people cope with stress.[10] One wanted to know how stress is processed. To some extent, it is even more important to know something about the strategies for coping with stress, rather than the stress itself, because it is the way in which one behaves in relation to stressful, strenuous, or even threatening events and situations that first determines the consequences of stress. Dealing with such situations requires the individual to exert him or herself on several levels:

- Problematic life situations usually require an active involvement of the person concerned to resolve the problem.
- The problem-solving action is usually preceded by a phase of thinking about the situation to find possible problem-solving strategies.
- The stress makes it necessary to come to terms with the increased emotional tension that frequently accompanies it. It is often the case that a strong psychological imbalance stands in the way of a rational solution to the problem.

Alongside coping strategies that promise success there are also ones that tend to prevent a resolution of difficult situations. Such strategies are of particular interest in the domain of applied psychology because one has to identify ineffective patterns of coping with stress before one can modify them (e.g., in so-called "stress-immunization training"[11]). Examples of such ineffective approaches are denial of the problem or resignation.

Which coping strategies a person applies in a specific situation depends, on the one hand, on the situation (the death of a close friend requires different processing mechanisms than the birth of a child) and, on the other hand, on the person him or herself. In the latter case, one can view the coping style as a more or less stable personality characteristic of the person concerned.[12]

Description and Assessment of Coping With Stress

The coping strategies of our respondents were assessed with a 27-item questionnaire.[13] The instructions were especially formulated so that we could assess the type of coping used at the current time. Therefore, we asked the respondents how they coped with stress in their current life situation, but not how they had coped with the critical life events assessed previously. It is important to mention this because, in the further course of the study, we examine whether and in what way the critical life events of the past 16 years have influenced the coping strategies at the time of the second wave.

On the basis of preliminary analyses of these data, we were able to categorize the replies to the 27 questions into seven general coping dimensions. These clearly differ from each other in terms of content, and meet the statistical criteria for scale reliability. Table 3.5 lists these seven strategies and presents two sample items from each scale.

It can be seen that our seven coping scales cover the levels of stress processing discussed above. Scales 1, 6, and 7 address the level of cognitive (i.e., mental) involvement with the problem. The search for possible solution alternatives, further information, as well as the attempt to look at the problem from another perspective lead directly toward the goal when coping

TABLE 3.5
Sample Items for Seven Coping Scales

Coping Scales	Sample Items
	When I have to deal with great strain...
Scale 1: Rational problem solving	... I work out a plan for solving the problems ... I actively undertake something to resolve the problem
Scale 2: Affect regulation	... I keep my feelings under control ... I cry
Scale 3: Resigned acceptance	... I come to terms with the fact that one can't change anything ... I am helpless in the face of the problem
Scale 4: Avoidance	... I try to ignore the problem ... I look for recognition in other domains
Scale 5: Social contact	... I talk to friends, acquaintances, or colleagues about how to solve my problem ...I get everything off my chest by talking to friends or acquaintances
Scale 6: Information search	... I find out how one can solve such problems ... I obtain information through books, newspapers, and television
Scale 7: Redefinition	... I try to see the positive sides of my situation ... I tell myself, things will soon get better

with difficult life situations. Scale 1 additionally covers the aspect of the subsequent action or activity.

Scales 2 and 3 refer to the level of emotional processing. Scale 2 ("Affect regulation") provides information on how far a person is able to accept the feelings that arise and express them, or how far they pull themselves together and suppress their emotions. This does not yet say which approach is more appropriate. Particularly here, the appropriateness of the reaction should be determined to a large degree by the type of situation involved.

In Scale 3, "Resigned acceptance," it is easier to say that such a procedure will lead to unsatisfactory coping regardless of the situation. As the sample items in the table show, a resigned attitude is always accompanied by a great degree of inactivity, which necessarily encourages the continued existence of the problem if it does not go away by itself.

Scale 4, "Avoidance," also covers a behavior that is not solution-oriented. This summarizes behaviors that represent an internal and external movement "away from the problem." However, in extremely stressful situations, it is nonetheless conceivable that such an approach, as a sort of protection from too much stress, can be thoroughly helpful as an initial reaction to a difficulty when it facilitates a subsequent, more solution-oriented coping approach.

Scale 5, "Social contact," refers to a behavior in which interpersonal resources are used to solve individual problems. Contact with friends and acquaintances, as well as their support in difficult life situations, certainly belongs to those coping strategies that can be labeled *effective.*

Coping With Stress in Generation and Gender Comparisons

The first stage of analysis is to inspect the means on the seven scales and compare them in terms of generation or gender membership. The range for all seven scales lies between the poles *rarely* (1) and *very frequently* (4). Figure 3.8 compares the parent with the children's generation; Fig. 3.9 compares the group of men with the group of women. These profiles indicate that the parents and children in our sample mostly use a series of coping strategies that were previously presented as more favorable, whereas those strategies that are probably less useful continuously have lower scores. We first look at the dotted curve for the total sample. This reveals the highest values for rational problem solving and affect regulation, followed by information search and redefinition. Thus, a rational coping style prevails, in which the solution is found on the widest possible information base, with cognitive flexibility, and under the least possible affective influence (higher scores on Scale 2 correspond to higher affect suppression). The lowest scores are on the scales "Resignation" and "Avoidance," which is also in line with a solution-oriented approach. At 2.2, the mean score for social contact indicates that crises tend to be tackled alone, and that less use is made of social support networks.

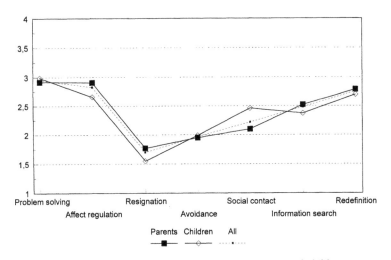

FIG. 3.8. Comparison of coping with stress in parents and children.

We turn to the differences between groups. The most conspicuous differ-ence is shown for the scale "Social contact." There is both a generation effect and a gender effect, revealing that women and members of the chil-dren's generation use more social contacts when coping with stress. Further generation effects indicate higher affect suppression, higher resignation, and more information search among the parents. One could interpret this as indicating that the parents' strategies are less effective than those of the children. At first glance, the finding that parents search for more information

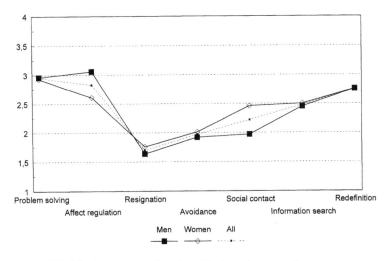

FIG. 3.9. Comparison of coping with stress in men and women.

may counter this interpretation, but this can also be considered to indicate that parents have a greater information deficit than their adult children. Such an information deficit could reinforce a resigned attitude to coping.

Significant gender differences are found for the scales "Affect regulation" and "Resignation." Women exhibit more emotion and more frequently try to avoid the problem with which they are confronted. With reference to the higher score for social contact mentioned earlier, the coping style of women reveals itself to be more emotional and more embedded in the social environment than that of men. This seems to be an approach that initially focuses on mental hygiene, in the sense of emotional balance, and shifts the actual problem to one side. In contrast, the men's approach is aligned far more toward a direct solution of the problem, although this possibly does not take sufficient account of the emotional side of the situation.

The theoretical ideas on the effectiveness of individual coping strategies mentioned previously cannot be confirmed empirically on the basis of the present data. We only have information on the frequency with which our respondents apply certain strategies, not how successfully they apply them. Finally, it should be noted that there are no differences for the scales "Rational solution" and "Redefinition" in either the generation or gender comparison.

RELATIONS BETWEEN CRITICAL LIFE EVENTS AND COPING WITH STRESS

Now that the current state of our sample has been described regarding their use of specific coping strategies, we tackle the task of looking for conditions in our respondents' past that could have contributed to the attainment of this current state. In other words, we asked ourselves whether the critical life events experienced up to now, for whose processing a person is dependent on his or her coping resources, impact on how our respondents cope with similar situations today. We assume here that a successful coping with critical life situations in the past contributes to better coping with similar situations in the future. It is just as conceivable that bad experiences in the past can have an unfavorable impact on coping with later life crises. The following examines whether and, if this is the case, how the critical life events of the past 16 years have influenced the coping styles of parents and children in the present.

The Number of Perceived Events and Their Impact on Coping Behavior

Analogue to the procedure used to describe the life events, we deal initially with the simple number of events experienced and then describe the impact of the perception of these events on current coping.

The Total Group of Events. It has been ascertained that there are small, but significant differences between the genders and generations regarding coping strategies. This means that persons' scores on the seven coping scales are partially determined by their gender and generation membership. We are additionally interested in whether the number of critical life events experienced also impacts on these scores. Table 3.6 reports the results of an analysis designed to check whether and, if so, which effects gender, age (which contains the information on generation membership), and the number of critical life events experienced have on current coping with stress. The variable "number of experienced events" was graded into three categories: 0–4 events were coded as "few," 5–10 as "intermediate," and more than 10 as "many." These results are summarized in Table 3.6.[14] In view of the complexity of the research question, this initially rather incomprehensible table is actually a very simple way to present the results. Therefore,

TABLE 3.6
Impact of Gender, Age, and Number of Experiences Events on
Current Coping With Stress

Variable	Significant impact?	On which scale?	Which impact?
AGE	NO	/	/
GENDER	YES		For women
		Affect regulation	↓
		Resignation	↑
		Social contact	↑
NUMBER OF EXPERIENCED EVENTS	YES		Many events
		Rational problem solving	↑
		Affect regulation	↓
		Social contact	↑
		Information search	↓
		Redefinition	↑

at this point, we explain how to read this table in some detail because the further presentation of results follows the same pattern.

The description follows the column headings: Column 1 presents the variables that have been studied. Column 2 reports whether each variable has a significant impact on any of the seven coping scales. If this is the case, as can be seen in Table 3.6 for gender and number of events, we want to know which of the seven coping strategies is involved. Very few variables impact simultaneously on all seven coping strategies. Column 3 lists the scales involved for each variable that has a total impact. For example, the variable "gender" has a significant impact (see Column 2), but this relates only to the three scales "Affect regulation," "Resignation," and "Social contact" (see Column 3).

The last question concerns the type of effect on the three scales involved. These results are reported in Column 4, which should be read in the following way: The starting point for the variable "gender" is the shaded field "For women" in the first line of the fourth column. The field below this (downward pointing arrow) then means: The score on the scale "Affect regulation" is lower for men than for women. The next field shows that the score for women is higher on the scale "Resignation" than it is for men. Finally, the score for "Social contact" is also higher for women than for men, which, in the two latter cases, is symbolized by an upward pointing arrow.

The descriptions of the impact of the variable "number of experienced events" can be read off in the same way: Persons who have experienced many events exhibit higher scores on the scale "Rational problem solving" than those who have only experienced a few events. The situation is reversed for the scale "Affect regulation": Persons who have experienced many events obtain lower scores on this scale than those who have experienced fewer events.

After this digression on the technique of table reading, we present a short summary of the results reported in Table 3.6. Whereas age has no impact on coping mechanisms, gender does, which is not surprising in light of the previously reported findings. However, this section is interested in the impact of experienced events. The table shows that the number of all experienced events has a statistically significant impact on the coping strategies. However, this does not tell which events are responsible for this effect because these reports only consider the total sum of all experienced events for each person. The next step should overcome this deficit.

Comparison of the Three Event Groups. A more precise and detailed analysis becomes possible when the information from the categorization of the events into three different groups is exploited and separate analyses are carried out for the number of events experienced from Group I, Group II, and Group III. If this reveals differences in the variables, we can use the group descriptions to make statements on which particular kinds of event have an impact on later coping mechanisms when they occur with a greater frequency.

The procedure is the same as that used for the total number of events. Gender is also taken into account here as an additional variable. Because the three event groups differ for the parents and children, Tables 3.7 and 3.8 report findings separately for the two generations.

TABLE 3.7
Parents: Impact of Gender, Age, and Number of Experienced Events on
Current Coping With Stress for the Three Event Groups

PARENTS - EVENT GROUP I (strokes of fate)			
Variable	Significant impact?	On which scale?	Which impact?
			For women
GENDER	YES	Affect regulation	↓
		Resignation	↑
		Social contact	↑
EVENTS	NO	/	/
PARENTS - EVENT GROUP II (personal problems)			
Variable	Significant impact?	On which scale?	Which impact?
			For women
		Affect regulation	↓
GENDER	YES	Resignation	↑
		Avoidance	↑
		Social contact	↑
			Many Events
EVENTS	YES	Affect regulation	↓
		Redefinition	↓
PARENTS - EVENT GROUP III (positive events)			
Variable	Significant impact?	On which scale?	Which impact?
GENDER	NO	/	/
EVENTS	NO	/	/

TABLE 3.8
Children: Impact of Gender, Age, and Number of Experienced
Events on Current Coping With Stress for the Three Event Groups

CHILDREN - EVENT GROUP I (strokes of fate)			
Variable	Significant impact?	On which scale?	Which impact?
			For women
GENDER	YES	Affect regulation	↓
		Resignation	↑
		Social contact	↑
EVENTS	NO	/	/
CHILDREN - EVENT GROUP II (personal problems)˙			
Variable	Significant impact?	On which scale?	Which impact?
			For women
GENDER	YES	Affect regulation	↓
		Social contact	↑
			Many events
		Affect regulation	↑
EVENTS	YES	Resignation	↑
		Avoidance	↑
		Redefinition	↓
CHILDREN - EVENT GROUP III (positive events)			
Variable	Significant impact?	On which scale?	Which impact?
			For women
GENDER	YES	Affect regulation	↓
		Social contact	↑
EVENTS	NO	/	/

The impact of the gender variable, which is also reported in both tables, is not discussed in further detail here because the dependence of coping strategies on gender has already been reported. Instead, we restrict ourselves to the impact of the number of events. A first glance shows that the results on the occurrence of event effects are identical for parents and children. Neither the events in Group I nor the events in Group III have an impact on coping with stress. The result for Group III seems particularly surprising. One could have anticipated that the experience of positive life events and their processing would have had a positive impact on later coping abilities. Perhaps, however, the low stress associated with these events did not confront respondents with any great challenge in terms of necessary coping work. The coping resources available at the time of the event were sufficient, therefore there was no need for change or an integration of new ways to deal with such events.

The circumstance that no significant effects can be confirmed for Group I is explained by the particular nature of the events summarized in this group. We have described them as "strokes of fate" that have to be simply accepted. Unlike the events found in Group II, it is hardly possible to exert any influence on their occurrence. It seems as if the fact of less control over the occurrence of these events is linked to the assumption that their consequences are also preprogrammed irreversibly. To some extent, one abandons oneself to one's fate and tries to use the available means to cope with it, without considering the possibility that a change in these means could at least ameliorate the negative consequences of critical life situations.

In contrast, the events in Group II show clear effects on later coping with stress in parents and children. It seems as if a certain degree of personal involvement and control beliefs have to be associated with a critical life event before the specific processing mechanisms become accessible to change. What types of effect can be ascertained here? For children, an increase in the number of experienced events in this category is accompanied by an increase in affect regulation (in the sense of a suppression of emotions), resignation, and avoidance or circumvention of the problem, whereas the score for the redefinition of the problem sinks.

In light of the previous results on effectiveness, these findings indicate that, although an increased number of experienced events of this kind is accompanied by a change in coping strategies, this change seems to be a shift toward less solution-oriented strategies. In parents, it is the scales "Affect regulation" and "Redefinition" that are affected here: Both show a tendency to decline. As far as affect regulation is concerned, parents and children seem to draw closer together. Parents admit increasingly more feelings, whereas children control their feelings more—although when doing this, as already mentioned earlier, they continue to exhibit less affect regulation than the parents.

The widespread assumption that personal growth and development is stimulated by crises and difficult life situations is not supported by our findings. It appears that the opposite is true: Personal crises seem, at least as far as the coping strategies that we have assessed are concerned, to have an inhibiting and negative impact on the development of a coping style that could be viewed as functional and "appropriate."

The Perception of Experienced Events and Its Impact on Coping Style

Up to now, we have looked at the impact of the pure number of life events experienced on the current way of coping with stress. Although this approach has already revealed informative effects, it is also extremely important, as mentioned earlier, to go beyond the pure number and find out something about how the persons have perceived and experienced the events they have been exposed to. This information was obtained through questions on predictability, ability to cope, duration of coping, former and current stress, as well as former and current gain. This now results in the following question: What impact do the answers to the seven perceptual questions have on the seven coping scales in the three event groups among parents and children? In view of the complexity of this question, it is initially simplified.

The seven questions on the perception and evaluation of events were used to form the groups used to describe the events. We tested whether these seven descriptive dimensions can be reduced to a small number of dimensions without losing too much information in the process. After detailed analyses for the various subgroups in our sample, we found that it was possible to reduce the number of dimensions to three dimensions describing independent characteristics of an event:[15]

1. *Negativity.* The questions on ability to cope, duration of coping, former stress, and current stress can be aggregated to form a score that provides information on how far an event represents a severe negative disruption in a person's life. Negativity combines high stress, long duration of coping, and negative ratings on ability to cope.

2. *Gain.* The two scores on former and current personal gain were aggregated to form a total gain score.

3. *Predictability.* During the efforts to reduce the number of dimensions, the predictability of an event proved to be a variable that could not be combined with any of the other dimensions.

This leaves us with three dimensions that can be tested for their impact on coping with stress. Tables 3.9 and 3.10 report these results separately for parents and children.[16] The construction of these tables follows the same

TABLE 3.9
Parents: Impact of Event Perception on Coping With Stress for Three
Event Groups

Event group	Variable	Significant impact?	On which scale?	Which impact?
				For high negativity
Strokes of	NEGATIVITY	YES	Affect regulation	↓
fate			Redefinition	↓
	GAIN	NO	/	/
				For high negativity
Personal			Social contact	↓
problems	NEGATIVITY	YES	Redefinition	↓
				For high gain
	GAIN	YES	Information search	↑
	NEGATIVITY	NO	/	/
Positive				For high gain
events			Rational problem solving	↑
	GAIN	YES	Resignation	↓
			Information search	↑

structure as that reported previously. A first glance shows that the variable "predictability" does not appear. The results of data analysis have shown that the degree of predictability has no significant impact on coping with stress in any of the event groups or in any of the subsamples. For this reason, this variable is not presented in the tables. The situation is completely different for the variables "negativity" and "gain." A glance at the results for Group I (strokes of fate) reveals clear effects of event perception on coping in both children and adults. Thus, whereas the mere number of events in this group—as confirmed in the previous section—has no impact, there is an effect of perception that is independent of the number of events. The effect occurs for negativity, but not for gain. This may be related to the fact that the gain from these events is so low that it does not lead to an improvement in coping strategies.

TABLE 3.10
Children: Impact of Event Perception on Coping With Stress for
Three Event Groups

Event group	Variable	Significant impact?	On which scale?	Which impact?
Strokes of fate	NEGATIVITY	YES		For high negativity
			Affect regulation	↓
			Resignation	↑
			Social contact	↑
	GAIN	YES		For high gain
			Rational problem solving	↑
Personal problems	NEGATIVITY	NO	/	/
	GAIN	YES		For high gain
			Rational problem solving	↑
			Avoidance	↓
Positive events	NEGATIVITY	YES		For high negativity
			Resignation	↑
			Redefinition	↓
	GAIN	NO	/	/

Among parents, a negative estimation of these events leads to reduced affect regulation and reduced redefinition. It is easy to understand why negative perception leads to a reduction in the ability to redefine. The redefinition of an event implies intrinsically the ability to adopt new perspectives, which is difficult for a perception that is fixed on negative aspects.

In addition, the quality of the events in Group I makes it much harder to perform a redefinition compared with events in Group II. In other words, it seems far more plausible to positively reinterpret a partnership crisis than a case of death or of economic difficulties. In the children, negative perception also leads to less affect control and more resignation and social contact. A picture arises of an attitude of helplessness that is caused by intensively negative experiences with fatelike events.

For Group II (personal problems), an impact of the number of events has already been reported. We found that the greater the number of events of this kind that were experienced, the more unfavorable the impact on coping strategies. The data on event perception qualify this impression somewhat, but only for the children. Although negativity has no effect, we find a clear impact of gain: The stronger the perception of gain, the higher the scores for rational problem solving and the lower the scores for avoidance. Although the impact of the number of events gave rise to the impression that the children also had to pay for their increased sensitivity toward events in this group with a deficiency in the development of their coping potentials, this is corrected by the present findings.

Among the parents, in whom the number of events already has a more unfavorable impact on coping, negative perception leads to an additional reinforcement of this effect, in that increasing negativity is accompanied by a decline in the application of the coping strategies "Social contact" and "Redefinition."

Group III (positive events) reveals contradictory effects for parents and children. In the parents, negativity has no impact, but gain does. If parents perceive the positive events of Group III as bringing gain, then this leads to an increase in rational problem solving and information search and a decrease in resigned attitudes. However, it has to be considered that the parents only reported low values for the gain from these events. Thus, if it were possible for the parents to shift their perspective on these events in a more positive direction when they were able to see the developmental potential of these family developments, then this could also increase the feeling of personal competence over the path of better processing mechanisms. For children, there was an effect of negativity: When these intrinsically positive events are nonetheless experienced as being very negative, this leads to an increase in resignation in dealing with these events, whereas the ability to redefine them declines.

CRITICAL LIFE EVENTS AND PHYSICAL HEALTH IN 1992

Psychological research has frequently confirmed the impact of stress on physical health.[17] Indeed, the contribution of long-term stress to the occurrence of so-called "psychosomatic illnesses" (e.g., stomach ulcers, headaches, etc.) is no longer just an accepted fact in scientific circles, but is also being integrated increasingly into the everyday health awareness of a broader public. Critical life events, particularly when they occur cumulatively within short periods of time, also induce stress, and thus influence mental and physical well-being. The following examines whether we can also confirm an impact of experienced critical life events on physical health in our sample at Wave 2.

Assessment of Physical Health

Within the predominantly psychological framework of our study, it was not possible to collect detailed information on physical illnesses and disorders. However, to enable us to make at least a few general statements on this topic, we gave both parents and children a list of 20 physical symptoms and asked them to report how frequently each of these symptoms had appeared over the course of the previous year on a 5-point scale ranging from *never* (1) to *very often* (5). The list of symptoms is presented in Table 3.11.[18]

Once again, we were in no way interested in a complete assessment of all possible physical symptoms. The main focus was to assess symptoms whose incidence or prevalence have a confirmed psychological component. Hence, although one can state that a person whose answers lead to a high score (i.e., has reported high ratings for a large number of the symptoms on the list) is not healthy, the opposite conclusion—that a very low score indicates physical health—is not permissible.

Physical Health: A Comparison
of Generations and Genders

We first look at the differences between generations and genders. The comparison is based on the mean score of each person's replies on the list of 20 symptoms. Instead of performing a differentiated analysis of individual symptoms of illness, we focus on this global score that reports how strongly a person has suffered from psychosomatic symptoms during the year before the survey. Figure 3.10 displays a gender and generation comparison of these scores.

The first conspicuous fact is that both parents and children report a low symptom stress. The mean for the total sample is 2.1, indicating that the subjects are scarcely exposed to permanent stress by the symptoms in our list. However, the comparison according to generation and gender reveals statistically nonrandom differences, although they are only in the domain of rather minor complaints. First, a generation affect can be determined (i.e., parents show continuously higher scores). Second, there is a gender effect (i.e., women report more symptoms than men). The generation effect is explained by the age difference. Many of the symptoms in our list occur more frequently among older persons than young ones (e.g., difficulties in recall, heart complaints). The gender effect may be due to the fact that women are generally more sensitive to physical changes, and also have a

TABLE 3.11
Items for Assessing Physical Symptoms

Headache
Difficulties in getting to sleep or insomnia
Muscular tension in back or neck
Stomach complaints
Shortness of breath without physical strain
Rash or itchiness
Diarrhea
Weariness or dizziness
Difficulties in recall
Racing heart or strong heartbeat
Chest pains
Teeth grinding
Light fatigue
Constipation
Dryness in the mouth or problems with swallowing
Decline in sexual interest
Lack of appetite
Overeating
Back pain (due to work)
Back pain (not due to work)

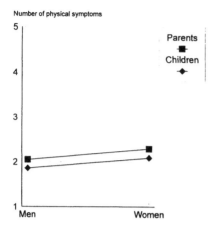

FIG. 3.10. Generation and gender differences in general physical stress symptoms.

stronger tendency toward psychosomatic reactions to problematic situations.[19]

Relation Between Critical Life Events and Physical Health

Even when the findings on physical symptoms presented earlier show that our subjects tend not to suffer too greatly from them, it is nonetheless worth investigating whether significant relations can be confirmed between the frequency of symptoms of illness in 1992 and the number of critical life events experienced over the previous 16 years. In other words, the question is: Is it possible to predict the level of the symptom stress score in 1992 on the basis of the number of events experienced? This should not be understood to imply that one can provide an exact prediction of the symptom load score purely on the basis of information on life events. Naturally, a host of other factors codetermine the occurrence of physical symptoms. We are far more concerned with testing whether the number of events experienced can provide a significant contribution to such a prediction.

Four variables were used to predict the symptom stress score in 1992: the number of events experienced from Groups I, II, and II, as well as the respondent's age. The analysis resulted in a percentage that reports what proportion of the variation in the value of the symptom stress in 1992 is predicted by individual differences on the four previously mentioned variables. In addition, each predictor variable's contribution to the total prediction is also reported. These values, called *beta coefficients*, can vary between −1.0 and +1.0. The closer to +1.0, the greater the variable's contribution to the prediction. Both the proportion of variance explained and the beta coefficients can be tested for significance. Table 3.12 reports the findings from this analysis for various subgroups in the sample.

TABLE 3.12
Relation Between Number of Experienced Events and Physical Stress Symptoms

Variables influencing stress symptoms	Parents (n = 401)	Fathers (n = 195)	Mothers (n = 206)	Children (n = 187)	Sons (n = 92)	Daughters (n = 95)
Group I	.25 *	.23 *	.32 *	.20 *	.06	.27 *
Group II	-.05	-.01	-.10	.26 *	.26 *	.23 *
Group III	-.08	-.13	-.07	-.11	-.16	-.15
Age	.04	.23 *	.00	.02	.05	.00
Percentage of explained variance	6*	2	8*	15*	10	18*

*p < .05.

We first look at the percentages of explained variance. These seem to be rather low, even when they are labeled as statistically significant (with an asterisk). However, two points should be noted: First, the number of events and age are only a small excerpt from the set of conditions that contribute to the occurrence of physical symptoms. Second, we are dealing with data on a high level of abstraction. For example, the symptom stress score is a mean based on 20 different symptoms. The reports on the frequency of events experienced also fail to cover which events these are, although a degree of differentiation is provided by the separation into three event groups.

Nonetheless, viewed against the background of these constraints, the results seem very informative: The children's values are continuously higher than those of their parents. Critical life events and their consequences seem to also have a direct impact on the physical level here. For the daughters, for example, it is possible to explain 18% of the total variance of symptom stress in 1992 solely on the basis of the number of life events experienced.

We can obtain more detailed information from the beta coefficients for the individual predictor variables. We first look at age. At least for the parents, it could be anticipated that the age variable would play a certain role in the occurrence of physical symptoms. However, our data confirm this only for the fathers (beta = .23). The group of parents and the group of mothers have beta values of approximately 0.00, which means that no relations exist. We find the same picture for the children—a result that is nonetheless in line with expectations here.

Which event groups are particularly significant for the symptom stress? Group I ("strokes of fate") reveals positive and statistically significant beta coefficients for all subsamples (except for the sons); that is, the more events of this kind experienced, the higher the symptom stress score. The frequency of events in Group II ("problems with a more personal involvement") reveals a different picture for parents and children. Among the children, these types of event seem to have the same effect as the events in Group I, and the scores are even higher. For the parents, in contrast, there are no statistically significant findings.

Earlier in this chapter, it was suggested that the parent generation may generally be less sensitive to personal problems in particular, whereas the children may be more prepared to face the demands of such life situations. If this is the case, these results reveal that the parents are so successful in suppression that they can even prevent this suppressed stress from resurfacing in the form of physical symptoms, which would, nonetheless, tend to contradict popular psychoanalytical theories.

There are interesting findings on Group III that summarize positively evaluated events. Although none of the coefficients is significant, there is an informative trend in that all values are negative. In other words, the more events of this kind that a person has experienced, the lower their symptom stress score. These findings tend to suggest that there are also critical life events whose effects promote health. However, this topic requires further and more differentiated data analyses.

In summary, the number of experienced events alone can already exert a certain effect on a later occurrence of psychosomatic symptoms. However, this effect does not necessarily have to strengthen symptoms; it can also hinder symptoms when the events are perceived as positive. However, it should not be overlooked that this assessment of critical life events and physical symptoms was carried out simultaneously. This particularly affects the retrospective assessment of critical life events. Thus, we cannot make any valid statements on the direction of the effects of these two variables. Indeed, it may be that persons who report more physical symptoms tend to report more critical life events. At the same time, it is also possible that certain personality characteristics, such as the level of neuroticism, predetermine the answer on the number of physical symptoms, as well as the answer on the frequency of critical life events in the same way. Although it would be possible to use our data to seek answers to such differentiated questions, we have decided to be content with the findings already presented in this chapter.

A BRIEF SUMMARY OF THE MOST IMPORTANT POINTS

- The average number of critical life events over the past 16 years is seven, and there are no differences between the parent and children's generations.

- The parent and children's generations differ in terms of the events that they experience most frequently (with the exception of "a death" and "vacation"), due to the particular stage on the family life cycle at which they are located.
- Alongside the mere number and kind of critical life event, the perception or experience of these events is particularly crucial. Compared with their wives, husbands experiences their critical life events as being less stressful in intensity and duration and easier to cope with. The children's generation and—independent of age—women in general also gain greater profit for their future lives through the confrontation with critical life events, compared with the parent generation or men.
- A comparison of two different life events that probably have a negative or positive quality ("a death" vs. "birth of a child") confirms, within the framework of an event-centered analysis, that the perception of events depends on personal factors, as well as the type of event.
- A statistical grouping of the events produces three categories for parents and three for children: (a) fatelike mishaps (e.g., death, illness), (b) personal problems (e.g., partnership problems, separation or divorce), and (c) positive events (e.g., birth of a child, special journeys).
- No relation can be found between the number of fatelike and positive events and coping with stress, whereas a higher number of personal problems in both parents and children is accompanied by a markedly lower ability to cope with such problems.
- In an event-centered analysis, three modes of perception are labeled as follows: (a) negativity (i.e., to what extent a certain event is experienced as being undesirable and aversive), (b) gain (i.e., how far the occurrence of a specific event has proved to be a benefit for later life), and (c) predictability (i.e., how far the occurrence of the event in question can be anticipated). For these three modes of perception, we have tested their impact on coping with stress separately for the parent and children's generations, and also separately for the groups of fatelike mishaps, personal problems, and positive events. This produced the following findings.

Fatelike mishaps. Strokes of fate that are experienced as particularly negative are accompanied by a notably lower affective control in the parents. In addition, the parent generation is less able to give such events a new, less stressful interpretation. The children's generation also finds it difficult to control feelings when strokes of fate are particularly severe. At the same time, such events are accompanied by an increased experience of resignation and helplessness, but also by the search for comfort and support through conversations with trusted persons.

Personal problems. For the younger generation, these are particularly problems with relationships. The more negative and disrupting the experience, the less children are prepared to take advantage of opportunities for discussion and support in their social surroundings. At the same time, their willingness to give serious personal problems a new and less stressful interpretation is only low. For the children's generation, this results in a less helpful and more problem-sustaining behavior when tackling personal difficulties, whereas this cannot be ascertained in the parent generation. The older generation, probably because of its greater experience of life, can gain a positive element from personal problems in the long-term that promotes their further development. As long as this is the case, such an experience is linked more closely to rational and constructive forms of coping.

Positive events. If, in the younger generation, events that are generally rated as positive (such as the birth of one's own child or entering a partnership) are associated with a negative perception, this reveals a clear increase in helplessness and resignation. In contrast, parents who draw a personal gain from positive events generally tend to have a more rational and less resigned form of coping with stress.

• Regarding the stress of physical symptoms (assessed with a series of selected complaints such as headache, sleep disturbances, stomach pains), there is a low score in the total sample. Nonetheless, gender and generation effects can be found within this low level of physical impairment, in that the parent generation and women exhibit a higher load of symptoms.

• In general, a higher stress through physical symptoms is linked to a greater number of critical life events. This relationship is much closer for the children's generation—above all, for the daughters—than for the parent generation, and thus indicates a particular risk potential for the younger generation.

END NOTES

1. Basic literature on life-span developmental psychology can be found in Baltes, Reese, and Nesselroade (1977) and Baltes (1987).
2. Some standard works on life-event research are Holmes and Rahe (1967) and Dohrenwend and Dohrenwend (1974, 1978).
3. The frequently complex methodological problems confronting research on critical life events are discussed in Perkins (1982). Some possible ways to assess critical life events are presented by Cochrane and Robertson (1973); Sarason, Johnson, and Siegel (1978); or Schwarzer (1993).
4. Our questionnaire also included a question on the time point when the critical event occurred. For example, it is likely that events located further in the past have a less dominant stress potential than those that are much closer to the present. However, this point is not dealt with any further because the replies that we received were so fragmentary that we could not aggregate them for data analysis.

5. Compare Rodgers and White (1993) and Schneewind (1995).
6. Compare Seligman (1992) and Schwarzer (1993).
7. The following studies present examples of the large amount of work on this aspect: Brown and Harris (1989); Cohen (1988); and Montada, Filipp, and Lerner (1992).
8. Bandura's (1986, 1992) work on social learning theory deals with this relation in more detail.
9. The statistical procedure used here was hierarchical agglomerative cluster analysis (Tryon & Bailey, 1970). Although analyses were performed for three, four, and five clusters, the three-cluster solution proved to be intrinsically most meaningful.
10. Each theoretical treatment of stress must start with a definition of the concept. Examples of such efforts can be found in Field, McCabe, and Schneidermann (1988) and Lazarus and Folkman (1984). From the enormous amount of literature on the topic of coping, we wish to mention Haan (1982), Lazarus (1991), and Lazarus and Folkman (1984), Finally, Pearlin and Schooler (1978) published one of the first major empirical studies.
11. Compare Meichenbaum (1985).
12. Lazarus (1991) described various aspects of coping (see also Schwarzer, 1993).
13. Our items are taken from a comprehensive instrument for assessing family stress and coping developed by Peterander, Bailer, and Henrich (1987). An overview of other possible methods of assessing coping behavior can be found in Schwarzer (1993).
14. The results reported in the table are based on a multivariate analysis of covariance (MANCOVA) using number of experienced events (in dichotomized form) and gender as dependent variables and age as the covariate. Only main effects were tested (cf. Guilford, 1965).
15. Separate factor analyses were computed for the three event clusters and for various subsamples. All analyses produced a consistent three-factor solution. On the method of factor analysis, see Cattell (1978) or Gorsuch (1974).
16. The values of the three modes of perception were dichotomized to the scale mean, and this recomputed value was entered as a variable into the analysis of variance here.
17. Relevant findings on this context can be found in Perrez and Reicherts (1992), Peterson and Bossio (1991), and Seligman (1992).
18. The questions on physical symptoms are taken from the Health and Stress Profile of Olson, Stewart, and Wilson (1989; see also Weiß, Schneewind, & Olson 1995).
19. Support for this hypothesis based on conversion symptoms can be found in Adler (1986).

4

CHANGES IN CHILDREARING

Complaints about the young are almost as old as human history. Even as far back as Homer, we can find warnings about the danger to society of declining morals in the young generation, and this topic has continued to crop up again and again across the centuries.[1] In the former Federal Republic of Germany, the last time this happened was as a reaction to the 1968 generation and its demands for a reorganization of society along antiauthoritarian lines. A countermovement arose, which tried to grapple excessive permissiveness by demanding that people rear their children properly. This simultaneously revealed the cause of the declining morals diagnosed in the following generation—namely, a deficit in appropriate "childrearing."[2]

This criticism particularly addresses the traditional institutions of childrearing and education—above all, the family and the school. A major role is generally assigned to the family—and here predominantly the parents—because this is nearly always the institution that provides the context in which children have their earliest, more or less intensive, and long-lasting experiences of learning and life. Although one can engage in splendid arguments about the "appropriateness" of individual goals and measures of parental childrearing, there seems to be a general consensus on the fundamental function of family socialization. Essentially, this fundamental function is to create the necessary personal preconditions in the following generation in the form of a desire and ability to "participate in social life and, if necessary, to contribute to its transformation."[3]

The study of the relations between parental childrearing behavior and the child's development into a capable individual member of society has a long tradition in psychology, educational science, and sociology. Usually, these disciplines have drawn on the background of the characteristic image of humanity in Western cultures, oriented toward guiding principles such as individual activity and autonomy. These disciplines have tried to trace the essential features of childrearing activity that help to approach this ideal. Generally, these are studies that have worked out relations between the socialization experiences of children and their personality structure cross-sectionally within a particular historical and socioecological context. However, longitudinal studies, or even those that examine developmental courses through comparisons across generations, are in short supply.[4]

This chapter tackles at least a part of this deficit by using a longitudinal approach and a comparison across generations to examine whether there have been changes in parental childrearing behavior during the 16 years covered by our study, and, if there have been changes, which direction they have taken. The goal of this chapter is kept within a modest framework: It attempts neither to confirm the relations between childrearing and childhood behavior nor to explain the possible time- and generation-dependent changes in parental childrearing measures. Instead, it is a mere description of parental childrearing behavior from the perspectives of the parental and filial generations. Nonetheless, such descriptive findings are highly informative because they reveal something about constancy, change, and the direction of parental childrearing in an epochal comparison, and they provide indications regarding whether, and to what extent, parent–child relations are handed down from one generation to the next.

THE ASSESSMENT OF PARENTAL CHILDREARING BEHAVIOR

Before dealing with changes in the content of parental childrearing behavior in detail, the assessment instruments used in this study must be introduced. These were part of the comprehensive battery of questionnaires developed to measure family relations at the first wave in 1976, labeled the Family Assessment Test System (FATS). The FATS is constructed in the form of modules, and assesses parent–child relations and relations between spouses and family climate.[5]

In the present context, we are only interested in the relations between parents and their children. In principle, there are two ways to assess these: by observing parent–child interactions directly and classifying these interactions into preset observation categories, or recording the subjective perception of parent–child relations from the perspective of the partners involved. The FATS is based on the latter approach. Therefore, it focuses on the parents' childrearing activities (i.e., those more or less intentional attempts at intervention that parents use to change or stabilize the behavior of their children). We have differentiated between three aspects of parental childrearing activity:

1. Childrearing Goals. These are demands referring to specific childhood behaviors that parents expect their children to comply with. Childrearing goals can be assessed verbally in the form of set demands that range from specific and currently important behaviors to more general and far-reaching expectations (e.g., "My child should empty the trash can," "My child should graduate from high school").

2. Childrearing Attitudes. These are attitudes that parents reveal in their dealings with their children, expressed in a series of beliefs in, for example, leniency versus severity or control versus trust. In verbal terms, such beliefs are found in the form of statements such as "I firmly believe in not giving in to my child's demands," or "I basically never check up on whether my child actually does what I ask him or her to do."

3. Childrearing Practices. These are concrete behaviors that parents fall back on to reward or punish their children. Childrearing practices can be assessed verbally as descriptions of behavior that parents use to respond to their children's positive or negative behaviors. Examples are: "When I feel that my child has done something particularly well, I show him how proud I am of him," or "If my child has done something that I disagree with completely, then I scold her."[6]

Up to now, we have indicated that the parents provide information on their childrearing behavior themselves. Therefore, this can also be called *self-perceived parental childrearing behavior.* Nonetheless, by making small adjustments in phrasing, the statements originating from the parents can also be assessed from the perspective of the recipients of parental childrearing efforts—that is, the children. They are then, for example, "My mother/father wants me to graduate from high school whatever else I do," "My mother/father doesn't let me get away with anything," or "If my mother/father feels that I have done something particularly well, she/he always shows me how proud she/he is of me." When the focus is on the perceptions of the children, it is termed *other-perceived* or, more precisely, *child-perceived parental childrearing behavior.* What is important here is that we are always dealing with a real dyad. This means that a mother provides statements about a specific child and, vice versa, this child's statements refer exclusively to his or her mother. This results in self- and child-perceived statements on parental childrearing behavior for four constellations of relationships: mother–son, mother–daughter, father–son, and father–daughter.

Another important point is that there is no reason that the parent and child perspective should agree. Empirical research has shown that they only agree to a greater or lesser extent.[7] Apart from the fact that perceptual discrepancies can be, in themselves, interesting indicators for the quality of the parent–child relation, the subjective perspective of the partners involved is particularly interesting from a psychological perspective. This focusing on the subjective perspective can be justified by the so-called "Thomas theorem," which states: "If people define situations as real, they are real in their consequences."[8] Applied to our current research issue, this means that it is each subjectively perceived reality of a parent–child relation that has more or less generalizable or long-term consequences for the perceptions and behavior of the partners involved. Chapter 5 takes up this hypothesis and tests whether the subjective perception of earlier parental childrearing behavior can be related to the current perception of parent–child relations. However, this chapter concentrates, as we have already said, on time- and generation-dependent change in subjectively perceived parental childrearing behavior.

Finally, it is worth mentioning that the various domains of parental childrearing behavior (i.e., childrearing goals, attitudes, and practices) each break down into different aspects of content that can, in turn, also vary in strength. In the full version of the FATS, there are, depending on the relationship constellation, up to 9 separate aspects of parental childrearing goals, up to 12 childrearing attitudes, and up to 7 childrearing practices. In all, this means that we can discriminate among up to 28 components of parental childrearing behavior.[9] We label the specific configurations of various aspects of the contents of childrearing goals, attitudes, and practices the *parental childrearing style*. This, in turn, can be perceived from the parent's or child's side, so that we can discriminate between a *self-perceived* and a *child-perceived childrearing style*. Finally, empirical methods can be applied to find different childrearing styles that are typical for certain parent–child relations, and thus permit a classification of concrete parent–child relations into *types of childrearing style*. We no longer pursue this approach to stylizing parental childrearing behavior, which has been adopted relatively frequently in the previous research literature, but concentrate on the change in individual components of parental childrearing style.

However, what are the components of childrearing style on which the following analyses are based? We have not drawn on all possible 28 aspects of content, but selected 10 features that—distributed across the three domains of childrearing behavior—reflect central dimensions of parent–child relations. Each of these dimensions consists of a scale composed of several statements that respondents have to judge on rating scales. The following presents a short description of the individual scales grouped according to the three domains of childrearing behavior. As an illustration, we present one sample item from each scale in the form used to assess self-perceived parental childrearing behavior.

Childrearing Goals

1. Orientation Toward Religious Norms. This concept assesses the extent to which parents want their children to orient themselves toward traditional religious ideals. It can be viewed as a useful indicator for a general commitment to norms. Sample item: "My son/daughter should attend church regularly."

2. Achievement Orientation. Parents who give positive ratings to statements on this scale want their children to exhibit dominant and achievement-related behavior, at school as well as at play. They should strive to belong to the "better" group, and they should also make this visible to the external world. Sample item: "My son/daughter should continuously try to improve his/her school grades."

3. Autonomy. This concept has a different character for boys and girls. In boys, the focus is on the aspect of autonomous decision making (Sample item: "My son should decide completely for himself what he wants to spend his pocket money on"), whereas for girls—particularly from the mothers' perspective—the goal is a female existence independent from a future partner that allows the daughter to be personally responsible for a wide range of her activities (Sample item: "My daughter should also go out by herself even when she is married").

4. Conformity. This scale assesses how far parents expect their children to exhibit socially desirable, deferential behavior guided by external forms. In general, this childrearing goal reflects a more or less obedient willingness to conform. Sample item: "My son/daughter should always be only friendly and kind to other people."

Childrearing Attitudes

1. Permissiveness. This concept focuses on how far parents are prepared to set limits for their children, and also particularly when they expressly disapprove of their children's behavior. In general, it means that children are given a large scope for testing out their own plans and action impulses, which is generally reflected in a childrearing attitude of low parental intervention. Sample item: "I allow my child to carry on doing things even when I disapprove of them."

2. Authoritarian Attitude. At its extreme pole, this scale characterizes a parental attitude that rigidly and adamantly insists on enforcing parental demands on the child, and thereby takes no account of the child's interests. Sample item: "If I do not agree with what my son/daughter is doing, then he/she always has to follow my will."

3. Emotional Expression. This concept expresses itself in different ways for mothers and fathers. In mothers, closeness to their child manifests itself in their openness in making their inner moods externally recognizable (Sample item [negatively poled]: "I strive to ensure that my son/daughter never knows what I am really feeling"). In contrast, for fathers, the aspect of affection is the most prominent indicator of emotional closeness to the child (Sample item: "I am pleased when my son/daughter is affectionate to me").

Childrearing Practices

1. Loving Attention. This concerns a specific form of parental recognition for positively evaluated child behavior that can be deduced particularly from emotional behavior. It is especially these nonverbal components of attention that should reflect a high degree of authentic emotional bonding, and thus have a high reinforcement value for the child. Sample item: "If I feel that my son/daughter has done something particularly well, then I beam with joy."

2. Corporal Punishment. This concept assesses the degree of violent aggression toward the child when he or she has done something for which he or she is to blame in the parents' eyes. The emotions that accompany corporal punishment are anger and rage. Sample item: "If my son/daughter has done something with which I completely disagree, then I slap his/her face out of rage."

3. Limited Praise. This scale addresses a reaction that parents intend as a reward for positive child behavior, although, conceptually, it takes an intermediate position between reward and punishment. It expresses a kind of "yes, but" attitude, in which one can see that, even when the parents approve of their child's behavior, they are unable to admit this without reservations. Here, parental recognition is linked to the condition that the children must not relax their willingness to achieve and make an effort. Sample item: "If I feel that my son/daughter has done something particularly well, then I tell him/her that he/she must make a strong effort to do just as well the next time."

Following this overview of the individual concepts of parental childrearing behavior focused on in the following sections of this chapter, we highlight whether and how these concepts have changed over time in the parent generation.

A SECOND CHANCE: IF PARENTS HAD
TO REAR CHILDREN AGAIN

"Imagine that you now have a daughter who is exactly the same age as your daughter was at the time of our first survey. The following statements refer to opinions, goals, and concrete childrearing situations. We want to know how you would reply to these statements if you were currently the mother of a 9- to 13-year-old daughter." These are the instructions that we used to ask the mothers of daughters to place themselves once more in their parental role 16 years after the first survey. With appropriate changes in phrasing, we also asked the mothers of sons, as well as the fathers of sons or daughters, to give a new rating on their childrearing behavior. It was expressly drawn to their attention that there have been numerous social, political, and societal changes over the past 16 years that could also have an impact on the topic of "childrearing." Hence, the goal of these instructions was to deduce the intensity and direction of a possible time effect from the discrepancies between the answers on the individual concepts of childrearing style that the parents gave in 1976 and 1992. In concrete terms, have, for example, parental demands that their children conform decreased between 1976 and 1992, or have they—and this possibility should also be expressly included—remained stable over this period?

Table 4.1 presents an overview of the mean changes in the individual childrearing components split according to the four possible constellations of parent–child relations. A quick glance at Table 4.1 reveals that change is more dominant than stability. More precisely, 28 of the 40 time-related comparisons show changes in childrearing behavior that are significant on at least the 5% level. For the remaining 12 comparisons, no statistically significant differences across time can be confirmed, providing support for the stability hypothesis. Another general finding is that the changes are distributed fairly equally across all four relationship constellations. This means that time effects occur with an almost equal frequency on all individual dimensions of childrearing style, regardless of the gender of the parent or child. However, this does not imply that these time effects occur in the same childrearing concepts for all relationship constellations.

A somewhat closer look at the findings reveals that those concepts of childrearing style whose weightings have changed across time have clearly followed a specific direction. This is revealed particularly impressively in the domain of childrearing practices. Both mothers and fathers would bestow a larger amount of loving affection on their children, they would less frequently discipline their children through corporal punishment, and they would—with the exception of father–son relations—less frequently give their children "achievement-spurring" feedback in the sense of a conditional recognition for positive behavior (e.g., according to the motto, "That was quite good, but you can do even better next time").

This last finding is supported by the fact that the domain of childrearing goals—once more, with the exception of father–son relations—reveals a clear drop in the achievement motivation demanded of children. Even more marked is the decline in the orientation toward religious norms that is equally strong across all four constellations of relations. In contrast, demands for conformity in the sense of a more or less unquestioning willingness to conform to society have declined exclusively in mothers with regard to both their sons or

TABLE 4.1
Parents: Comparison of Childrearing Styles in 1976 and 1992

CHILDREARING STYLE SCALES	Mother-Son (n = 111)			Father-Son (n = 112)		
	1976	1992	p	1976	1992	p
Childrearing goals[1] Orientations toward religious norms	2.59[4] .83	2.32 .80	***	2.61 .73	2.43 .86	***
Achievement orientation	2.23 .62	2.03 0.58	***	2.74 .56	2.65 .52	
Autonomy	2.71 .73	2.80 .70		3.25 .41	3.33 .46	
Conformity	2.88 .57	2.72 .52	***	3.10 .45	3.04 .47	
Childrearing attitudes[1] Permissiveness	2.59 .43	2.79 .45	***	1.96 .55	2.14 .49	***
Authoritarian attitude	2.36 .60	2.13 .53	***	2.43 .65	2.25 .57	**
Emotional expression (openness, affection)[3]	2.70O .60	2.73O .54		3.03A .86	2.88 .71	*
Childrearing practices[2] Loving attention	3.84 .72	3.86 .57		3.16 .74	3.33 .68	**
Corporal punishment	1.47 .48	1.38 .41	***	1.55 .54	1.34 .42	***
Limited praise	2.68 .82	2.52 .74	**	2.74 .68	2.84 .75	

(table continues)

TABLE 4.1
(Continued)

CHILDREARING STYLE SCALES	Mother-Daughter (n = 112)			Father-Daughter (n = 98)		
	1976	1992	p	1976	1992	p
Childrearing goals[1] Orientation toward religious norms	2.56[4] .80	2.31 .81	**	2.57 .90	2.33 .89	***
Achievement orientation	2.92 .60	2.78 .61	***	1.90 .54	1.74 .43	**
Autonomy	2.80 .66	3.10 .61	***	3.36 .46	3.31 .47	
Conformity	2.77 .61	2.58 .59	**	3.13 .56	3.05 .47	
Childrearing attitudes[1] Permissiveness	2.56 .48	2.58 .44		2.53 .47	2.45 .47	
Authoritarian attitude	2.23 .66	2.07 .49	**	2.37 .59	2.14 .51	***
Emotional expression (openness, affection)[3]	2.85O .69	2.86O .61		3.40A .64	3.16A .66	***
Childrearing practices[2] Loving attention	3.84 .72	4.09 .58	**	3.43 .80	3.68 .62	**
Corporal punishment	1.47 .48	1.21 .29	***	1.28 .39	1.15 .26	***
Limited praise	2.68 .82	2.45 .79	*	2.52 .80	2.68 .72	*

Note. * $p < .05$. ** $p < .01$. *** $p < .001$. 1: Scores ranging from 1 to 4. 2: Scores ranging from 1 to 5. 3: O = Openness. A = Affection. 4: Upper entry = mean. Lower entry = standard deviation.

130

daughters, whereas there has been no change in this area among fathers. Expectations of more autonomy can be found only in the mother–daughter relation, although it has to be recalled that this concerns a specifically female concept of autonomy reflecting the social advances in the process of female emancipation. Accordingly, the findings in the domain of childrearing goals indicate a general weakening of normative commitments and a lowering of achievement- and conformity-related behavior standards.

This picture is supplemented by the findings on childrearing attitudes. Here there is a clear decline across the board in authoritarian childrearing attitudes, and this holds for all relationship constellations. In other words, parents insist far less than they did in 1976 on imposing their demands exclusively in line with their own ideas, which simultaneously means that they grant their children more say in things. Another aspect of this stronger consideration of the child as an autonomous person is the degree of leniency toward childish behavior impulses. It seems to be particularly sons who profit from this because both mothers and fathers grant them more freedom than they do to daughters, even when they take liberties of which their parents basically disapprove. Finally, it can be ascertained that fathers are much more successful than they were 16 years before in visibly expressing their affection for their sons and daughters in the form of physical affection, at least on the level of attitudes. This finding fits in with the increased level of loving attention that, as was already seen, can be confirmed particularly for fathers in the domain of childrearing practices.

All in all, a specific picture of the change in childrearing behavior from the parents' perspective begins to take shape. It is characterized by (a) a lower level of demands to conform to religious, achievement-related, and social behavior standards; (b) more say in things, leniency, and overtly expressed affection; and, finally, (c) a stronger emphasis on positive emotionality as a response to desired child behavior accompanied by a simultaneous decrease in aggressive corporal measures of discipline and in conditional forms of recognition for children's efforts.

Of course, there are also differences in emphasis for individual components depending on the constellation of relations inspected. For example, the aspect of leniency is stronger in mothers; in fathers, the expression of emotional affection is stronger. Nonetheless, on the whole, the pattern of change in parental childrearing behavior is relatively constant. In all, the time effect appearing in the parent generation suggests that a stronger, emotionally based consideration of childhood individuality and a more liberal approach to the child can be plotted over the course of the years.

It has to be noted that these findings are based on mean changes. As the standard deviations from the means also reported in Table 4.1 show, there are notable interindividual differences on nearly all features of parental childrearing behavior, and these have remained more or less constant in size across the two waves. In other words, just as there were already parents with a very authoritarian or a less authoritarian attitude toward their children in 1976, parents also show similarly clear differences in attitudes in 1992. It is certain that then, just as now, such differences are also reflected in the children's actual behavior and their perceptions of relations. Once again, it is necessary to refer to the findings that are presented in more detail in chapter 5.

Another question is how far individual differences in parental childrearing behavior have remained constant over time. To investigate this, we correlated the individual scores of parents on each of the 10 childrearing style concepts in 1976 and 1992, and thus obtained a measure of the relative stability of features of childrearing style—completely analogue to the procedure used in chapter 2 to test the relative stability of personality characteristics. These correlations are presented in Table 4.2.

All correlations are statistically significant, and the mean correlation of $r = .48$ indicates that a comparatively high 16-year stability has been retained across all features of childrearing style and relationship constellations. However, there are a few concept- and parent-specific differences that should not be overlooked. For example, the childrearing goal "Orientation toward religious norms" has the highest stability across time. This obviously addresses a clearly discernable behavior standard (e.g., "My child should attend church regularly"). Despite that there has been a clear decline in this childrearing goal, it is still easy for parents to report whether this is an important or less important demand that they place on their children.

However, the childrearing attitude "Permissiveness" exhibits a lower differential stability across time. It is particularly mothers who have changed their attitudes here—or, more precisely, for those mothers who showed a lower level of leniency in 1976, it is relatively difficult to predict whether they have retained this attitude in 1992 or whether they have become more lenient toward their children.

In summary, it can be seen that the relatively abstract childrearing attitudes that are formulated in behaviorally less proximal terms have a lower relative stability than the more strongly behavior-oriented childrearing goals and practices. Nonetheless—also in light of the relatively low number of items used to assess the individual concepts of childrearing style—it is astonishing that parents, although they have performed quantitative shifts, broadly repeat the same pattern of childrearing that they already practiced toward their children 16 years before.[10]

WE'LL DO IT DIFFERENTLY—OR? IDEAS ON CHILDREARING IN THE YOUNG GENERATION

How do the parents' ideas on childrearing differ from those of their now grown-up children in 1992? In other words, is there a generation difference in childrearing? This is the question addressed in this section. In addition,

TABLE 4.2
Parents: Relative Stability of Variables of Childrearing Style From 1976 to 1992

CHILDREARING STYLE SCALES	M-S ($n = 111$)	F-S ($n = 112$)	M-D ($n = 112$)	F-D ($n = 98$)	Mean correlation
Childrearing goals					
Orientation toward religious norms	.65	.65	.62	.73	.67
Achievement orientation	.59	.33	.59	.48	.51
Autonomy	.58	.32	.35	.54	.33
Conformity	.59	.43	.47	.49	.54
Childrearing attitudes					
Permissiveness	.22	.47	.19[1]	.44	.34
Authoritarian attitude	.47	.36	.35	.37	.39
Emotional expression (openness, affection)[2]	.35O	.52A	.29O	.54A	.43
Childrearing practices					
Loving attention	.45	.64	.43	.40	.49
Corporal punishment	.46	.42	.41	.48	.45
Limited praise	.47	.43	.61	.62	.54
Mean correlation	.49	.47	.44	.52	.48

Note. M-S = Mothers of sons. F-S = Fathers of sons. M-D = Mothers of daughters. F-D = Fathers of daughters.
1: $p < .05$; all other correlations: $p < .01$. 2: O = Openness. A = Affection.

this section also examines the relation between the childrearing style of the children's generation and the childrearing behavior that their parents practiced 16 years before.

Generation Differences in Childrearing

To expose generation differences in childrearing behavior for 1992, we compared two sets of data. First, we took the results of the survey of parents following the mode of data collection presented in the last section. It can be recalled that parents were asked to place themselves once more in the role of rearing a child today who is the same age as their son or daughter was 16 years before. Second, we asked the adult sons and daughters of these parents to tell us what sort of childrearing attitudes they would have toward a son or daughter if this child were to be the same age as they were 16 years ago. The actual instructions given to the young adults were: "Imagine yourself in the same situation as your father/mother 16 years ago, and that you have a son/daughter who is the same age as you were then. How would you reply to the following statements on childrearing with regard to your own 9- to 14-year-old child?"[11]

The young adults completed the same inventory for assessing parental childrearing goals, attitudes, and practices as their parents. This makes it possible to compare two family-linked generations on the basis of the same childrearing concepts. Two things have to be taken into account here. First, because special instructions were used to rule out the time effect in the parent generation, the goal of this research question is to ascertain a generation effect that applies at one point of time in 1992. Second, our main interest is to find out whether the childrearing behavior of sons toward their own sons is influenced by the corresponding behavior of their fathers. Naturally, this also applies in the same way for adult daughters (i.e., how far does their behavior toward their own daughters include the childrearing that they experienced from their mothers?). In other words, in this three-generation perspective, we are only interested in same-gender parent–child relations following the pattern: "Mother → Daughter → Daughter's Daughter" or "Father → Son → Son's Son." In line with this, Table 4.3 presents mean scores and standard deviations for the 10 childrearing style concepts for only same-gender constellations.

A glance at the table reveals that both genders show some major childrearing differences between the generations. Essentially, these differences take the same direction as that found in the previously mentioned analysis of time effects for the parent generation, although the weights take a slightly different distribution. The most marked generation differences are in the domains of childrearing goals and childrearing practices.

Childrearing goals reveal a markedly lower orientation toward religious norms and a marked decrease in the demands for conformity in the younger generation. For mother–daughter constellations, there is also a marked increase in expectations of autonomy in favor of the next generation, whereas the young fathers reveal a lower level of achievement-related demands on their sons.

In the domain of childrearing practices, the children's generation shows a notable increase in their willingness to respond to positive behavior in their children, with a high degree of attention and affection. In addition, compared with the parents, the younger generation applies limited praise far less frequently as an appropriate means of rewarding desired child behavior. There are no statistically significant differences for corporal punishment as a

TABLE 4.3
Comparison of Current Childrearing Style of Parents and Children in 1992
(Same Gender, Parent-Child Dyads Only)

CHILDREARING STYLE SCALES	Father-Son (n = 95)			Mother-Daughter (n = 96)		
	Father	Son	p	Mother	Daughter	p
Childrearing goals[1] Orientation toward religious norms	.2.42[4] .86	1.89 .77	***	2.31 .81	1.72 .70	***
Achievement orientation	2.65 .52	2.44 .49	*	2.78 .61	2.65 .69	
Autonomy	3.33 .46	3.43 .40		3.10 .61	3.52 .50	***
Conformity	3.04 .47	2.73 .47	***	2.58 .54	2.27 .53	***
Childrearing attitudes[1] Permissiveness	2.14 .49	2.30 .43	*	2.58 .44	2.68 .44	
Authoritarian attitudes	2.25 .57	2.32 .56		2.07 .49	2.00 .56	
Emotional expression (openness, affection)[3]	2.88[A] .71	3.26[A] .65	***	2.86[O] .61	2.99[O] .64	
Childrearing practices[2] Loving attention	3.33 .68	3.95 .57	***	4.09 .58	4.49 .43	***
Corporal punishment	1.34 .42	1.33 .38		1.21 .29	1.19 .27	
Limited praise	2.84 .75	2.43 .61	***	2.45 .79	1.99 .77	***

Note. *p < .05. *** p < .001. 1: Scores ranging from 1 to 4. 2: Scores ranging from 1 to 5. 3: O = Openness. A = Affection. 4: Upper entry = mean. Lower entry = standard deviation.

means of discipline, although it has to be considered that the mean scores on this feature of childrearing style are, in any case, very low in both generations.

The domain of childrearing attitudes reveals the lowest differences between the generations. Nonetheless, it is worth mentioning that young fathers are much more prepared to accept or express affection in their relations with their sons. In addition, young fathers tend to be more lenient than their own fathers—a finding that is not reciprocated in the mother–daughter relationship. In all, the change in the pattern of childrearing in the intergeneration comparison particularly reveals less commitment to norms and less pressure to conform in the younger generation, as well as a stronger willingness to express positive emotions in contacts with their children.

Despite these differences between the generations, is it still possible to find common features within families in terms of the individual features of childrearing style? This is the next question. Once again, we compare two data sets—namely, the individual scores of the fathers and their sons or of the mothers and their daughters on each feature of childrearing style. As in the previous chapters, we use correlation coefficients to measure the agreement between each pair of representatives for the two generations. The results of these comparisons are presented in Table 4.4.

The first impression is that there is no or only a slight agreement between the parent and children's generations for most concepts of childrearing style. However, two exceptions should be noted. First, the childrearing goal of "Orientation toward religious norms" obviously shows clear family-determined differences. Second, it is conspicuous that the demands for autonomy that young women make for their own daughters—even when they are, on average, stronger than those of their mothers—still show a relatively close relation to the corresponding goal concepts of the mothers. It should be recalled that this childrearing goal concerns a specific female expectation of emancipation that is directed particularly toward a later partnership. It seems as if this childrearing concept reveals a more or less strongly marked awareness for female emancipational needs that is reflected in a relatively high consensus between mothers and daughters. In other words, as in the generally ascertainable family differences in religious behavior, a woman-specific childrearing goal is revealed here that is obviously handed down from one generation to the next.

However, these findings should not obscure the fact that—viewed as a whole—intergenerational agreements on childrearing behavior are not particularly high. Admittedly, it should not be forgotten that we are dealing with a comparison of two perceptual perspectives originating from different persons, even when these persons belong to the same families. Therefore, we could ask ourselves whether these relations would look different if one and the same person was to adopt different perspectives. This is the topic of the next section.

TABLE 4.4
Correlations Between Current Parental Childrearing Style and Current
Children's Childrearing Style (Same Gender, Parent-Child Dyads Only)

CHILDREARING STYLE SCALES	F-S (n = 95)	M-D (n = 96)	Mean correlation
Childrearing goals			
Orientation toward religious norms	.50 ***	.70 ***	.61 ***
Achievement orientation	.29 **	.27 **	.28 **
Autonomy	-.02	.45 ***	.25 **
Conformity	.14	.11	.13
Childrearing attitudes			
Permissiveness	.12	.25 **	.19 *
Authoritarian orientation	-.07	.12	.10
Emotional expression			
(openness, affection)[1]	.02 A	.13 O	.08
Childrearing practices			
Loving attention	.06	.02	.04
Corporal punishment	.02	.06	.04
Limited praise	.09	.30 **	.20 *
Mean correlation	.14	.26 *	.20 *

Note. F-S = Father- Son, M-D = Mother-Daughter. * $p < .05.$ ** $p < .01.$ *** $p < .001.$
1: O = Openness. A = Affection.

The Children's Own Childrearing Style
and Their Retrospective Assessment
of Their Parents' Childrearing Style

In an additional set of instructions, we asked the young adults to place
themselves in the role of their parents and to rate the statements on diverse
aspects of childrearing behavior in the way that they consider their parents
would have rated them 16 years ago. The actual instructions were: "Sixteen
years ago, your parents gave us information on how they were bringing you
up. Now, we want to ask you to place yourself in the position of your parents
16 years ago, and then to fill out the questionnaire in the way that you

believe your father filled it out 16 years ago when we asked him how he was rearing you." With appropriate alterations to the instructions, daughters were also asked to give retrospective ratings on the childrearing behavior of their mothers.

If we use this way to contrast retrospectively perceived parental child-rearing style with the childrearing behavior that the younger generation expresses prospectively with regard to its own children if they were of a comparable age, the discrepancy between these two scores results in a special kind of change effect. This consists of an aggregation of time and generation differences from the perspective of the children. Therefore, we can also call this the children's *time and generation effect*. Although it has to be noted that this is a measure of discrepancy based exclusively on the subjective perception of differences in parental childrearing, this is why it is of great psychological interest. Two issues are the focus of attention here. The first concerns the size of the discrepancies between the childrearing style attributed to the parents and the children's own childrearing style, and, particularly, what direction these discrepancies take, if any discrepancies can be found. The second issue is to test how far individual differences in the retrospective perception of parental childrearing style relate to the young generation's own childrearing behavior. This question reveals that we are addressing the topic of *intergenerational transfer*.

We first deal with the first question on the extent and direction of possible discrepancies between retrospectively assessed parental childrearing style and the children's own childrearing style from the perspective of the younger generation. Table 4.5 reports the corresponding means and standard deviations, although, once more, only the scores for same-gender parent–child constellations are presented because of the implicit three-generation perspective.

It is immediately conspicuous that there are significant differences beween own childrearing style and retrospectively assessed parental child-rearing style on all 10 concepts, and for both female and male respondents in the children's generation. Apart from two comparisons with a weaker significance, these differences are very strong, and thus document that the young adults generally distance themselves distinctly from their parents in terms of their childrearing behavior.

Regarding the direction of this change, the same picture found in the previous analyses on the time effect for parents and the generation effect can be confirmed, only this time the differences are particularly strong. In all, a pattern of change in parental childrearing style is corroborated; it is characterized by a lowering of normative and socially conformist expectations, paired with less authoritarian control and the granting of a greater scope of freedom. In addition, the "new" parents place more value on children's autonomy, as well as reduced achievement expectations, which

TABLE 4.5
Children: Comparison of Own Current Childrearing Style With Retrospectively
Perceived Childrearing Style of Same-Gender Parent

CHILDREARING STYLE SCALES	Sons (n = 95)			Daughters (n = 96)		
	Son for own son	Son for father retro	p	Daughter for own daughter	Daughter for mother retro	p
Childrearing goals[1] Orientation toward religious norms	1.89[4] .77	2.54 .94	***	1.72 .70	2.43 .93	***
Achievement orientation	2.44 .49	2.86 .47	***	2.65 .69	2.99 .54	***
Autonomy	3.43 .40	3.11 .45	***	3.52 .50	3.00 .67	***
Conformity	2.73 .47	3.13 .39	***	2.27 .53	2.75 .47	***
Childrearing attitudes[1] Permissiveness	2.30 .43	2.19 .51	*	2.68 .44	2.46 .50	***
Authoritarian attitude	2.32 .56	2.67 .62	***	2.00 .56	2.19 .60	***
Emotional expression (openness, affection)[3]	3.26[A] .65	2.62[A] .71	***	2.99[O] .64	2.65[O] .64	***
Childrearing practices[2] Loving attention	3.95 .57	3.10 .69	***	4.49 .43	3.90 .70	***
Corporal punishment	1.33 .38	1.72 .73	***	1.19 .27	1.42 .55	***
Limited praise	2.43 .61	2.84 .76	***	1.99 .77	2.55 .87	***

Note. * p < .05. *** p < .001. 1: Scores ranging from 1 to 4. 2: Scores ranging from 1 to 5. 3: O = Openness. A = Affection. 4: Upper entry = mean. Lower entry = standard deviation.

are expressed, among others, by a broad renunciation of achievement-spurring childrearing practices. Finally, the young adults introduce a larger degree of emotional affection and commitment toward their children into their parental role compared with their own childhood experiences.[12]

If we want to find a common denominator for this pattern of change, we can generally talk about an increasing intimacy and liberalization in parental childrearing behavior. As a rule, parent–child relations no longer function in terms of superiority and subordination. Instead, parents view their children as autonomous partners with a large number of equal rights in a more or less egalitarian relationship. Succinctly, a childrearing determined by parents has turned into a partner relationship.[13]

However, as the standard deviations in Table 4.5 reveal, there are also notable individual differences. In other words, despite an undeniable trend toward more liberalness among the younger generation, some follow this trend particularly strongly, whereas others are far more hesitant. This leads us to the second issue in this section—namely, how far individual differences in own childrearing behavior can be predicted on the basis of the childrearing style that the children's generation experienced 16 years before. To study this, we correlate the individual scores on own childrearing style with the corresponding scores on the features that the members of the young generation attribute to their parents in retrospective. These findings are reported in Table 4.6.

At first glance, it is conspicuous that the relations between own and retrospectively ascertained parental concepts of childrearing style are equal in content, as well as highly significant. The mean correlation is $r = .43$, with hardly any differences between sons and daughters. The highest correlations are for the domain of childrearing goals. This is followed by childrearing practices, whereas the correlations for childrearing attitudes are generally somewhat lower.

What do these findings mean? First, it should be recalled that these correlations are based on two different judgment perspectives that nonetheless originate from one and the same person. In contrast to the findings in the last section, which were based on information from two persons—namely, the parent and the accompanying child (see Table 4.4)—the present findings refer exclusively to the members of the children's generation. This means that, in each case, only one set, person-specific judgment scheme is activated by the different instructions for assessing own and retrospectively attributed parental childrearing style. This is certainly a major reason that the corresponding correlations in the previous section are clearly lower than the ones reported here.

However, the findings in Table 4.6 are quite informative. They provide a picture that reveals that young adults view their ideas on childrearing, at least to some extent, as a function of the childrearing behavior they consider

TABLE 4.6

Children: Correlations of Own Current Childrearing Style With
Retrospectively Perceived Childrearing Style of Same-Gender Parent

CHILDREARING STYLE SCALES	SS-SF ($n = 95$)	DD-DM ($n = 95$)	Mean correlation
Childrearing goals			
Orientation toward religious norms	.50	.60	.45
Achievement orientation	.46	.40	.43
Autonomy	.40	.48	.44
Conformity	.51	.43	.47
Childrearing attitudes			
Permissiveness	.38	.47	.37
Authoritarian attitude	.26	.47	.37
Emotional expression (openness, affection)[1]	.34A	.20O2	.27
Childrearing practices			
Loving attention	.39	.43	.41
Corporal punishment	.33	.36	.35
Limited praise	.52	.49	.51
Mean correlation	.41	.44	.43

Note. SS-SF = Son for own son - Son for father retrospectively. DD-DM = Daughter for own daughter -Daughter for mother retrospectively. 1: O = Openness. A = Affection. 2: $p < .05$. All other correlations: $p < .01$.

they were confronted with 16 years before. Here it is not so important whether the childrearing approach that their parents used with them "actually" happened in the way that they perceive it in retrospective. What is far more important is how they reconstruct the purported childrearing behavior for themselves, and what effects the outcome of this reconstruction process has on their own ideas on childrearing.

In fact, the findings indicate, as stated, that the attributed parental childrearing style influences the children's own ideas on childrearing, despite the generally considerable shift toward more liberalness confirmed in the younger generation. This is clarified with an example: A roughly 30-year-old son who experienced a comparatively restrictive upbringing when he was 14 will certainly treat his own son—to some extent, in line with the spirit of the times—more liberally than his father had done before him. Nonetheless, in comparison with his current contemporaries, he will be one of the less liberal fathers. In other words, despite a time- and generation-determined change in childrearing, there is still a handing down of the style of parental childrearing behavior from one generation to the next that is anchored in subjective experience.

THE SPIRIT OF CONTEMPORARY CHILDREARING: WHO IS CLOSER, MOTHERS OR FATHERS?

In the previous section, we have ascertained a general shift toward more liberalness in childrearing behavior when focusing on the perceptions of the younger generation. The question now is whether the older generation is sensitive to this change that, to a certain extent, reflects the current "spirit" of childrearing.

We tested this by asking the mothers and fathers in the parent generation to answer the various statements in the childrearing questionnaires under special instructions. Similar to the way in which the adult sons and daughters had to place themselves in the roles of their parents and rate their childrearing style retrospectively, the present research question asked the parents to place themselves in the role of their children as parents, and to report how their children, if themselves mothers and fathers, would probably rear their own children. The actual phrasing of the instructions was as follows: "When filling out this questionnaire, imagine that your son/daughter is in the same situation as you were 16 years ago, that is, he/she is the father/mother of a son/daughter of the same age as he/she was 16 years ago. How do you think that he/she would answer these questions?" If the information from the parent generation obtained in this way is compared with the reports on the childrearing style that the younger generation attributes to itself, we can ascertain how well the parent generation is able to predict the probable childrearing behavior of the children's generation.

Because, in the given context, mothers and fathers had both been asked to rate the childrearing behavior of their sons and daughters, we want to pay particular attention in the following to whether fathers and mothers differ in the mean precision of their predictions. The corresponding means and standard deviations for the individual childrearing style scales are reported in Table 4.7.

To interpret these findings, it is first necessary to visualize what the significant differences marked with asterisks mean. When the difference between sons or daughters and their mothers and fathers is statistically

TABLE 4.7
Comparison of Current Childrearing Style of Children With the Childrearing
Style Attributed to Them by Both Parents

CHILDREARING STYLE SCALES	Sons ($n = 91$)			Daughter ($n = 93$)		
	Son	Mother for son	Father for son	Daughter	Mother for daughter	Father for daughter
Childrearing goals[1]						
Orientation toward religious norms	1.89[4] .77	2.12* .81	2.02 .90	1.72 .70	1.93* .85	1.93* .85
Achievement orientation	2.44 .49	2.54* .52	2.62* .51	2.65 .69	2.68 .67	2.91** .52
Autonomy	3.43 .40	3.36 .40	3.30** .48	3.52 .50	3.33* .65	2.99*** .53
Conformity	2.73 .47	2.88** .45	2.87* .99	2.27 .53	2.43 .60	2.63 .43
Childrearing attitudes[1]						
Permissiveness	2.30 .43	2.33 .47	2.15* .53	2.68 .44	2.59 .47	2.47** .40
Authoritarian attitude	2.32 .56	2.38 .51	2.46* .50	2.00 .56	2.24** .48	2.19** .47
Emotional expression (openness, affection)[3]	3.26[A] .65	3.35[A] .51	3.12[A] .68	2.99[O] .64	2.82[O] .63	2.98[O] .51
Childrearing practices[2]						
Loving attention	3.95 .57	3.81 .64	3.64** .74	4.49 .43	4.24** .56	4.06** .62
Corporal punishment	1.33 .38	1.33 .37	1.28 .37	1.19 .27	1.23 .33	1.20 .30
Limited praise	2.43 .61	2.83** .65	2.87** .76	1.99 .77	2.41** .82	2.47** .70

Note. * $p < .05$. ** $p < .01$. *** $p < .001$. 1: Scores ranging from 1 to 4. 2: Scores ranging from 1 to 5. 3: O = Openness. A = Affection. 4: Upper entry = mean. Lower entry = standard deviation.

significant, for a specific childrearing concept, this means that there is a significant difference between the parent's and child's perspective. In other words, the more significant differences there are in individual features of childrearing style, the greater the distance between the parents' and their children's ideas on childrearing.

In this light, we can first test whether such differences can be confirmed more frequently in either the mothers or fathers. The result is clear: From 20 possible comparisons, there are 14 significant differences for the father–son or father–daughter constellation, compared with only 9 in the corresponding comparisons for the mothers. If we also consider the direction of these differences in light of the clear liberalization of parental childrearing indicated in the previous section, we can state that mothers seem to be more sensitive toward this pattern of change than fathers. To a certain extent, they have grasped the current "spirit of childrearing" better, irrespective of whether their children are sons or daughters.

Particularly in the domain of childrearing practices, fathers in the parent generation seem to find it particularly difficult to perceive a higher level of nonverbal affection and the renunciation of limited praise as important elements in the current concept of childrearing, although the latter also applies to mothers. Also with regard to features of childrearing such as achievement motivation and permissiveness, fathers are further removed from the childrearing concept of the younger generation than mothers.

We still have to ask whether the generally confirmed greater closeness of mothers to the childrearing concepts of their children is also revealed on the level of individual differences. Once more, this question can be examined with the methodological help of correlation coefficients, which tell us something about how far the relative position of the mothers or fathers agrees with that of their children for the individual features of childrearing style. These findings are reported in Table 4.8. To complete the picture, this table also reports how far the parents agree with each other in their views on the current childrearing style of their children.

First, it can be deduced from the mean father–child or mother–child correlations that there are no marked differences between fathers and mothers in the differential precision of predictions. Thus, on the level of individual differences, we are unable to confirm the significant finding in the mean comparison—namely, that mothers are closer to the concept of childrearing in the younger generation. It is far more the case that mothers and fathers reveal a higher level of agreement among themselves than they do in relation to their child—a finding similar to that already ascertained in chapter 2 for personality judgments. The comment there was that parents have a longer experience of situations at their disposal in which they exchange information on the behavior of their children.

Apart from this, it is also mentionable that all relationship constellations show a high level of agreement on the extent of religious norm orientation.

TABLE 4.8
Correlations Between Current Childrearing Style of Children and Childrearing
Style Attributed to Them by Both Parents

CHILDREARING STYLE SCALES	Sons (n = 92)			Daughters (n = 94)		
	S-MS	S-FS	MS-FS	D-MD	D-FD	MD-FD
Childrearing goals Orientation toward religious norms	.53 ***	.50 ***	.68 ***	.70 ***	.51 ***	.52 ***
Achievement orientation	.33 ***	.29 **	.36 ***	.27 **	.09	.27 **
Autonomy	.18 *	-.02	.12	.45 ***	.27 **	.40 ***
Conformity	.22 *	.14	.20 *	.11	.01	.47 ***
Childrearing attitudes Permissiveness	.22 *	.21 *	.24 **	.10	.23 *	.49 ***
Authoritarian attitude	.11	.26 **	.35 ***	.07	.12	.24 *
Emotional expression (openness, affection)[1]	.23ZA*	.09A	.36A ***	.18O *	.07O	.20O *
Childrearing practices Loving attention	.14	.27 **	.37 ***	.07	.29 **	.39 ***
Corporal punishment	.14	.21 *	.42 ***	.19 *	.34 ***	.33 ***
Limited praise	.07	.16	.48 ***	.35 ***	.23 *	.37 ***

Note. S-MS = Son for own son -Mother for Son. S-FS = Son for own son -Father for Son. MS-FS = Mother for Son -
Father for Son. D-MD = Daughter for own daughter -Mother for Daughter. D-FD = Daughter for own daughter -Father
for Daughter. MD-FD = Mother for daughter -Father for daughter. * $p < .05$. ** $p < .01$. *** $p < .001$. 1: O = Openness.
A = Affection.

This finding is also just as familiar as the relatively high correlations for the woman-specific dimension of childrearing style "Autonomy." The analysis of generation effects in the previous section revealed correlations of a similar size. For the case of religious norm orientation, we attributed this high intergenerational agreement to the concrete and close-to-behavior formulation of the ideal demands, and we attributed the specific female emancipation demands to a gender-specific understanding between mothers and daughters on a topic that has received much attention in the public debate.

All in all, it can be stated that mothers generally can predict the probable childrearing behavior of their children better than fathers, and thus they have also adapted themselves better to the current "spirit of childrearing." However, no significant differences can be found in the differential precision of prediction between mothers and fathers. On the individual level, the extent of agreement between the generations seems to be determined more strongly by content-specific conditions.

WHICH DIRECTION IS CHILDREARING TAKING?
TIME AND GENERATION DIFFERENCES COMPARED

The previous sections of this chapter have compared the different perceptual perspectives of the parent and children's generations on questions of childrearing. In each case, we focused on a particular aspect of the comparison, such as the temporal change in childrearing style in the parent generation or the current difference between generations. We now want to piece the various perceptual perspectives together into a total picture.

In our first study in 1976, we assessed a complete series of parental childrearing style aspects in the fathers and mothers, in which each question referred to a particular child. In 1992, we gave the same questions to the mothers and fathers for a second time under two different instructions: First, they had to imagine that their child was currently the same age as he or she was in 1976 (i.e., between 9 and 14 years), and then report how they would raise their child under today's circumstances. Second, they had to place themselves in the position of their now adult son or daughter and imagine how they would raise a 9- to 14-year-old child under today's circumstances.

Likewise, we also presented the questions on parental childrearing style to the adult sons and daughters under two sets of instructions: First, they had to report how they would rear a child of the same gender and the same age as they had been at the time of the first wave (i.e., 16 years ago) under today's circumstances. Second, they had to place themselves in the role of their mothers or fathers and answer the various questions on childrearing style in the way that their parents would probably have answered them 16 years before with reference to themselves.

By comparing parents and their children, we can now ascertain time and generation effects for the individual features of childrearing style as well as combined time-and-generation effects. Admittedly, this sounds a little confusing. Therefore, we try to show what we mean with an example. This is taken from the domain of childrearing goals—and for girls. Its contents deal with an aspect already addressed several times, and on which there is probably a high consensus that much has happened over the last years: autonomy or, more precisely, female emancipation. Figure 4.1 presents detailed information on how we have assessed this concept as a childrearing goal.

For each of the four statements, respondents had to report their agreement with it on a 4-point scale, from *I disagree fully* (1) to *I agree fully* (4). These data can be used to ascertain an individual score for each person. These individual scores can then be further processed for the individual samples and instruction conditions into the usual statistical measures, such as means and standard deviations. The outcome for our example can be seen in Fig. 4.2.

An initial look at the means labeled *M* shows that agreement with the childrearing goal of "female emancipation" has grown increasingly in the mothers' generation from 1976 to 1992 and—drawn on the year 1992—in the mothers' and daughters' generations. It should be noted that all differences between means are highly significant.

For simplicity's sake, we assume that the means represent the individual scores of an actual mother–child pair (e.g., a 54-year-old mother and her 28-year-old daughter who were 38 and 12 years old, respectively, in 1976). As can be seen, if the mother had to raise her 12-year-old daughter once more under current conditions, one of her goals would have been more emancipation. We label this increase in emancipation, which can be observed from 1976 to 1992, as a *time effect in the mothers.* We can also see that if today's 28-year-old daughter had a 12-year-old daughter to raise, she would demand an even

Items for the scale:
"Autonomy/Female Emancipation"

- She should also go out by herself even when she is a married woman
- As a married woman, she should also sometimes take a vacation by herself
- When she is older, she should feel free to go to a bar or go dancing
- She should be financially independent from her future husband

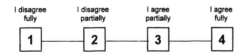

FIG. 4.1. Operationalization of the childrearing goal: "Autonomy/female emancipation."

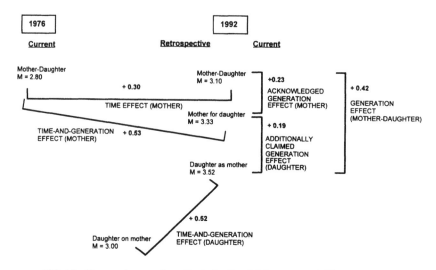

FIG. 4.2. Time and generation effects for the childrearing goal: "Autonomy/female emancipation."

greater degree of emancipation from her. We label the difference between the mean emancipation demands of the daughters and their mothers that can be ascertained in 1992 a *generation effect between mother and daughter*. Interestingly, however, when we ask the mothers to place themselves in their daughters' shoes (i.e., to imagine how their daughters would raise a 12-year-old daughter today), their emancipation demands are even higher. In other words, the mother knows, to some extent, that today's younger generation has other ideas on childrearing and recognizes this by increasing her demand for emancipation. We call this portion the *generation effect acknowledged by the mother*. However, this portion does not account for the entire generation effect (i.e., the mother underestimates her daughter's demand for emancipation). To cover the complete generation effect, there is still a remainder, which we call the *additionally claimed generation effect in the daughter*.

The time effect in the mother and the generation effect that she acknowledges can be aggregated into one value. This is the *time-and-generation effect from the mother's perspective*. There is also a *time-and-generation effect from the daughter's perspective*, which is computed from the difference between the daughter's estimated emancipation score for her mother in the 1976 retrospective and the amount of emancipation that she would wish for her own daughter under today's conditions.

Following this pattern, we examined all 10 features of childrearing style for time- and generation-determined changes. As already reported in the previous sections, these changes document a clear trend toward an increasing liberalization and emotionalization of parent–child relations. We summarize again: Normative commitments are in decline, achievement and conformity demands are reduced, limits are being set less clearly, individual scope is becoming larger, and emotional forms of expression more overt. What has caused this trend toward liberalization and emotionalization? Is it a time effect that has more or less crept up over the past 16 years? Is it a generation effect that the younger generation uses to distinguish itself from the older generation? Or is it a combination of the two (i.e., of time and generation effects) that is expressed in the different perspectives of older and younger generations? To answer these questions, we have used a specific methodological procedure to compute the effect sizes of time and generation effects, as well as separate time and generation effects for parents and children.[14] Table 4.9 reports the results of these analyses.

This table presents the mean effect sizes for the various aspects of childrearing goals, attitudes, and practices on which this chapter has concentrated separately for mother–daughter and father–son constellations. The more the mean effect sizes differ from zero, the more support they provide

TABLE 4.9
Effect Sizes of Time and Generation Differences for Parental Childrearing Style

DOMAINS OF CHILDREARING STYLE	Time effect parents	Generation effect parent-child	Time + Generation effect parents	Time + Generation effect child
Childrearing goals				
Father-son	.19	.49	.41	.83
Mother-daughter	.33	.54	.68	.80
Childrearing attitudes				
Father-son	.15	.25	.14	.56
Mother-daughter	.10	.19	.00	.43
Childrearing practices				
Father-son	.12	.49	.32	.77
Mother-daughter	.39	.44	.46	.62
All domains of childrearing				
style	.15	.41	.29	.72
Father-son	.27	.39	.38	.62
Mother-daughter				
Total	.21	.40	.34	.67

for the diagnosed shift toward increasing liberalization and emotionalization. It can be seen that this change effect is stronger for childrearing goals and practices than for childrearing attitudes, and essentially irrespective of whether relations are between mothers and daughters or fathers and sons.

A look at the last line of the table gives a total impression of the importance of the individual change effects. This makes it clear that the generation effect is almost twice as strong as the time effect. It can also be seen that the combined time-and-generation effect from the perspective of the young generation is almost exactly twice as large as the corresponding value for the older generation. In other words, the shift toward liberalization and emotionalization is much stronger in the younger generation than in their parents, although the parents, as has been shown, award their children a quite considerable generation bonus.

How can we interpret this shift toward more liberalization and emotionalization in family childrearing? Although this chapter is not concerned with the possible consequences of changes in childrearing, as mentioned earlier, nonetheless the chapter closes with a few comments on this. First of all, it can be ascertained that a liberal upbringing does not, in itself, have positive or negative effects on the personality development of young persons. In the childrearing domain as well, extended personal scopes can help to strengthen a certain autonomy in children and adolescents, particularly when they are accompanied by a stimulating and emotionally positive family climate. However, extended freedoms can also lead to a lack of orientation and disturbed social behavior when there is a lack of parental guidance and no willingness to set limits.

Therefore, we may well have something to think about when today's young parent generation identifies more frequently with the following statements than their parents do: "I basically never check up on whether my child actually does what I ask him/her to do" or "I allow my child to carry on doing things even when I disapprove of them." These, by the way, are statements from the childrearing attitude scale on permissiveness, which, as was shown, has exhibited clear increases in approval over the generation comparison. If one agrees with such statements without reservations, this is no longer a question of liberal childrearing, but a flagrant deficit in childcare and limit setting. In this case, there certainly is an urgent need for people to have the courage to rear their children properly.

A BRIEF SUMMARY OF THE MOST IMPORTANT POINTS

- *Parental childrearing style* has changed over the course of the years. In general, if parents had to take on childrearing tasks again today, they would (a) place lower demands to conform on their children regarding religious, achievement-related, and social behavior standards; (b) grant their children more say in their upbringing and treat them more leniently; and (c) be more emotionally accessible for their children and praise them more or punish them less. Fathers hardly differ at all from mothers in this respect, regardless of whether sons or daughters are concerned.

• Despite this shift toward increasing liberalization and emotionalization, individual differences in childrearing style have been retained over the 16-year time interval. In other words, parents who already demanded less achievement motivation and were more lenient and emotionally open compared with other mothers and fathers in 1976 exhibit a similar, although more strongly marked, childrearing pattern in 1992. Likewise, those mothers and fathers who practiced a more strict childrearing style in 1976 belong to the comparatively "strict" parents 16 years later, even if their attitude has become somewhat more relaxed over the years.

• Comparisons between the parent and children's generations reveal that the young adults have an emotionally more open, egalitarian, and less norm-oriented concept of childrearing than their parents.

• Although the mothers in the parent generation are, on average, closer to the current "spirit of childrearing" than the fathers, an inspection on the level of individual differences reveals that they tend to agree more with their spouses than with their children.

• In general, more liberal and more emotionally toned parent–child relations can be traced back to a far greater extent to differences between the parent and the children's generation than to a mere time effect. In other words, the younger generation seems to have succeeded in asserting a childrearing ideal that is principally oriented toward more equality and overt emotional expression.

• Despite this strong generation difference, it can also be confirmed clearly that parental childrearing behavior is handed down from one generation to the next: Children who have become acquainted with a more liberal childrearing style through their parents orient themselves—nonetheless to a greater extent than their parents—toward their parents' childrearing concept. Vice versa, young adults whose parents demanded more achievement, let them get away with less, and more frequently used punishments as disciplinary measures orient themselves toward the model of their parents, although somewhat less strongly, in their own childrearing behavior.

END NOTES

1. The indication that even Homer was dissatisfied with youth can be found in Delbrück (1893, p. 28).
2. Authors who have tackled the topics of "the courage to rear children properly" or "appropriate" childrearing include Maccoby (1992), Baumrind (1991), and Steinberg et al. (1995).

3. See Lüscher and Fisch (1977, p. 19).

4. Information on the results of research on family socialization can be found in Belsky et al. (1984), Maccoby and Martin (1983), Luster and Okagaki (1993), and Schneewind (1994).

5. Compare Schneewind (1988a) and Schneewind, Beckmann, and Hecht-Jackl (1985).

6. Information on the formal structuring of parental childrearing style can be found in Lukesch (1975) and Schneewind (1980). See also Darling and Steinberg (1993).

7. Compare here the methodological considerations and empirical findings in Tein, Roosa, and Michaels (1994); Johnson, Shulman, and Collins (1991); and Schwarz, Barton-Henry, and Pruzinsky (1985).

8. See Thomas (1928, p. 572).

9. The conception of FATS takes account of various types of relations (e.g., mother–son, father–daughter) with, in part, specific aspects of the content of childrearing style. As a consequence, each childrearing style is not assessed completely identically across all relationship constellations.

10. However, it should be considered that, when parents were confronted directly with childrearing issues and problems in 1976, their involvement in this topic was probably stronger than under the "artificial" instructions in 1992, at a time when they had left the "business" of childrearing behind them.

11. In contrast to the suggestion regarding the parent generation in Note 10, we can assume that the children's generation has a much stronger personal interest in the topic of childrearing because most of them still have to face this task in the future.

12. Compare the findings on temporal change in childrearing goals in Germany in Noelle-Neumann and Piel (1983) and Gensicke (1994). Similar findings have been reported for the United States (e.g., Alwin, 1988).

13. See the hypothesis of increasing child-centeredness in families in Germany proposed by, among others, Schütze (1988). For a discussion of this topic in the United States, see Demo (1992).

14. The computation of effect sizes is based on the technique of meta-analysis (see Glass, McGraw, & Smith, 1981) that is used particularly frequently in psychotherapy research. Meta-analysis is based on the principle of standardizing intervention-induced differences. In the simplest case, for the measure of change under consideration, the mean differences between experimental groups and controls are related to the standard deviation of the control groups' scores. In our case, we took time course and generation membership as "interventions," and defined the values for the wave in 1976 or the membership of the parent generation as the "control group scores" in each case.

5

RELATIONS BETWEEN PARENTS AND THEIR ADULT CHILDREN

The quality of parent–child relations is not just of great importance while the next generation is passing through childhood and adolescence. Even when children are grown up, the way that the generations relate to each other continues to play an important role in the well-being of both. A series of studies have confirmed that satisfying and harmonious contacts between parents and their adult children impact positively on their physical and mental well-being.[1] However, it also has to be taken into account that relations between the younger and older adult generations possess a history whose roots lie in early parent–child relations. Therefore, one of the questions tackled in this chapter is whether and to what extent we can trace back the quality of the current relationship between parents and their children (i.e., as assessed in the year 1992) to the earlier pattern of relations in 1976. This first calls for a brief description of the instrument constructed to survey current parent–child relations.

THE ASSESSMENT OF CURRENT PARENT–CHILD RELATIONS

The instrument for assessing current parent–child relations was specially developed for this study. We particularly wanted to operationalize two basic ideas: (a) to assess the most important aspects of parent–child relations from a psychological perspective as economically as possible, and (b) to ascertain which contribution the parent or child makes to the formation of the various aspects of the relationship within a specific parent–child dyad. The latter called for a specific survey format that is described briefly in the following.

Let us assume that a mother is asked to describe her relationship with her adult son. To assess the aspect of the relationship entitled "Conflict," she is given, alongside other questions related to conflict, the question displayed in Fig. 5.1. Unlike the usual relationship-oriented assessment instruments, this response format does not just require the mother to make a statement on the degree of differences of opinion that exist between herself and her son from her perspective, but also to report how far these differences of opinion are caused by her son or herself. This permits a clear discrimination between one's own contribution and another person's contribution to a specific aspect of a relationship. The son can also be surveyed using the same procedure. Thus, his perspective on how far he or his mother is involved in bringing about differences of opinion can also be distinguished. In all, this can be used to derive a complex pattern of self and other components of specific relationship aspects from the perspectives of both partners involved.

Drawing on theoretical findings from research on the psychology of relationships, we have concentrated on four central relationship dimensions that are each assessed with six items in the response format described earlier.[2] These dimensions are: (a) "Emotional closeness versus distance," (b) "Communication," (c) "Control versus acknowledged autonomy," and (d) "Conflict." Table 5.1 presents two sample items for each of these four relationship dimensions (not including the response format).

Total scale scores on each of the four relationship aspects were computed for all relationship constellations (i.e., mother–son, mother–daughter, father–son, father–daughter), as well as for each self- and other contribution from the perspective of the respondent. This resulted in 16 scale scores for each relationship aspect based on four relationship constellations: two perspectives (parental and filial generation) and two components (self and other). The scales proved to have a satisfactory reliability, as the internal consistency coefficients reported in Table 5.2 confirm. Therefore, for clarity's sake, we did not differentiate any further in terms of relationship constellations.

The scales are interrelated to a varying degree. In particular, "Closeness" and "Communication" have high positive intercorrelations (the mean correlation is $r = .79$), whereas "Conflict" correlates negatively with "Closeness"

How frequently do differences of opinion crop up between you when you are together for a longer period of time?

	Hardly ever	Rarely	Sometimes	Frequently	Very frequently
Those caused by my son	1	2	3	4	5
Those caused by myself	1	2	3	4	5

FIG. 5.1. Response format in the questionnaire on the current relationship between parents and their adult children.

TABLE 5.1
Sample Items for the Four Relationship Scales

Closeness versus distance
- How much affection is there between you?
- How much indifference or lack of interest is there between you?

Closeness versus distance

- How much affection is there between you?

- How much indifference or lack of interest is there between you?

Communication

- Do you like talking to each other?

- Do your conversations tend to be boring and superficial?

Control versus acknowledged autonomy

- How far is your relationship shaped by set rules and expectations?

- How much autonomy and personal freedom do you each allow the other?

Conflict

- How much conflict and strife do you experience in your relationship?

- How often are you annoyed and angry with each other?

TABLE 5.2
Reliabilities of the Four Relationship Scales for the Parent and Children's
Generations Taking Account of Own and Other Contributions

Relationship scales	Parents ($n = 426$)		Children ($n = 198$)	
	Own contribution	Other contribution	Own contribution	Other contribution
Closeness	.73	.79	.88	.84
Communication	.74	.77	.84	.82
Control	.63	.61	.60	.71
Conflict	.72	.76	.93	.83

Note. All coefficients: $p < .001$.

155

and "Communication" (mean correlations of $r = -.67$ and $r = -.54$, respectively). In contrast, "Control" shows a slight overlap with the other three scales (mean correlations of $r = -.35$ with "Closeness," $r = -.27$ with "Communication," and $r = .54$ with "Conflict").

These findings were also confirmed on the item level through a series of factor analyses.[3] These various analyses, based on different constellations of relationships, perspectives, and contributions to relationships, generally produced three highly interpretable factors with the items from the scales "Closeness" and "Communication" loading on one factor and the items from the scales "Control" and "Conflict" each forming a separate factor.

These findings indicate that our efforts to assess current parent–child relations are constructed on a relatively sound methodological base. Hence, we can now turn to some questions that provide information on the quality of relations between adult children and their parents.

DIFFERENCES BETWEEN PARENTS' AND CHILDREN'S PERCEPTIONS OF CURRENT RELATIONS

First of all, we want to examine whether differences can be found among the individual raters (i.e., mothers, fathers, sons, and daughters) regarding their own and the other person's contribution to the relationship. An appropriate measure for studying this is the correlation coefficient between the assessments of own and other contributions to the individual relationship aspects. Table 5.3 reports the corresponding values for each of the four relationship constellations, in each case, from the perspective of both partners.

The generally high to very high correlations indicate that the weightings of own and other contributions in the rating of the relationship mostly take the same direction for all partners. The only conspicuous exception is that the relationship aspect "Control" reveals lower correlations between own and other components among sons and daughters, compared with fathers and mothers. Otherwise, there is an astonishingly high overlap between these two aspects of relationship ratings. Therefore, in the following, we use the mean of the own and other contribution to characterize the relationship quality from the perspective of one partner.

We first provide an overview of the mean ratings on the current quality of the relationships between parents and children from the perspective of each partner involved. Table 5.4 reports the corresponding means and standard deviations. A more detailed inspection of these findings, which is also confirmed by analysis of variance (ANOVA),[4] permits the following conclusions:

1. The data indicate clearly that relations between parents and their adult children are generally rated positively on both sides. The degree of mutually

TABLE 5.3
Correlations Between Own and Other Contribution From the Perspective of the Relationship Partner

Relationship scales	Mother on son (n = 111)	Son on mother (n = 95)	Mother on daughter (n = 102)	Daughter on mother (n = 95)	Father on son (n = 112)	Son on father (n = 94)	Father on daughter (n = 101)	Daughter on father (n = 80)
Closeness	.66	.80	.82	.84	.83	.77	.82	.88
Communication	.76	.88	.83	.86	.87	.89	.95	.87
Control	.84	.58	.82	.61	.83	.63	.81	.70
Conflict	.86	.91	.91	.94	.94	.87	.95	.89

Note. All coefficients: $p < .001$.

TABLE 5.4
Means and Standard Deviations of the Four Relationship Scales From the
Perspective of the Relationship Partners

Relationship scales	Mother on son (*n* = 111)	Son on mother (*n* = 95)	Mother on daughter (*n* = 102)	Daughter on mother (*n* = 95)	Father on son (*n* = 112)	Son on father (*n* = 94)	Father on daughter (*n* = 101)	Daughter on father (*n* = 80)
Closeness	4.14[1] .46	4.00 .61	4.28 .45	4.21 .64	4.01 .54	3.70 .62	4.19 .49	3.87 .80
Communication	3.88 .54	3.67 .64	4.12 .49	4.00 .67	3.77 .58	3.37 .70	3.95 .62	3.39 .73
Control	2.01 .50	2.16 .55	2.04 .55	2.30 .60	2.02 .52	2.17 .53	1.93 .48	2.20 .58
Conflict	2.00 .54	2.28 .68	2.07 .55	2.37 .76	1.99 .57	2.35 .66	1.95 .52	2.39 .70

Note. 1: Upper value = mean. Lower value = standard deviation.

perceived closeness and communication is high, whereas the tendency toward mutual control and level of conflict in the relationship both tend to be rated as low.

2. Despite this generally positive picture, there are also more differentiated findings. First of all, it is conspicuous that, on all relationship dimensions, the older generation concedes a more favorable rating of the relationship than the younger generation. In other words, in their relationship with their sons and daughters, mothers and fathers generally experience more affection and more satisfying communication, but less control and differences of opinion than the children report in their own ratings. This clear generation effect is a general indication that the young adult generation has a more distanced attitude toward their parents than that revealed in the parents' perception of their relationship with their children.

3. However, this generation effect is not equally strong for all relationship aspects. It is strongest for the perceived level of conflict in the relationship and for the quality of communication between the two generations, whereas the discrepancies between the generations regarding the extent of mutual closeness and control are generally weaker.

4. However, even this statement has to be qualified when a more detailed analysis based on the relationship constellations is performed. For example, the relationship between mothers and their adult children is characterized continuously by a greater degree of closeness and communication. This applies particularly to mother–daughter relations. Interestingly, mothers and daughters have not only the highest scores on closeness and quality of communication, but also the lowest discrepancy between their perspectives. To a lesser extent, this also holds for mother–son relations. In contrast, relations between fathers and their children are clearly more distanced, with children—above all, adult sons—reporting that they have a much lower degree of psychological access to their fathers than the fathers assume themselves. Because fathers hardly differ from mothers in their perceptions of the closeness and quality of communication in their relationships to their children, the more distanced relationship between fathers and their adult children is due predominantly to children's perceptions of relations. One possible explanation for this generation-specific difference in perception in socioemotional relationship behavior is a gender role effect. Mothers, it would seem, are still perceived as specialists in interpersonal warmth, affection, and sociability by adult children, compared with fathers.

5. A gender role effect may also provide an explanation for the finding that young adult daughters perceive their fathers and mothers as being much more controlling than adult sons do. Here as well, there are no differences between the perspectives of the mothers and fathers, regardless of the adult child's gender. Once more, it is the children's perspective that is decisive. How far the relations to their parents of adult women in the younger

generation represent a continuation of the stronger parental monitoring tendency that is characteristic for girls cannot be clarified here.[5]

As Table 5.4 reveals, mean ratings on the quality of current relations between parents and their adult children are positive across all relationship constellations. Nonetheless, as the standard deviations from the means reveal, there are quite substantial interindividual differences, and this applies equally to both generations. In other words, parents and children deviate more or less strongly from the mean rating in terms of the quality of their relations. Some rate their relationship more positively than average; others, in contrast, have a clearly less favorable view. This raises the question of whether and to what extent the individual differences in perceived relations are similar for both members of a relationship dyad. To give an example, if an adult son experiences a low level of emotional closeness in his contacts with his father, does the same also apply to his father? Vice versa, if the father expresses a particularly high level of affection toward his son, will this also be reciprocated by his son?

Answers to these questions are provided by the intrafamilial correlations for the individual content dimensions of current parent–child relations displayed in Fig. 5.2. These are reported separately for families with sons and families with daughters. The figure also displays the correlations between mothers and fathers for their ratings of relations with the same child. The size of these correlations reveals something about how far both parents agree in their judgment on the relationship to their child. Thus, the triangular form of the intrafamilial correlations in the figure provides an impression of the level of agreement on current parent–child relations that exists within the familial triad of relationships.

The findings first show that relations take the same direction across all relationship aspects and can be confirmed statistically for all relationship constellations. This indicates a certain level of agreement between the individual partners regarding the weighting of individual aspects of relationships. Hence, there exists something like a mutually confirmed definition of relationship quality that manifests in the at least partially overlapping perspectives of the partners involved.

Nonetheless, the rather moderate size of these correlations also indicates that agreement on the perception of relations among individual family members is in no way perfect. This is particularly the case in families with daughters for the relationship aspect "Control versus acknowledged autonomy," which generally produces the lowest intrafamilial correlations. Here, adult daughters and their two parents perceive a comparatively low level of agreement on this aspect of relationships that is so particularly important for personal individuation. In addition, parents also report little agreement among themselves regarding their personal relations with their daughters. When it is also considered that, as mentioned earlier, adult daughters per-

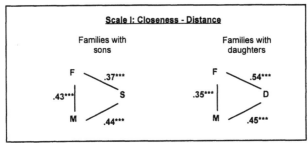

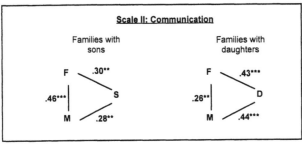

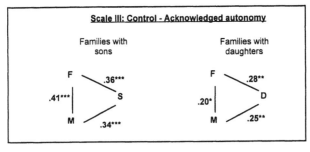

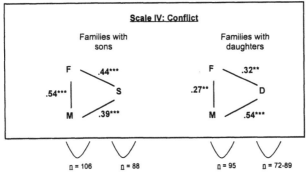

n = 106   n = 88   n = 95   n = 72-89

* ρ < .05. ** ρ < .01. *** ρ < .001. F = Father, M = Mother, S = Son, D = Daughter.

FIG. 5.2. Intrafamilial correlations for the four scales on the current relationship between parents and their adult children.

ceive their relations to both parents as more controlling than sons do, and, in addition, that the parents' perspectives do not differ, the impression is strengthened that young women have developed a particular sensitivity toward the potential constraints on their autonomy involved in their relations to their parents. It cannot be ruled out that this can also form the breeding ground for current disagreements in parent–daughter relations.

A further interesting finding that also concerns the parent–daughter relation, although indirectly, is that parents of daughters generally agree far less on their relations with their daughter than parents of sons. However, this stands in no recognizable relation to the level of agreement in perception that is found in the individual relationship aspects for each parent–child constellation. Therefore, there is no indication for specific parent–child coalitions (e.g., that a low level of agreement between parents is simultaneously accompanied by a higher or lower level of agreement with one particular parent).[6] It is far more the case that the lower levels of agreement between parents regarding daughters in comparison with sons have to be evaluated as an indication that mothers and fathers tend to develop relationships with their daughters within the family context that are less dependent on the perspectives of their spouses, and thus more autonomous compared with their relationships with sons.

PREDICTING CURRENT PARENT–CHILD RELATIONS FROM PARENTAL CHILDREARING STYLE

Can the quality of relations between parents and their adult children be predicted on the basis of the childrearing style practiced by the parents 16 years before? This is the question tackled in the following. We answer it by focusing on two approaches. The first addresses the perspective of the children's generation. In other words, can the differences that young men and women perceive in their current relations with their parents be traced back to how they rated the childrearing behavior of their parents when they were still children or young adolescents? The second addresses the perspective of the parent generation (i.e., whether and to what extent the parents' current perceived relationships to their adult children can be predicted on the basis of the childrearing style that they practiced before). We first look at the corresponding findings for the children's generation.

Current Relations and Childrearing Style: The Children's Perspective

As reported in detail in chapter 4, parental childrearing style can be broken down into three domains. These are childrearing practices (i.e., concrete behaviors such as praise or blame that parents use to reward or punish their child), childrearing attitudes (i.e., the general attitude that parents take toward their children that expresses itself in either being firm or giving in to the child's wishes), and childrearing *goals* (i.e., precepts and rules such as demands for conformity that children are expected to comply with under greater or lesser pressure). In addition, we have differentiated between self-perceived childrearing *style* (i.e., the behavior that parents attribute to themselves in their dealings with their children) and other-perceived childrearing *style*. The latter takes the perceptual perspective of another person who is not identical to the parent. What is particularly important here is the perceptual perspective of the receivers of parental childrearing efforts—namely, the children.[7]

Do children who have experienced their parents' behavior as strict and severe during their childhood and adolescence perceive more distance or conflict in their current relationship with their parents? Vice versa, does the earlier experience of parental affection and empathy express itself through a greater degree of closeness and communication in the current relationship? These are the types of question that guided our data analysis.

We correlated the various aspects of parental childrearing style as perceived by the children in 1976 with the relationship scales for current parent–child relations in 1992. Because we repeatedly found differences between specific relationship constellations when examining other research issues, these analyses were also performed separately for the basic four relationship types (i.e., son–mother, daughter–mother, son–father, daughter–father). The results can be summarized as follows.

1. In general, correlations between parental childrearing style as perceived by the children in 1976 and current parent–child relations tend to be low, when any of them actually do take a nonrandom pattern. This applies particularly to the current relationship aspects of "Control" and "Conflict," which reveal only weak relations for isolated childrearing style scales and types of relationship. Therefore, at least as far as these two relationship aspects are concerned, no reliable prognosis of current parent–child relations can be made on the basis of the earlier perception of parental childrearing style.

2. The picture looks somewhat different for the two relationship dimensions "Emotional closeness versus distance" and "Communication." Correlative patterns crystallize here for at least some relationship types, indicating a moderately high relation between the childrearing style perceived by children and current parent–child relations. As ascertained at the beginning of this chapter, closeness and communication reveal a psychological affinity that also expresses itself in high intercorrelations. In other words, persons who feel an emotional bond with their father or mother also like talking to them. In addition, the extent of emotional closeness or distance is a funda-

mental relationship dimension that probably forms relatively early as a basic trend in parent–child relations, and will tend to remain stable across time.

3. Despite these considerations, it is only from the daughters' perspective that the dimension "Closeness versus distance," in particular, reveals a moderately strong relation to previously perceived parental childrearing style. This holds, although also with slight shifts in the content accentuated, for both daughter–mother and daughter–father relations. Daughters who perceived their mothers as (a) lovingly attentive, (b) less angry and depreciative, and (c) simultaneously understanding during their childhood and early adolescence report more closeness and stronger ties in the current relationship to their mothers as young adult women. The interaction of these three aspects of perceived parental childrearing behavior produces a multiple correlation of $R = .42$, which indicates that at least 15% of the difference in the daughters' current perception of relationships can be traced back to the early perception of maternal childrearing behavior.[8]

4. The currently perceived closeness toward the fathers from the daughters' perspective cannot be predicted so well. When fathers previously had tried to discipline their daughters less by withdrawal of their affections and sought more intensive contact with them, the daughters now continue to perceive their relationship to their fathers as being close and warm-hearted. However, with a multiple correlation of $R = .38$ ($R^2 = .12$), this relation is weaker than that between mothers and daughters. Nonetheless, these findings indicate that, at least for the daughters, the psychological approachability of their parents at a time when they were still children is reflected in an emotionally positive relationship to them in early adulthood. We cannot explain why it is not possible to make a similar statement about the sons. However, it would seem—as shown in the following findings—that the failure to confirm substantial relations between parental childrearing style and current perceptions of closeness in contacts with parents is not due to a specific lack of sensitivity in the sons.

5. The relationship aspect "Communication" reveals a statistically significant pattern of relations among sons as well, particularly in the son–mother relationship. However, these findings are also rather unexpected. Namely, those sons whose mothers punished undesired behavior by withdrawing their affection and commented on positive behavior according to the basic principle "That was quite good, but the next time you can do even better" report that they have closer and more satisfying communication with their mothers in young adulthood.

Alongside these childrearing practices, specific childrearing goals also leave their traces. On the one hand, these are high maternal expectations regarding their sons' academic and occupational achievement, accompanied, on the other hand, by a low encouragement of child-appropriate interests. This particular pattern of maternal childrearing style—which, with a

multiple correlation coefficient of $R = .41$, actually predicts 13% of the sons'
current perceptions of communication—reflects a strongly achievement-oriented component of childrearing behavior, particularly in academic terms,
that is typical for an upwardly mobile, middle-class mentality. It is particularly the mothers who are responsible for asserting these achievement
goals, which is also why it is not surprising that this pattern is less recognizable in son–father relations. In childhood, those sons who now report
good communication with their fathers were particularly exposed to a
greater degree of withdrawal of affection as a disciplining technique ($R =
.32; R^2 = .09$). It is particularly interesting that this "slave-driver syndrome"
cannot be found at all when the sons are asked to rate the former childrearing behavior of their parents from their current perspective. We return to
this point in more detail later.

6. Hence, an achievement-spurring childrearing behavior is a better predictor of the quality of current communication in sons, whereas the picture
for daughters—although only in daughter–mother relations—is more in line
with general expectations. Young women perceive current communication
with their mothers as more satisfying the more that they had perceived
their mothers' behavior as lovingly attentive and contact-seeking when they
were children ($R = .34; R^2 = .10$). Therefore, a clear difference manifests in
childhood, particularly in relation to the mother, which depends on the
gender of the child. The common denominator seems to be a strong experience of communicative bonding between child and mother. Communication with sons is established through achievement-related topics, whereas
in daughters it is particularly aspects of the socioemotional relationship that
predict later communication behavior.

Despite these informative detailed findings, it must be pointed out once
more that the predictability of the current relationship between adult children and their parents is generally shaped only moderately by the perception of earlier parental childrearing style. It seems that, over the course of
the 16 years, which covers an extremely eventful period from childhood to
young adulthood in the children's generation, major changes in development have taken place. These changes permit only a low precision in the
prediction of current parent–child relations on the basis of an early selective
assessment of the children's perception of parental childrearing style. In
other words, the internal schemata for perceiving and evaluating parental
childrearing behavior had not yet consolidated sufficiently in the children
to remain uninfluenced by later experiences of relationships.

If this interpretation is accepted, we have to ask whether we would gain
different results if we were to take the perspective of the parents. Findings
reported in chapters 2 and 4 indicate that parents already developed a more
stable picture of their children and their childrearing behavior at the time

of the first wave in 1976, and that this also has a stronger impact on their perceived relationships with their children in the here and now. If this proves to be true, it must also be reflected in a higher predictability of current parent–child relations on the basis of the assessment of childrearing style made 16 years before. The next section examines whether it is possible to confirm this assumption.

Current Relations and Childrearing Style:
The Parents' Perspective

We point out in advance that our data completely confirm the prior assumption. All four relationship dimensions and all paired parent–child constellations show more or less close relations between current perceived relationships and self-perceived parental childrearing style. Therefore, we now present the individual findings separately for each of the four relationship dimensions, and we analyze the gender-specific differences in individual parent–child constellations.

We begin with the relationship aspect "Emotional closeness versus distance," as reported by the parents in their perception of their current relationship with their children. Table 5.5 summarizes the bivariate or multiple correlations between the "closeness versus distance" dimension and the features of self-perceived parental childrearing style assessed 16 years before. The table reports only statistically significant correlations, and distinguishes among childrearing practices, attitudes, and goals. This makes it easy to see the domains of parental childrearing style in which predictability is focused, and to what extent the individual domains of childrearing style interact and are reflected as a specific pattern of childrearing style in currently perceived closeness versus distance. As a measure of the strength of these relations, the last row in the table presents the multiple correlations (R) and the differences in the current perception of closeness versus distance explained by the multiple correlations (R^2) for the individual parent–child constellations.[9]

A first glance at the table reveals that, in all four relationship constellations, at least two of the three domains of childrearing style relate significantly to currently perceived closeness versus distance. The closest link is found for father–daughter relations ($R = .44$; $R^2 = .16$). A high degree of loving attention, paired with the need for affection and a patient approach to the daughter, but also high academic aspirations, are the essential features of paternal childrearing style that also characterize the experience of emotional closeness to the daughter in 1992 from the father's perspective. Less strong, but following a similar basic trend, is the relation between maternal childrearing style and current closeness to the daughter. Although the component of maternal attention that could be traced back to childrearing

TABLE 5.5

Parents: Prediction of the Scale "Closeness Versus Distance" From Parental Childrearing Style in 1976

CHILDREARING STYLE	Mother-Son ($n = 111$)	Mother-Daughter ($n = 102$)	Father-Son ($n = 112$)	Father-Daughter ($n = 101$)
PRACTICES	Corporal punishment ($r = -.27$)	/	Corporal punishment ($r = -.30$)	Loving attention ($r = .36$)
ATTITUDES	Experimenting ($r = -.22$)	Impatience ($r = -.22$) Composure/ Sovereignty ($r = .18$)	Impatience ($r = -.28$)	Affection ($r = .33$) Impatience ($r = -.23$)
GOALS	/	Sociopolitical commitment ($r = .20$)	/	(School) qualification demands ($r = .20$)
Multiple correlations	$R = .35***; R^2 = .10$	$R = .34**; R^2 = .09$	$R = .34***; R^2 = .10$	$R = .44***; R^2 = .16$

$** p < .01; *** p < .001.$

167

practices is lacking, patience and calmness are the central predictors, joined on the level of childrearing goals by the desire for the daughter to be socially active and show solidarity with her peers. This expresses a stronger relationship-oriented behavioral expectation in mothers in comparison with the achievement-related goals in fathers, which once more reflects a typical gender role difference.

Mother–son or father–son relations also reveal highly similar patterns of childrearing styles that are each formed by a specific component of childrearing behavior in the domains of practices and attitudes. It is conspicuous that, in both fathers and mothers, the clear renunciation of corporal punishment as a means of discipline is an early indicator for perceived closeness in adulthood. This is joined in the attitude domain by the mothers' conscious renunciation of the use of a manipulative approach toward their sons, whereas the fathers attribute themselves with a higher level of patience or a lack of irritation with their sons.

A psychologically similar pattern of parental childrearing style is found for the relationship aspect "Communication." These results are summarized in Table 5.6, which is constructed along the same lines as Table 5.5. Two things are conspicuous when looking at this table. First, the domain of childrearing goals, with one exception, makes no relevant contribution to the prediction of the current quality of communication. Second, in contrast to the other relationship constellations, current mother–daughter communication can be predicted through only one feature of maternal childrearing style, and this only to a slight extent. Nonetheless, this concerns the scale "Loving attention," which—as an indicator of mental and physical closeness—also qualifies as a feature of parental behavior that favors communication in mother–son and father–daughter relations.

This aspect of childrearing style is most conspicuous in father–daughter relations, being joined by the element of affection in the attitude domain. In mother–child relations, loving, attentive behavior is supplemented by a considerate and simultaneously less manipulative childrearing attitude that links up in the domain of childrearing goals with a low demand to comply with religious norms.

The three relationship constellations described so far have focused on reward situations for the child, in which a high measure of positive emotionality predicts the later quality of communication, whereas in the case of father–son relations, the focus is on the renunciation of punishment, particularly the renunciation of punishment through withdrawal of privileges such as watching television. This is joined by a high measure of patience and interestingly—although it makes only a slight contribution to predictions—the fact that the son is a planned or wished for child. It is precisely this last finding that, in contrast to the other findings, reveals that the prediction of current parent–child relations can feed on a high diversity of nonetheless plausible sources of early parental childrearing style.

TABLE 5.6

Parents: Prediction of the Scale "Communication" From Parental Childrearing Style in 1976

CHILDREARING STYLE	Mother-Son ($n = 111$)	Mother-Daughter ($n = 102$)	Father-Son ($n = 112$)	Father-Daughter ($n = 101$)
PRACTICES	Loving attention ($r = .19$)	Loving attention ($r = .21$)	Withdrawal of material privileges ($r = -.27$)	Loving attention ($r = .33$)
ATTITUDES	Permissiveness ($r = .25$) Experimenting ($r = -.23$)	/	Impatience ($r = -.29$) Planned birth ($r = .19$)	Affection ($r = .31$)
GOALS	Religious norms ($r = -.22$)	/	/	/
Multiple correlations	$R = .45^{***}; R^2 = .17$		$R = .38^{***}; R^2 = .12$	$R = .35^{***}; R^2 = .10$

*** $p < .001$.

169

As a third qualitatively differentiable aspect of current parent–child relations, we now turn to the dimension of "Control versus acknowledged autonomy," which primarily concerns the perceived measure of power and influence in the shaping of the relationship between the parents and their adult children. From the perspective of the children—as reported in the last section—no substantial relations can be confirmed between the childrearing style perceived by the child and the current perception of control in the relationship to the parents, whereas the situation looks completely different from the parents' perspective. Table 5.7 reports these findings in a condensed form.

Even a quick glance at the table reveals that, apart from one single relationship constellation (mother–daughter), all three domains of childrearing style provide a more or less strong contribution to predicting current control perceptions. The closest relations, even compared with the other dimensions of current parent–child relations, are to self-perceived childrearing style.

This applies particularly to mother–son or father–son relations. The multiple correlations attain $R = .52$ and $R = .56$, respectively, and predict 23% and 27% of the extent of current perceived control.

When interpreting these findings, it is first necessary to recall that the special response format for assessing current parent–child relations allowed us to differentiate how far the occurrence of a certain weighting on the corresponding relationship dimension was perceived as being caused by oneself or by the relationship partner. This idea applies, in principle, to all four of the relationship dimensions focused on in this chapter. In the case of parental perception of control, the correlation between one's own and the other person's contribution proved to be extraordinarily high (see the findings presented in Table 5.2). Therefore, we can assume that the following findings also apply particularly to that portion of relationship control that the parents attribute to themselves in their contacts with their children. This is important because the level of control, or of acknowledged autonomy in a given relationship, has to be viewed as a reciprocal process involving both relationship partners. With regard to relations with the self-perceived parental childrearing style assessed 16 years before, what is particularly interesting is the portion of control or acknowledged autonomy that the parents attribute to themselves in the current relationship to their children.[10]

Mother–son or father–son relations reveal a pattern of childrearing style that is similar in its essential elements, although there are slight differences in emphasis. This style is characterized by severe reward and punishment techniques, a strong monitoring tendency, and marked normative demands. In detail, mothers with a strong current inclination toward control tended more readily to punish their sons by withdrawing their love and to reward them by granting material favors. They simultaneously exhibited a strong

TABLE 5.7
Parents: Prediction of the Scale "Control" From Parental Childrearing Style in 1976

CHILDREARING STYLE	Mother-Son (n = 111)	Mother-Daughter (n = 102)	Father-Son (n = 112)	Father-Daughter (n = 101)
PRACTICES	Material reward (r = .37) Withdrawal of love (r = .27)	/	Corporal punishment (r = .30) Material reward (r = .27)	Withdrawal of material privileges (r = .25)
ATTITUDES	Protectiveness (r = .34) Impatience (r = .22)	Experimenting (r = .18) Protectiveness (r = .21)	Protectiveness (r = .39) Impatience (r = .26)	Protectiveness (r = .24)
GOALS	Achievement motivation (r = .33)	Solidarity (r = -.20)	Religious norms (r = .31) (School) qualification demands (r = .20)	Solidarity (r = .23)
Multiple correlations	$R = .52***; R^2 = .23$	$R = .34**; R^2 = .09$	$R = .56***; R^2 = .27$	$R = .36**; R^2 = .10$

$** p < .01; *** p < .001$.

171

protective tendency, coupled with increased irritability in daily childrearing, and this was additionally coupled with strong achievement demands in the domain of childrearing goals. Thus, this solidifies into a picture of a strongly controlling, simultaneously overprotective and achievement-oriented childrearing style that is more interested in asserting the mother's own, relatively rigid childrearing principles than in the needs of the child.

Father–son relations can be viewed in a similar light. Fathers who tend to take a controlling attitude in their current relationship to their adult sons previously used more corporal punishment and, in cases of reward, material benefits as a form of discipline. They also, much like the mothers, revealed a severely protective and simultaneously impatient attitude toward their sons. Their normative expectations were directed toward the more or less strict compliance with religious or Christian demands, as well as the achievement of high academic and other qualification standards. Thus, here as well, the parental childrearing pattern is characterized by a high level of control and influence, and takes little account of childhood claims for autonomy. Despite the plausibility of this retrospective interpretation, we were impressed by how far this syndrome of features of early childrearing style still influences the present striving of mothers and fathers to take a controlling attitude in their dealings with their adult sons.

As already mentioned, these relations are particularly marked for parent–son relations. The picture is less clear for parent–daughter relations, although the individual characteristics of childrearing style found in the contacts with sons are also visible. This applies particularly for an increased monitoring tendency in the sense of a strongly protective attitude that ensures the physical closeness of the daughters. In mothers, this is also accompanied by a manipulative component, coupled with low expectations of solidarity toward peers. The latter can be understood as indicating that mothers want to protect their daughters from becoming overinvolved in complicated social relationships that may turn out to be disadvantageous for them. In contrast, fathers tend to punish their daughters by withdrawing material and other privileges, as well as exhibiting a basically protective attitude. However, unlike mothers, fathers expect their daughters to show solidarity toward their peers, which, in this case, can certainly be rated as a sign of normative social behavior.

Finally, we take another look at the question of whether the extent of perceived conflict in the relation between parents and their adult children can be traced back to features of earlier childrearing style. These findings are summarized in Table 5.8. Apart from the fact that the domain of childrearing goals is completely irrelevant for the conflict dimension, the picture is relatively consistent across the various parent–child constellations. It is conspicuous that, on the level of childrearing practices—with one exception—it is exclusively punishment techniques that predict the degree of

TABLE 5.8
Parents: Prediction of the Scale "Conflict" From Parental Childrearing Style in 1976

CHILDREARING STYLE	Mother-Son (n = 111)	Mother-Daughter (n = 102)	Father-Son (n = 112)	Father-Daughter (n = 101)
PRACTICES	Corporal punishment (r = .29)	Depreciation (r = .40)	Depreciation (r = .39) Material reward (r = .16)	Depreciation (r = .22)
ATTITUDES	Impatience (r = .25) Planned birth (r = -.18)	Impatience (r = .37)	Impatience (r = .31)	Impatience (r = .27) Low involvement in childrearing role (r = .25)
GOALS	—	—	—	—
Multiple correlations	$R = .39***; R^2 = .13$	$R = .43***; R^2 = .17$	$R = .45***; R^2 = .18$	$R = .41***; R^2 = .14$

**** $p < .001$.

173

current conflict in parent–child relations. A high level of depreciation or harsh verbal expression of anger when punishing undesired child behavior almost continuously makes a strong contribution. It is only in mother–son relations that this component turns into the even more severe disciplinary measure of corporal punishment. In addition, all parent–child constellations show that an irritated and impatient approach to children contributes to the prediction of current tensions in relations to the now adult children. Mother–son relations are additionally stressed when mothers reported that the birth of their sons had been unplanned and unwelcome. In contrast, fathers of unplanned daughters reveal low regard and an impatient attitude to their daughters, as well as a low commitment to their paternal role.

Thus, in all, we find a specific pattern of antecedent childrearing styles for the current level of conflict in parent–child relations as well. In contrast to the other relationship dimensions, this pattern—consisting of, in particular, the components of depreciation and emotional instability—is relatively consistent across the various parent–child constellations. Here, we have uncovered a common source for current tensions in parent–child relations that feeds on earlier biographical experiences of relationships, and has at least a partial influence on the current relationship situation.

When summarizing the findings on the impact of parental childrearing style on current parent–child relations, we sometimes gain a differentiated picture. Results differ depending on the perspective of the person surveyed, the aspect of relationships concerned, and the specific parent–child constellation. However, the most conspicuous finding is that we obtain a far better prediction of the parental view of their current relationship to their children from the features of childrearing style assessed in them 16 years before than we do when we take the children's perspective. We attribute this to stronger biographical changes and less stable relationship schemata on the side of the children.

If the latter hypothesis is correct, and we are able to confirm that the adult children have now developed a sufficiently stable picture of their parents' earlier childrearing behavior, even when this does not necessarily correspond to the reality at that time, it must be possible to find closer relations between current parent–child relations and the children's retrospectively assessed ratings of parental childrearing style. This issue is investigated in more detail in the next section.

CURRENT RELATIONS AND RETROSPECTIVE CHILDREARING STYLE FROM THE CHILDREN'S PERSPECTIVE

As already discussed in detail in chapter 4, one of the things we asked the young adults in the children's generation in 1992 was to imagine how their mothers and fathers had probably answered the various statements and questions on childrearing given to them 16 years before. Thus, the young adults' task was to "put themselves in their parents' shoes" retrospectively and then reproduce their parents' childrearing style. Therefore, in precise terms, this is the retrospectively assessed, self-perceived childrearing style of the parents from the perspective of their adult children. To prevent complication, we simply talk about the retrospective childrearing style from the children's perspective in the following.

In presenting the results, we have once more computed separate correlations between the four relationship dimensions and the retrospectively assessed features of childrearing style for all possible parent–child dyads. We also retained the discrimination into different domains of childrearing style (i.e., practices, attitudes, and goals).

It can be stated in advance that this research question has proved to be extraordinarily productive. This is not only because the relations studied produce respectably high values for psychological studies in this field, with multiple correlations between $R = .45$ and $R = .69$, but also because, in terms of content, they have led to informative findings. We consider later how such relatively close relations can be explained in more detail. First, however, we present an overview of the individual findings.

We start with the relationship aspect "Emotional closeness versus distance." Relations with the various features of retrospective childrearing style are summarized in Table 5.9. The first thing to note is the high multiple correlations. Particularly for son–mother and daughter–father relations, the resulting values indicate that 44% of the differences in currently perceived closeness versus distance to parents can be traced back to a specific constellation of parental childrearing style. For example, sons who retrospectively attribute to their mothers (a) a high level of loving attention and few irritable reactions to undesired behavior, (b) leniency and a less rigid insistence on their childrearing principles, and, finally, (c) a low pressure to conform and achieve report that they currently have a much closer relationship with their mothers. This reveals a good fit between a content-specific mixture of childrearing practices, attitudes, and goals and the current bonds, in which the central elements of this pattern of childrearing style are positively experienced maternal emotionality, high childrearing flexibility, and low normative pressure.

A similar pattern of relations can also be found in daughter–father relations, although this does not involve the normative component from the domain of childrearing goals. Instead, daughters do not just attribute their fathers with a less authoritarian attitude to childrearing, but also a high level of protection accompanied by a low tendency to manipulate. It is interesting to see how daughters interpret protection as a positive feature of paternal behavior that expresses their desire for closeness and contact. This is in direct contrast to the meaning that fathers and mothers attribute

TABLE 5.9
Children: Prediction of the Scale "Closeness Versus Distance" From Retrospectively Perceived Parental Childrearing Style in 1976

CHILDREARING STYLE	Son-Mother (n = 91)	Son-Father (n = 90)	Daughter-Mother (n = 94)	Daughter-Father (n = 89)
PRACTICES	Verbal anger expression (r = -.34) Loving attention (r = .39)	Withdrawal of material privileges (r = -.27) Loving attention (r = .39)	Loving attention (r = .52) Corporal punishment (r = -.38)	Loving attention (r = .47)
ATTITUDES	Permissiveness (r = .41) Authoritarian rigidity (r = -.45)	Affection (r = .43)	Similarity (r = .44) Openness (r = .40)	Permissiveness (r = .07; β = -.34) Authoritarian rigidity (r = -.35) Protectiveness (r = .47) Experimenting (r = -.16)
GOALS	Conformity (r = -.42) Achievement motivation (r = -.47)	—	—	—
Multiple correlations	R = .69; R² = .44	R = .52; R² = .25	R = .65; R² = .39	R = .69; R² = .44

Note. All multiple correlations: $p < .001$.

to the feature "protection" reported in the last section. From the parents' perspective, protection tends to mean surveillance that can be best achieved through ensuring the child's physical closeness, which, for this reason, means that it also predicts a controlling attitude in the present day.

Daughter–mother relations reveal not just childrearing practices that—as in all other parent–child constellations as well—indicate loving attention and the expressed renunciation of corporal punishment as a form of discipline, but, in the attitude domain, somewhat different indicators that, nonetheless, have a plausible relation to perceived current closeness to the mother. On the one hand, this is the degree of similarity that the daughters attribute to the mothers in the relationship to them, and, on the other hand, the willingness that the daughters perceive in their mothers to be open about their own personal thoughts and feelings. Because this aspect of childrearing style is exclusive to the daughter–mother constellation, it seems to be a specifically female relationship component, indicating a willingness to engage in emotional disclosure, and therefore it represents an important element in the current experience of closeness and trust between daughters and mothers.

In son–father relations, retrospectively assessed childrearing style is the poorest predictor of current perceived closeness in comparison with the other parent–child constellations. Alongside loving attention in cases of reward and renunciation of the denial of material privileges as a means of punishment in the domain of attitudes, a high level of affection is a further significant indicator of currently perceived closeness. Unlike daughter–mother relations, in which maternal readiness to disclose her internal mental well-being tends to be an important indicator of closeness, in son–father relations, sons perceive the father's ability to create positive physical contact as the major aspect promoting closeness.

The relationship dimension of a more or less positive communication between adult children and their parents—that is associated closely to perceived current closeness versus distance—reveals a pattern of relations that has some similarities to the retrospectively attributed current childrearing style. However, there are also a few notable differences, as the findings reported in Table 5.10 reveal. Once more, the most striking findings are on son–mother relations. The features of childrearing style attributed to mothers explain 40% of the variance in current communication behavior. In the domain of childrearing practices, it is the renunciation of corporal punishment as a means of discipline that makes an important contribution to satisfactory communication with mothers from the sons' perspective. However, even more powerful predictors can be found in the domains of childrearing attitudes and goals. Alongside a low assertion of maternal childrearing principles, it is particularly perceived similarity to the son and the lack of an inconsistent and thus hardly predictable childrearing behavior

TABLE 5.10
Children: Prediction of the Scale "Communication" From Retrospectively
Perceived Parental Childrearing Style in 1976

CHILDREARING STYLE	Son-Mother ($n = 91$)	Son-Father ($n = 90$)	Daughter-Mother ($n = 94$)	Daughter-Father ($n = 89$)
PRACTICES	Corporal punishment ($r = -.27$)	Depreciation ($r = -.30$) Loving attention ($r = .36$)	Corporal punishment ($r = -.25$)	Loving attention ($r = .42$)
ATTITUDES	Authoritarian rigidity ($r = -.36$) Similarity ($r = .36$) Inconsistency ($r = -.25$)	—	Protectiveness ($r = .30$) Openness ($r = .41$)	Authoritarian rigidity ($r = -.33$) Protectiveness ($r = .45$) Orientation toward self-experienced childrearing style ($r = -.01$; $\beta = .22$)
GOALS	Conformity ($r = -.48$) Achievement motivation ($r = -.53$)	—	—	—
Multiple correlations	$R = .66; R^2 = .40$	$\underline{R} = .46; R^2 = .19$	$R = .51; R^2 = .23$	$R = .61; R^2 = .34$

Note. All multiple correlations: $p < .001$.

that sons experience as being supportive of communication. Of particular importance, as for perceived current closeness earlier, is the lack of conformity- and achievement-related maternal expectations. Thus, whether sons can have satisfactory and stimulating conversations with their mothers in the present day seems to depend on whether they feel that their mothers had not "pushed" them expressly in the direction of achievement and conformity.

Interestingly, this normative component of parental childrearing style is not a significant indicator of the quality of current communication in any other parent–child constellation. For daughter–mother relations, alongside the renunciation of corporal punishment, it is, above all, perceived maternal openness that is a relevant feature of childrearing. This fits in well with the ideas already presented on the closeness dimension. In addition, the perceived maternal tendency to protect—also interpreted here by the daughters as maternal interest in their well-being and less as surveillance—is also indicative of positive daughter–mother communication.

This last interpretation also seems to apply to daughter–father relations. Here, as well, paternal protectiveness, combined with a low tendency toward authoritarian behavior, proves to be an aspect of paternal childrearing style that encourages communication, whereby a loving approach to the daughters in reward situations also fits in well with this pattern. Interestingly, this is accompanied by the belief that the fathers are guided in their contact with their daughters by the way they had been brought up themselves. This implies either that the daughters actually have or had good contacts with their grandparents or at least received a positive picture of their grandparents through hearsay.

The least revealing results, as far as current communication behavior is concerned, are those on son–father relations. Significant findings are found only in the domain of childrearing practices, although these all take the expected direction. From the sons' perspective, their relationship to their fathers encourages communication particularly when they were loving toward them in reward situations and behaved less deprecatingly and irritably in punishment situations. Despite this finding, which also completely fits the picture in other parent–child constellations, it is notable that the sons perceive a much broader repertoire of features of childrearing style as significant predictors of current communication behavior in their relationship with their mothers. This suggests that sons generally have better communication with their mothers than with their fathers. This surmise is strengthened by returning to the findings presented in an earlier section of this chapter, and by looking at the results in Table 5.4 on the mean rating of current communication between sons and their two parents. This shows that, from the sons' perspective, communication with their mothers is generally far more satisfactory than that with their fathers.

Next, we turn to the results on the relationship dimension "Control versus acknowledged autonomy." Alongside the aspects of closeness and communication, this is a particularly important feature that shapes the relationship between young adults and their parents. What it means is how far adult "children" still perceive themselves as being "tied to their parents' aprons strings," or whether their parents have granted them the degree of autonomy that is characteristic for a fairly egalitarian relationship between adults. For this reason, it is particularly informative to find out which features of prior childrearing style young adults attribute to their parents as a possible "explanation" for the amount of currently perceived control. Table 5.11 presents an overview of these relations.

It is conspicuous that three out of four parent–child constellations reveal that a strong measure of parental depreciation and a tendency to anger in response to undesired child behavior, as well as a generally high level of impatience and irritation in dealing with the child, represent the core of a parent–child relationship that the children continue to perceive as strongly controlling even today.

Depreciation and impatience determine, to a particularly strong extent, the relations that sons have with their mothers as far as the degree of perceived control in the current relationship is concerned. In addition, sons seem to regard the fact that their mothers reacted with material privileges in reward situations as negative in retrospective. This is probably because they would have preferred emotionally more valuable forms of attention, such as recognition and a clear expression of pride in their sons. Finally, sons retrospectively perceive their mothers as impatient, as well as oriented toward principles and achievement-demanding. Interestingly, the fact that sons consider that their mothers express this control pattern from the position of perceived similarity to their child also plays a role.

In daughter–father relations, too, depreciation and anger as disciplinary techniques, as well as a generally impatient attitude, are central characteristics of a childrearing style that leads to a controlling relationship in the present. The link to self-perceived childrearing style seems to express a traditional normative attitude here. This is also supported by the paternal attitude that daughters should orient themselves toward religious behavioral guidelines and values.

Sons also attribute a high measure of depreciation and anger expression to their fathers' reactions to the sons' undesired behavior. Sons associate this with a strong tendency to control in the current relationship. In the same way, sons tend toward a negative perception of paternal rewards based exclusively on material privileges, as already seen in the relationship with their mothers. Instead of impatience, they attribute to their fathers a lack of composure and sovereignty in everyday childrearing, which is linked in a plausible way to greater strictness in the sense of an authoritarian and rigid attitude.

TABLE 5.11
Children: Prediction of the Scale "Control" From Retrospectively Perceived Parental Childrearing Style in 1976

CHILDREARING STYLE	Son-Mother ($n = 91$)	Son-Father ($n = 90$)	Daughter-Mother ($n = 94$)	Daughter-Father ($n = 89$)
PRACTICES	Material reward ($r = .18$) Depreciation ($r = .38$)	Depreciation ($r = .21$) Material reward ($r = .29$)	Withdrawal of love ($r = .33$) Loving attention ($r = -.26$)	Depreciation ($r = .31$)
ATTITUDES	Impatience ($r = .37$) Authoritarian rigidity ($r = .37$) Similarity ($r = -.01; \beta = .20$)	Composure/ Sovereignty ($r = -.27$) Authoritarian rigidity ($r = .30$)	Permissiveness ($r = -.32$) Impatience ($r = .34$)	Impatience ($r = .36$) Orientation toward self-experienced childrearing style ($r = .36$)
GOALS	Achievement motivation ($r = .42$)	/	/	Religious norms ($r = .30$)
Multiple correlations	$R = .63; R^2 = .35$	$R = .48; R^2 = .20$	$R = .48; R^2 = .20$	$R = .54; R^2 = .26$

Note. All multiple correlations: $p < .001$.

Daughter–mother relations reveal a slight shift in accent, but a similar psychological baseline. From the daughters' perspective, impatience and lack of leniency are the most important features of childrearing style in the attitude domain that continue to determine a higher measure of control in the present-day relationship with their mothers. Beyond this, they perceive a deficit in maternal attention in the childhood years, as well as frequent recourse to punishment through withdrawal of love as further features of a maternal childrearing style that lead to limited autonomy in the current relationship.

Although with differences in shading, this generally reveals a relatively consistent picture across the various parent–child constellations, according to which the current perception of control from the perspective of the young adults is characterized predominantly by a high measure of negative emotionality on the part of the parents, as well as through their inflexible attitude in dealing with their children.

It can be suspected that such a constellation of features of parental childrearing style relates not only to the measure of control, but also to the amount of conflict in current parent–child relations. Therefore, we examine this aspect of the current relationship between adult children and their parents in terms of probable antecedents in parental childrearing behavior. The relevant findings are summarized in Table 5.12.

First, it can be ascertained that the childrearing style features of depreciation or verbal anger expression, as well as an impatient attitude in dealing with the child, are the most striking predictors of the measure of current conflict in parent–child relations, and they are also equally significant across nearly all parent–child constellations. This relation is even clearer than that for the aspect of "Control versus acknowledged autonomy." This is also in line with the self-perceptions of the parents reported in the previous section. However, the relations reported there are based on prospective data; that is, the measure of depreciation and impatience reported by parents in 1976 is reflected 16 years later in a conflictual relationship to their children (see the findings summarized in Table 5.8). In contrast, the results discussed here, like all findings presented in this section, are based on the retrospective reports of young adults.

Once more, the clearest pattern is found for son–mother relations. Sons who have a highly conflictual relationship with their mothers assign them a higher tendency to anger, and are unable to see signs in their mothers of loving attention in situations in which they had done something particularly well as children. In addition, sons consider that their mothers did not just exhibit a general lack of patience, but also a less protective attitude, a more traditional attitude to childrearing, and high achievement demands.

The latter also play a role in the daughters' perspectives when they rate the level of conflict in their relationship to their fathers. As in the other

TABLE 5.12
Children: Prediction of the Scale "Conflict" From Retrospectively Perceived
Parental Childrearing Style in 1976

CHILDREARING STYLE	Son-Mother ($n = 91$)	Son-Father ($n = 90$)	Daughter-Mother ($n = 94$)	Daughter-Father ($n = 89$)
PRACTICES	Loving attention ($r = -.33$) Verbal anger expression ($r = -.42$)	Depreciation ($r = .40$)	Loving attention ($r = -.34$) Verbal anger expression ($R = .57$) Corporal punishment ($r = .42$)	Withdrawal of love ($r = .25$)
ATTITUDES	Impatience ($r = .43$) Protectiveness ($r = -.23$) Orientation toward self-experienced childrearing style ($r = .27$)	Composure/Sovereignty ($r = -.29$) Authoritarian rigidity ($r = .31$) Impatience ($r = .33$)	Impatience ($r = .43$)	Impatience ($r = .40$)
GOALS	Achievement motivation ($r = .49$)	/	/	Achievement motivation ($r = .26$)
Multiple correlations	$R = .69; R^2 = .44$	$R = .50; R^2 = .21$	$R = .55; R^2 = .26$	$R = .45; R^2 = .17$

Note. All multiple correlations: $p < .001$.

183

parent–child constellations, this is accompanied by a high measure of paternal impatience, as well as a tendency to react with withdrawal of love in punishment situations.

In the relationship to their mothers, daughters report impatience and irritability as a general characteristic of maternal childrearing behavior and the tendency to anger that is also typical of a conflictual relationship, as well as a lack of maternal attention and—what can be viewed as a particularly serious sign of disregard—a greater use of corporal punishment to avenge undesirable child behavior. In all, this reveals a strong dominance of aversive maternal childrearing practices in the daughters' perceptions that not unsurprisingly forms the background for a conflictual relationship to the mothers in the present day.

The domain of childrearing practices is emphasized more strongly in the relationship between daughters and mothers, whereas it is specific childrearing attitudes that gain more weight in son–father relations. Alongside the continuously ascertainable impatience in contacts with the son, it is particularly the lack of paternal composure, as well as a rigid adherence to prior childrearing principles, that appear to be conflict-inducing features of childrearing style in current son–father relations.

If we disregard the differentiations that can be confirmed for the individual types of relationship, then the conflict dimension also reveals a highly unified pattern of relevant influences of parental childrearing style that, from the perspectives of the young adults, has a more or less close relation to the degree of currently perceived conflict in the relationship to their parents. A particularly important role is taken by indicators reflecting a strong lack of emotional control and, particularly in mothers, a lack of emotional closeness. Once these signs of parental childrearing style have established themselves in the perceptions of the young adults, it must be difficult to resolve tensions and conflicts in their relationships with their parents.

Finally, a word on the question raised earlier—namely, why, in general terms, are there such strong relations between retrospectively assessed childrearing style and the current relationship to the parents in the young adults? When comparing the findings on prospectively assessed childrearing style from the perspective of the parent and children's generations, we argued that the relatively low predictive value of childrearing style perceived from the child's side could be traced back, on the one hand, to strong, developmentally determined changes in the period from childhood to young adulthood, and, on the other hand, to the fact that childhood judgment schemata are still rather unconsolidated. Although we can assume that the retrospectively assessed childrearing style from the perspective of adult children is now based on a sufficiently stable picture of relationships to their parents, we additionally suspect, particularly in comparison with the ratings on the childrearing behavior of their parents made 16 years before, that another process is at work, which is described briefly in the following.

We consider that the findings on retrospective childrearing style clearly reveal that the young adults' retrospective ratings on childrearing behavior are strongly codetermined by their current perception of the relationship with their parents. In other words, when we asked the now adults sons and daughters to "put themselves in their parents' shoes" and actualize the childrearing behavior practiced 16 years before, they did this, to a large extent, against the background of their current relationship to their parents.

This does not necessarily mean that the experiences gained in earlier contact with the parents have absolutely no impact on the current relationship. Earlier in this chapter, we showed that interesting findings have also been found on the level of prospective data for at least some relationship constellations and some relationship aspects. For example, it can be recalled that young women experience their current communication with their mothers as more satisfying when they had already rated their mother's behavior as lovingly attentive and contact-seeking when they were children. This pattern of relations also corresponds largely with the adult daughters' current retrospective view of their mothers' childrearing behavior, and thus suggests a degree of continuity in the daughters' perception of relationships.

However, there are also findings that contradict such a continuity hypothesis. For example, the son–mother constellation reveals that sons who perceived their mothers as being strongly achievement-spurring 16 years before currently report a more satisfactory relationship with their mothers. However, the exact opposite applies to the retrospective judgment of maternal childrearing style. The less sons consider that their mothers used to place much value on achievement and normative behavior, the better they can communicate with their mothers today.

The internal structure of retrospectively perceived childrearing style seems to be determined largely by current ratings of relationships, regardless of whether we are dealing with a continuously or discontinuously extrapolated relationship perspective. Thus, it is assumed that the retrospectively attributed childrearing style gains the quality of an explanatory concept that can be used to understand why the current relationship with the parents is perceived as being closer or more distanced, more or less satisfying in communicative terms, controlling, or conflictual. In this sense, current experiences of relationships and their "explanations" founded on earlier child–parent relations amalgamate into a subjectively plausible pattern of interpretation, and it is this that explains the size of these correlations.[11]

If this interpretation holds, it has implications for the status of retrospectively assessed data that psychological research on childrearing style uses so frequently as a substitute for real-time longitudinal studies. Put succinctly, such data tell us more about the perception of current parent–child relations and their subjective foundations than about the parental childrearing style that was "actually" practiced, or also perceived, at the time.

A BRIEF SUMMARY OF THE MOST IMPORTANT POINTS

• In 1992, both generations give a generally positive view on the current relationship between parents and their adult sons and daughters. The degree of perceived closeness and communication is generally high, whereas control and conflict are markedly lower.

• Despite this generally favorable picture of their relationship reported by both generations, some differences between the generations cannot be overlooked. Parents rate the relationship more positively than their children; the relationship between mothers and their adult children is characterized by a higher measure of closeness and communication in comparison with the fathers; above all, sons have a particularly distanced relationship with their fathers; in contrast, daughters perceive their relationship to both parents as more controlling in comparison with their male peers.

• Parents agree far less on the relationship with their daughters than on that with their sons. In contrast, daughters produce similar findings in their rating of their relationship with their mothers and fathers; that is, when they have a good relationship with their mothers, the same applies for their fathers; if they have a poor relationship with their mothers, this also applies for their fathers. However, there is one important exception here: On the topic of "autonomy," daughters agree just as little with their parents as the parents among themselves—a finding that points to the obvious lack of family consensus on rearing girls, which also corresponds with the high measure of parental control that daughters report in their contacts with their mothers and fathers.

• Current parent–child relations can be predicted, to a notable extent, on the basis of the parental childrearing style assessed 16 years before. This produces specific patterns of relations, depending on the relationship aspect in question: The more competent and confident parents were in dealing with their children in 1976, the greater the interpersonal closeness perceived by parents and children 16 years later. Loving attention on the part of the parents prepares the ground for positive communication between parents and their adult children. A high measure of parental protection in childhood and adolescence predicts a controlling attitude in later parent–child relations. Strong conflict in the relationship between parents and their adult sons and daughters has its antecedents in an increased tendency toward parental anger and less confidence in rearing their children.

• There is a particularly close relation between current parent–child relations in 1992 and the way in which young adults rate the childrearing style of their parents retrospectively. With even greater precision in terms of content, this confirms the previously described pattern of relations for the individual aspects of the relationship between parents and their adult children.

• In all, findings suggest that the current form of the relationship between parents and children is influenced, on the one hand, by the previously practiced parental childrearing style. On the other hand, the retrospective rating of parental childrearing style by the young adults makes a major contribution to how they rate the quality of the current relationship with their parents.

END NOTES

1. In this context, Braiker (1992) talked about "poisonous relationships." See also the psychoimmunological research program of Kiecolt-Glaser et al. (1988).
2. Compare the approaches to structuring important concepts in the psychology of relationships in Schneewind (1991) and Wynne (1984).
3. Representative treatments on factor analytic methods can be found in Cattell (1978) and Gorsuch (1974).
4. On the method of analysis of variance, see Guilford (1965).
5. The later section of this chapter on current relationships and childrearing style from the parents' perspective reports that an increasing degree of parent-perceived protectiveness is accompanied by greater control in current parent–child relations.
6. The alliance or coalition problem is a particularly important topic in structural family therapy (see Glick, Clarkin, & Kessler, 1987; Minuchin, 1974).
7. On the conception and diagnostic transformation of the FATS, see Schneewind (1988a), as well as Schneewind, Beckmann, and Hecht-Jackl (1985). All content concepts of the FATS were used in the present context (see Schneewind & Ruppert, 1992).
8. On multiple correlation/regression and the explanation of variance using the multiple determination coefficient R^2, see Cohen and Cohen (1983) and Berry and Feldman (1985).
9. In this case, the basis is hierarchical regression analyses, in which the diverse indicators of childrearing goals, attitudes, and practices are each entered into the regression model as blocks in this given sequence (see Cohen & Cohen, 1983).
10. In fact, this would have made it necessary to use the "own" contribution in the analyses. However, empirically, there were no differences in the findings when the "own" contribution or the mean of the "own" and "other" contributions were used.
11. Such an interpretation is in line with explanations based on attribution theory and action theory (see Weiner, 1990; Smedslund, 1988).

6

MARITAL OR PARTNER RELATIONS IN PARENTS AND CHILDREN

A study like ours, which takes an ecopsychological approach to the study of family development, and thus is oriented toward a model extending from the level of the individual across increasingly more all-encompassing systems up to the societal context, is faced with an extended number of possible units of analysis. This becomes particularly clear in the progression from the individual to the dyadic relationship. Our study separates the conceivable dyadic relations within the family into three, qualitatively differentiable groups:

1. Parent–Child Relations Against the Background of the Childrearing Context. Particularly at the first wave, when the children were ages 9–14, parent–child relations were defined primarily through the specific pattern of parental childrearing behavior toward the child. The child's role in this process, which was often underestimated or even ignored in earlier research, is not just the passive acceptance of parental childrearing measures, but can also be described as active. Mediated by the subjective perception of parental childrearing behavior, children certainly have the possibility of taking an active role in codetermining the relationship with their parents, just like their parents do. Regardless of what this interactive process between parents and children may look like, during this life phase, its content is negotiated predominantly through topics that can be summarized under the heading "childrearing" in the broadest sense.

2. Parent–Child Relations Against the Background of an Egalitarian Model of Relations. This type of dyadic relationship, which is no different from the first in terms of the persons involved, attains its autonomy through the state of development achieved by the family at the second wave. The children are now between the ages of 25 and 30, and thus find themselves in the phase of young adulthood. The individuality and autonomy that the children have developed over this time shifts the pattern of relations to their parents from a constellation marked by gaps in power between parents and children toward a more egalitarian relationship between two autonomous individuals. However, this is in no way a claim that parent–child relations always develop toward egalitarianism. As reported in detail in chapter 5, relations between adult children and their parents can also be dominated by conflicts and striving for control, which have their roots in the childrearing phase. Nonetheless, when attempting to assess such parent–child relations empirically, it is important to note that this stage no longer focuses on topics whose content is taken from the domain of "childrearing." Although it may be that the parents' or one parent's relation to a 30-year-old child is still shaped by the effort to "rear" the child, it should not be forgotten that this is a relationship between two adults.

3. The Parents' Marital Relations. When previously considering fathers and mothers, we reported on how they relate to the child as "parents." We were dealing with the parent system. However, there is also another level of relations on which fathers and mothers function as spouses or, in more general terms, as partners. Although the marriage system is closely related to the parent system because it involves the same persons, it has to be looked at separately. The quality and development of marital relations is subject to influences from all other dyadic relations within the family, while requiring a degree of demarcation from them so that it does not completely dissolve within the parent system. This need to discriminate also justifies the separate appraisal of marital relations in this chapter.

4. The Children's Marital or Partner Relations. Another possible dyadic constellation of interest here concerns partner relations in the filial generation. Although this necessarily goes beyond the borders of the actual family, it is conceivable that the characteristics of these relations will relate, at least in part, to the child's experiences of relationships gained while growing up within the family of origin. For example, one question is whether the parents' marital relations serve as a model for the child's own relations. These and other questions are considered in this chapter.[1]

Thus, this chapter focuses on the description and perception of own partner relations in both parents and children. Previous chapters have also presented an additional approach: the perception of the same relationship constellation by different persons (e.g., the perception of mother–son relations by both mothers and their sons). We also use this approach here. Thus findings on the parents' marital relations are based not just on the reports of fathers and mothers, but ratings on these relations are also available from each child surveyed. The same also applies to the children's partner relations. Their own ratings can be compared with those of the fathers and mothers.

PERCEPTION OF ONE'S OWN MARITAL RELATIONS

The first part of this chapter focuses on the perceptions of one's own partner relations in both generations. Particularly for the filial generation, the chapter links the current partner relationship to the experiences of relations within the family of origin.

Description of One's Own Partner Relationship

The simplest way to describe a partner relationship, which also marks the historical beginnings of research on partner relations, is simply to ask people how satisfied they are with it. However, such a concept of marriage satisfaction cannot do justice to the wealth of aspects within a relationship. This has led to the development of numerous procedures that permit a more differentiated description of marital relations.[2] As a result, any empirical study has to choose between a host of assessment instruments. Luckily, this problem was avoided because we already developed the Family Assessment Test System (FATS) while working on the first phase of the PCR project.[3] As well as describing dyadic parent–child relations in the childrearing context (see chaps. 4 and 5) and the family as an entire system using family climate scales (these are the topic of chap. 7), this test battery for the psychological assessment of family systems also contains an instrument for the multidimensional description of marital relations: the Marital Relationship (MR) System. To permit a comparison of data across two waves, this instrument was also used at Wave 2. It consists of a questionnaire containing 16 statements designed to assess four concepts. The questionnaire takes two forms because the original scale construction produced versions in which a few statements differed for men and women. The four concepts for assessing the quality of marital relations are:

1. Affection. Items on this scale address the mutual exchange of affection and sexual satisfaction within the relationship. They also address the feeling of a harmonious interplay between the two partners (Sample item: "I like being together with my husband/wife").

2. Conflict. This scale assesses the extent and frequency of conflicts ranging in strength from bad moods and tensions to loud and hefty confrontations (Sample item: "My husband/wife and I often have rows").

3. Resigned Dissatisfaction. This covers two aspects of perceived relations with complementary effects: on the one hand, lack of positive stimulation within the relationship; on the other hand, avoidance or concealment of conflict-laden topics. Taken together, these produce a passive, merely tolerated (i.e., resigned) dissatisfaction (Sample item: "There's not much sense in talking to my husband/wife about things I would like to be different. It doesn't change anything anyway").

4. Repression. This scale differs for men or women. However, for both genders, it contains the aspect of feeling repressed by the partner, as well as a personal tendency to provide additional reinforcement to this repression by giving up one's own desires (Sample item: "I can't do what I would actually like to do within our relationship").

Factor analysis and psychometric tests were also applied to check the reliability of this constellation of scales.[4] Table 6.1 presents the scale reliabilities of the MR System for the second wave and for various subgroups within our sample. As can be seen, with values ranging from alpha = .80 to alpha = .88, the scales "Affection," "Conflict," and "Resigned dissatisfaction" have satisfactory reliabilities. In comparison, the reliabilities for "Repression," which could not be computed across the entire sample because of the use of different items for men and women, are much lower.

Marital Relations in the Parent Generation

As in previous chapters, two approaches are used here to ascertain whether certain psychological features have changed or not over the course of time—that is, whether there is stability or a tendency toward change. The one approach addresses absolute stability, which provides information on possible changes in the means of a sample. The other addresses relative stability, which reveals whether there have been recognizable shifts in the

TABLE 6.1
Reliabilities of the Marital (Partner) Relations Scale

Marital (partner) relations scales	Total ($n = 580$)	Parents ($n = 421$)	Children ($n = 159$)	Father ($n = 208$)	Mother ($n = 203$)	Son ($n = 72$)	Daughter ($n = 87$)
Affection	.84	.85	.82	.85	.85	.83	.81
Conflict	.86	.86	.85	.87	.84	.80	.88
Resigned Dissatisfaction	.81	.81	.82	.81	.80	.85	.81
Repression	/	/	/	.44	.47	.57	.44

Note. All coefficients: $p < .001$.

strength of a particular feature within the sample. In the following, both approaches are now applied to marital relations in the parent generation.[5]

Absolute Stabilities in Parental Marital Relations. To ascertain whether the means on the marital relations scales have changed across the 16 years between the two waves, it is first necessary to determine what marital relations looked like at Wave 1. Figure 6.1 shows the means on the four scales for both fathers and mothers separately as well as for the total group. Results indicate that the marital climate was generally very positive. The highest values are found on the scale "Affection," which can be viewed as an indicator of positive marital relations. In contrast, the values on the scales "Conflict" and "Resigned dissatisfaction" are much lower—both being aspects of relations in which a low score is a sign of a marriage that is perceived to be positive and harmonious. The scale "Repression" has the highest mean among those scales addressing more negative aspects of relations. However, in relation to the breadth of the scales, there is some indication that the patterns of marital relations tapped by this scale tend to be rather infrequent. Thus, for the first wave, we were able to ascertain that marital relations in the parent generation reveal a clear predominance of marital affection and harmony, in comparison with the more negative areas of conflict, dissatisfaction, and repression.

What does this profile of marital relations look like 16 years later? Figure 6.2 plots the two mean profiles together for Waves 1 and 2 to highlight any changes. It can be seen that the two profiles take a similar course. The scale

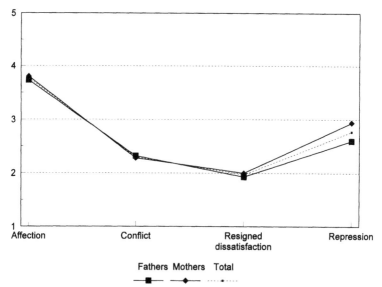

FIG. 6.1. Parents' marital relations in 1976.

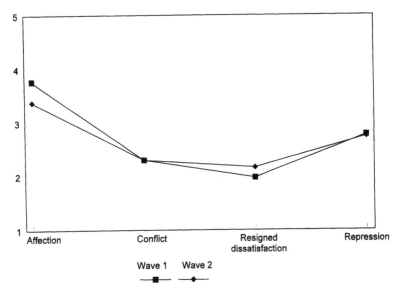

FIG. 6.2. Comparison of parents' marital relations in 1976 and 1992.

"Affection" continues to dominate in comparison with the negative indicators. Nonetheless, one cannot overlook that changes between the two waves
have reduced this dominance of positive compared with negative marital
features. This is revealed particularly in two scales whose values differ
significantly between the two waves. First, there is a clear drop in the mean
for affection. Shared affection, sexual satisfaction, and living together in
harmony are now rated less positively. Second, there is also an equally
strong increase in resigned dissatisfaction, which includes increased monot-
ony, a lack of stimulation, and problem avoidance.

If we consider what these results mean, a family life-cycle perspective
would suggest that our respondents do not seem to have coped very well
with the redefinition of marital relations, which is the developmental task
facing them in this life phase. A life phase during which the children are
getting ready to leave the family home, if they have not done so already,
and in which the parents are simultaneously facing retirement from occupational life also requires a redefinition of how to live together in the future
partnership. Successful coping with this developmental task should generally lead to an increase in affection and a decrease in resigned dissatisfaction
and repression. The present findings tend to suggest that the opposite is
the case.

Results presented so far refer to the total group of respondents in which
men and women are aggregated. It is possible that the changes found are
gender-specific. However, this hypothesis is clearly dismissed by the data
presented in Fig. 6.3, which plots the changes between the two waves sepa-

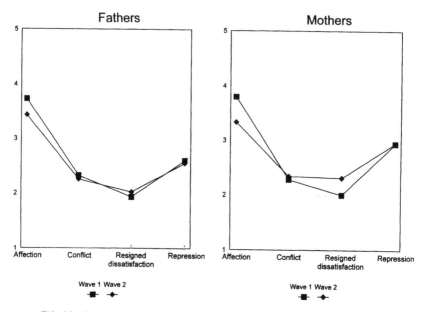

FIG. 6.3. Parents' marital relations from the mother's and father's perspectives: a comparison between 1976 and 1992.

rately for both genders. Although the differences between the two waves are clearer in women, changes in the men take the same direction and they attain statistical significance in both genders.

Therefore, the negative change in the perception of one's own marital relationship can be observed to the same extent in men and women. The situation looks different again when men and women are each compared at one wave. There are indications at both waves that women have a notably more negative perception of at least some aspects of marital relations. In 1976, women reported a significantly higher degree of repression within their marital relations. The same difference, as well as a markedly higher level of resigned dissatisfaction, is also found 16 years later. In summary, both genders have roughly the same perceptions of changes across time, but women rate their marital relations less favorably than men at both waves.

Relative Stabilities in Parental Marital Relations. The changes discussed previously only provide information on how the parent generation as a whole has changed during the intervening period. However, it is possible that, although the means have remained the same at both time points, individual persons reveal more or less marked changes in their estimation of their marital relations. The degree of this is expressed by the correlations between Waves 1 and 2 for the four marital relations scales. These are reported in Table 6.2.

TABLE 6.2
Relative Stabilities of the Marital (Partner) Relations Scales for Parents

Marital (partner) relations scales	Total ($n = 411$)	Fathers ($n = 208$)	Mothers ($n = 203$)
Affection	.62	.61	.65
Conflict	.59	.55	.64
Resigned Dissatisfaction	.51	.54	.49
Repression	.44	.38	.41

Note. All coefficients: $p < .001$.

In general, values indicate a moderate stability in marital relations. There are somewhat higher values for affection and conflict in comparison with resigned dissatisfaction and repression. If the findings reported in chapter 3 are recalled—and it is borne in mind what a variety of decisive individual and familial change events the respondents have been exposed to between the two waves—it is difficult to anticipate that these should have had no impact on marital relations. Marital relations are at the center of family life and are more or less affected by all events. From this perspective, it is certainly an important finding that it is specifically the scales "Affection" and "Conflict," which are the most conspicuous indicators for estimating the own relationship, that have remained relatively stable. If this is related to the mean scores on these scales (see Fig. 6.2), there are several indications that, in 1976, the respondents' marital relations were sufficiently well established to render them highly capable of coping with the dynamic processes of change within the family in the years to come. These stand in contrast to the less stable concepts of "Resigned dissatisfaction" and "Repression," which tap more subtle processes of marital relations, and are probably subject to more frequent oscillations across time. Furthermore, the values reported in Table 6.2 reveal that there are no mentionable differences between men and women in the stabilities of the individual scales. In other words, there appears to be no gender-linked sensitivity in perceiving changes within the own marriage.

Nonetheless, the stability coefficients confirm that changes have occurred. However, they do not reveal what kind of changes these have been. For example, for the scale "Repression," a high stability can be confirmed for the means, whereas the relative stability is very low at $r = .41$. Therefore, it would be interesting to find out more about the distribution of these changes within the sample. This information is provided in Fig. 6.4. Using the scores at the two waves, a value was computed for each person that reports whether scores on the individual dimensions of marital relations have increased, decreased, or remained unchanged over the prior 16 years. Figure 6.4 shows this distribution for the four dimensions separately for fathers and mothers, as well for the

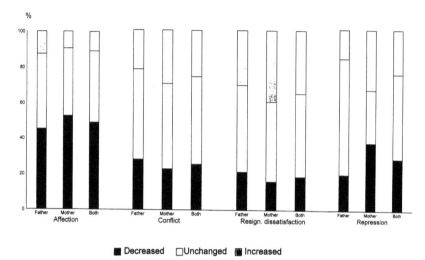

Decreased □Unchanged **Increased**

FIG. 6.4. Direction of change in parents' marital relations between 1976–1992.

total group. When classifying the differences between the first and second wave into the three values "decreased," "increased," and "unchanged," cases in which differences deviated only marginally from zero were also assigned to the "unchanged" category.

For each of the three samples, the percentages of persons who report an increase, decrease, or no change in their estimations of their marital relations were added up to 100%. This provides a differentiated picture of the information given by the stability coefficients. On all four scales, there is a relatively high percentage of persons in whom no change in their estimation of their marital relations can be ascertained. This is in line with expectations based on the stability coefficients. However, a comparison of increases and decreases on the individual scales is more informative.

1. Affection. The percentage of those for whom the degree of affection has decreased over the years is clearly the highest. Forty-nine percent of the respondents report a clear decrease, compared with 11% reporting a clear increase. If men are discriminated from women, the relation between increase and decrease in women reveals a much stronger movement toward a decrease in affection.

2. Conflict. For the total group, increase and decrease are in balance, whereas a separate inspection of the genders produces an opposite result to that on the dimension "Affection." Among women, the degree of conflict has tended to increase rather than decrease, whereas among men, a relatively larger decrease in perceived marital conflict can be seen.

3. Resigned Dissatisfaction. This reveals the same findings as perceived conflict, except that the percentage increase of 25% in perceived marital conflict now rises to 34%. When change occurs on this scale, it more clearly takes the direction of an increase in resigned dissatisfaction.

4. Repression. The most conspicuous finding concerns perceived repression in marital relations. For the total sample, the distribution of the three change categories corresponds roughly to the findings for perceived conflict, whereas a comparison of men and women reveals marked differences. For both increase and decrease, mothers show percentages that are almost twice as high as those of fathers.

Thus, there have been strong changes in both directions among mothers, which can certainly be anticipated on the basis of the low stability coefficients. However, it is astonishing that the proportion of those who perceive an increase in repression is just as large as the proportion of those who report a decrease. The next question is, why, among the fathers, whose stability coefficients are just as low as those of the mothers, is the proportion who fall into the increase and decrease categories so much lower? What causes the low stability in this case? The answer is that, as mentioned earlier, the "unchanged" category also contains small changes that can have a cumulative influence on the stability coefficients.

In summary, the following statements can be made on the basis of the distributions displayed in Fig. 6.4: When changes in the perception of the quality of marital relations occur, the perception of deteriorated marital relations is dominant, and this is expressed in a decrease in affection and an increase in conflict and resigned dissatisfaction. Although increase and decrease in the perceived change in repression in marital relations balance each other out, there are clear differences between men and women. Women seem to be particularly sensitive to this aspect of marital relations. In general, it can be seen that a larger proportion of women report negative change compared with men.

Agreement Between Partners. Up to now, we have treated men and women as separate groups, and differences between these groups have been traced back to general gender-specific features, without taking account of the fact that the respondents are married couples. However, the internal dynamics of a marriage only become recognizable when the analysis is shifted onto the level comparing husband and wife. We are particularly interested in whether and how far husbands and wives agree in their views on diverse aspects of their relations. Table 6.3 reports correlation coefficients at both waves.

The levels of agreement differ greatly across the individual scales. It is conspicuous that the agreement on "Affection" and "Conflict" is somewhat stronger than on "Resigned dissatisfaction" and "Repression." "Affection"

TABLE 6.3
Agreement Between Parents on the Marital (Partner)
Relations Scales at Both Waves

Marital (partner) relations scales	Wave 1 (n = 198)	Wave 2 (n = 198)
Affection	.50***	.71***
Conflict	.63***	.57***
Resigned Dissatisfaction	.30**	.52***
Repression	.01	.18*

*p < .05. **p < .01. ***p < .001.

and "Conflict"–the two scales emphasized as particularly relevant dimensions of marital relations–show the highest agreement between spouses. In contrast, the result for the scale "Repression" is notable. There was absolutely no relationship between the perspectives of husbands and wives at the first wave, whereas a correlation of r = .18 is found at the second wave. However, despite its statistical significance, this correlation tends to indicate a clear divergence in the perceptions of spouses. When it is borne in mind that women perceive far more repression in their marriages at both waves than men, then one possible explanation is that these are marriages in which women feel themselves to be repressed and men are the repressors. If this hypothesis is true, the correlation coefficients should be negative. Because this is clearly not the case, it would seem that an individual's perception of repression in marital relations seems to be largely independent of the perspective taken by the partner.

The comparison across the two waves indicates that spouses draw closer together during the course of their shared lives and in their perceptions of their marriage. Computation of the differences between the similarity coefficients for both waves confirms this assumption for three of the four scales. These differences lie between r = .17 and r = .22, and indicate that a clear mutual coordination of perceptions has occurred. Only the agreement on perceived conflict in the marriage decreases slightly across time, although it still attains a correlation of r = .57 at the second wave. It is possible that no increase occurs here because the level of agreement at Wave 1 was already relatively strong at r = .63.

Partner Relations in the Filial Generation

When talking about marital relations among the parents, these were also real marriages (i.e., married couples). In the filial generation, one of the phenomena reflecting the change in the spirit of the times over the last 20 years is that children who provide information on their own relationships are not necessarily married to their partners. The marked increase in non-married partnerships is also reflected in the data on our sample. Seventy-nine percent of the approximately 190 members of the filial generation we were able to survey live with a permanent partner. However, only half reported that they were married (see the corresponding data in chap. 1). As a result, we no longer talk about marital relations in this section, but the children's partner relations.

However, is it acceptable to throw the group of married and unmarried into "one pot"? Frequently, opting for a partnership without a marriage certificate is motivated by a desire to avoid the rigidity and restrictions of the conventional concept of marriage, and to live according to an alternative concept that will hopefully lead to a more fulfilling relationship. This has led an alternative "lifestyle" to become recognized as an autonomous life-style in the social sciences, although still not in politics and law, that is singled out from conventional marriage.

Although we cannot say anything about the motivation of our nonmarried respondents, we could test whether these two groups differ in their percep-tions of their partner relations. One of many possible hypotheses on plau-sible differences between married and unmarried partners is that nonmar-ried relationships could be characterized by a higher level of conflict. The more open basic principle underlying nonmarried relationships could mean that both partners are more able to face up to conflicts and deal with them.

Led by this and further plausible hypotheses, we compared means be-tween the two groups. The surprising result is that we could not find a tendency toward a difference on any of the scales. One has to ask whether this means that all assumptions and hypotheses regarding qualitative dif-ferences between these two groups are just an outcome of flowering scien-tific fantasy, and whether those involved in such relationships are also simply chasing an illusion.

Looking at our sample, it is probably another fact that is decisive—namely, the duration of the relationship. The proposed differences between married and nonmarried couples are probably only manifest within their relationship after several years. However, the maximum possible duration of the relationships of the children in the filial generation is necessarily too short for such differences to be confirmed at this time. Therefore, we per-formed no further separate analyses of partner relations among these two groups of children.

Figure 6.5 shows the means for the filial generation separately for sons and daughters. The general picture of partner relations is just as positive as that reported previously in the parent generation: a high level of affection as an indicator of positive relations, compared with markedly lower values on the scales "Conflict," "Resigned dissatisfaction," and "Repression." It can

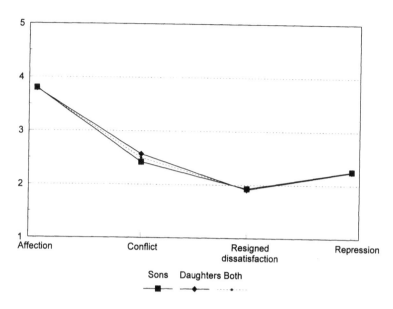

FIG. 6.5. Children's partner relations in 1992: comparison between sons and daughters.

also be seen that the filial generation exhibits no major gender differences. In the parent generation, women clearly report more dissatisfaction and repression than men at Wave 2, whereas the children's generation shows only a slightly higher value on the scale "Conflict" among women.

The similarity between the children's and parents' mean profiles was mentioned already. However, there are some interesting differences, as shown in Fig. 6.6. This compares the means of children and parents at the second wave. Despite the similarity in the profile across all scales, there are significant differences that provide information on generational differences in perceived partner relations. Somewhat more affection and conflict and a recognizably lower measure of resigned dissatisfaction and repression characterize the filial generation in comparison with the parent generation. In all, the results suggest that the children's generation has achieved a more functional and effective relational concept than the parents. This conclusion is supported by the following findings:

1. Affection as the equivalent of a general measure of partnership satisfaction is clearly dominant among the children. The emotional basis of their relationships generally seems to be stronger than in parents.

2. The relation between conflict and resigned dissatisfaction is important for the functionality of the relationship. This is confirmed particularly in the way in which conflicts are dealt with, or in the fact that conflicts are not

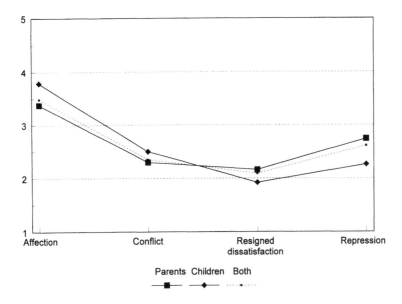

FIG. 6.6. Comparison of partner relations between parents and children in 1992.

ignored and partners practice a minimum degree of openness. In the parents, these two values are almost equal. In contrast, in the children, dissatisfaction is clearly lower than in the parents, whereas conflict is markedly higher. However, it is precisely this low value for dissatisfaction that shows that it would be wrong to interpret a high measure of conflict as negative. It is far more the case that more conflict can be assumed to lead to a greater ability to cope with it. By dealing constructively with the conflicts that arise, it is possible to prevent resigned dissatisfaction from smoldering at the roots of the relationship.

3. Much less repression within the children's partnerships indicates a relationship concept that is directed toward equal rights in both partners. In addition, relationship patterns that reflect traditional gender role stereotypes, such as the higher values on the "Repression" scale in mothers compared with fathers among the parent generation, cannot be found in the children's generation.

All in all, findings on the intergenerational comparison of partner relations reveal that the younger generation has an emotionally more intensive, more open, more egalitarian, but in no way less conflictual relationship than their parents. Another question is admittedly whether this relationship concept can be maintained over time. The parent generation generally revealed a slight erosion in the quality of marital relations across 16 years. The younger generation still has to show whether it will be able to manage their alternative relationships with equally minimal signs of wear and tear in the long term.

Variables Impacting on Partner Relations in the Filial Generation

This section attempts to identify some variables that impact on partner relations in the filial generation. This is restricted mostly to the interplay between various relations and perceptions of relations.[6] The target concept is the children's partner relations. Proceeding from basic assumptions in social learning theory, it can be anticipated that most of the children's knowledge about relationships has been gained within the environment of their own family.[7] As a consequence, the children's own partner relations should be oriented more or less toward the models of relationships provided in their family of origin.

The first idea that comes to mind is that the parents' marital relationship serves as a model or orientation point for the child's own partnership. There are basically two options here. On the one hand, the parents' relationship can serve as a positive model to which one orients oneself, in the sense that one tries to shape one's own relationship in a similar way to that of the parents. On the other hand, it may also serve as a negative model, with the result that one's goal is to do one's best to avoid repeating the "mistakes" of one's parents.

However, in the system of family relations, it is not just the parents' marital relations that can be effective here. For the children, their own relationship to their parents has a much more direct and important impact on social learning and the development of basic relationship competencies. Here, we are dealing with basic relationship skills that are reflected in all social contacts and, as a result, also in one's own partnerships.

Impact of Parents' Marital Relations on Partner Relations in the Filial Generation. The impact of the parents' marital relations on the partnerships of the children can basically be studied in two ways, as far as perceptual data are concerned. First, one can ask persons about relationships in which they are personally involved. Although the resulting description is subject to subjective evaluation and distortion processes, it is as close as one can get to what is actually happening, and thus provides the most precise picture possible of this relationship. Second, one can ask persons to describe a relationship in which they are not personally involved (i.e., one that they only observe as outsiders). Here as well, the outcome is naturally not "objective reality," but a subjective interpretation.

Both of these descriptions are available for the parents' marital relations: first, from the perspective of the parents, and, second, from the perspective of their children. Now, which of these two approaches has the strongest impact on the children's partnerships? On the one hand, it is plausible to assume that the parents' view of their own marriage will have less impact on the children than the children's view of this relationship. On the other hand, it also cannot be denied that, over the many years that they have lived together, the parents must have conveyed their own personal idea of their marital relationship to their children. Therefore, what needs to be explained is whether the impression of the parental marriage conveyed by the parents over many years or the children's own direct impression as outsiders has a stronger impact on the children's partnerships. We tested this question with the method of multiple regression analysis discussed many times before in this book. This procedure allows us to predict the children's partnership from the various reports on the parents' marital relations.

The potential impact of parents' perceptions of their own marital relations on the partner relations of their children has been described as a variable with a long-term impact. Our data provide only two so-called "stills" from these continuously effective inner-family events: the parents' reports in 1976 and, once again, in 1992. Because, as the reported stability coefficients confirm, we can assume that there are at least some differences in the parents' perceptions at these two time points, their data at both waves are used as predictor variables. We also have estimations from fathers and mothers, and these are both entered separately into the regression analysis. Each of the four partner relations scales of the children are related to the paternal and maternal marital relations data at two waves, thus they are related to 16 predictor variables. The analyses are performed separately for sons and daughters to detect potential gender-specific effects.

Table 6.4 reports the results. It gives the following information on the regression equation obtained for each of the four partner relations scales separately for sons and daughters: significant predictor scales and their accompanying beta coefficients,[8] which scale is involved, on which perspective it is based (father or mother), and at which wave (1 or 2) the information was gathered. Finally, the R^2 value reports the percentage of variance in the respective partner relations scales for the children that can be predicted by the specific parental scales on marital relations.

We now describe the results reported in Table 6.4 in terms of the most important questions raised.

1. Are there any relations at all between the children's partner relations and the ways in which parents describe their marital relations 16 years ago and today? The findings summarized in the table clearly support the exist-

TABLE 6.4
Relations Between the Children's Self-Perceived Partner Relations and the
Parents' Self-Perceived Marital Relations at Both Waves

Children: Own partnership	SONS (n = 60)		DAUGHTERS (n = 73)	
Affection	Conflict Father-II	.27	Resigned dissatisfaction Father-I	-.28
	$R^2 = 6$		$R^2 = 7$	
Conflict	Conflict Father-II	.33	Resigned dissatisfaction Father-II	.25
	$R^2 = .10$		$R^2 = .10$	
Resigned dissatisfaction	Resigned Dissatisfaction Mother-I	.26	Repression Mother-I	.25
	$R^2 = .05$		Resigned Dissatisfaction Father-I	.26
			$R^2 = .12$	
Repression	Repression Father-II	.29	Resigned dissatisfaction Mother-I	-.45
	$R^2 = .07$		Resigned dissatisfaction-Mother-II	.55
			$R^2 = .21$	

Note. I = Wave 1 (1976). II = Wave 2 (1992).

ence of such relations. For both sons and daughters, there are significant relations for all four scales, confirming that the quality of the parents' marital relations impacts on their children's partner relations.

2. What can be said about the closeness of these relations? This can be measured with the r^2 or R^2 values. Although the explanations of between 5% and 21% of variance reveal that parents' marital relations are not the only variable impacting on children's partner relations, these relations are strong enough to justify an interpretation of their content. It is conspicuous that, with the exception of the scale "Conflict," relations are much closer for daughters than for sons.

3. Are there any indications for a dominance of same-gender patterns of influence? This be confirmed only for sons: Apart from the scale "Resigned dissatisfaction," all dimensions of sons' partner relations are influenced only by the father's perceptions of parent marital relations. In contrast, for daughters, the paternal and maternal perspectives play equally strong roles.

4. Is the impact of parental perceptions of their own marital relations more short or long term? It is particularly interesting here to see whether parents' marital relations as perceived 16 years ago also impact on the children's partner relations, or whether this impact is more or less covered over or neutralized by the current situation. The findings indicate a combination of long- and short-term effects. Here as well, there seem to be differences between sons and daughters, in the sense that the current paternal influence is particularly dominant for sons, whereas the picture is more heterogeneous in daughters.

We now summarize the most important content-related findings that can be derived from the results.

1. Only the negative indicators of parents' marital relations seem to predict partner relations in the filial generation. For example, the degree of affection has no impact on children's partner relations. This is possibly because this aspect of the parents' relations is private, and therefore is not communicated very much in dealings with the children.

2. Conflict in parental relations is a powerful predictor only in the father–son constellation. A surprising finding is revealed here: The higher the amount of conflict perceived by the fathers, the more conflict sons also report in their partnerships. At the same time, paternal marital conflict also predicts a higher degree of affection in the sons' partnerships. It seems as if a paternal willingness to engage in conflict encourages sons to express conflict in their own relations, and to become involved more strongly in the positive sides of their partnerships.

3. The level of resigned dissatisfaction in the parents is the most important predictor of the children's partner relations, and particularly in daughters. In line with the failure to confirm an impact of parental affection, it would seem that the parents' marital relations predominantly impact on the children as negative examples. The picture of both parents patiently accepting a dissatisfying marriage seems to have the strongest impact on the way children shape their own relations. This impact is conveyed over both the mothers and the fathers. It should also be mentioned that these are, in part, long-term processes; that is, parental perceptions of dissatisfaction at the first wave show a strong impact on the current partner relations of the children. Earlier, we described resigned dissatisfaction—in contrast to affection and conflict—as a concept whose strength in a relationship is not expressed directly on a behavioral level. It is more of a conglomerate of rather subtle and covert aspects of the quality of parental relations. However, when this dimension exercises such a strong effect on the children, it would seem as if children have already developed a strong sensitivity toward difficult situations in their parents' relations at the time of the first wave. In any

case, a transfer process has occurred for precisely this aspect of relations. Without the parents noticing it, and probably against their wishes, its effect is that children shape their relations in the same way as their parents do. This finding shows how important it is to clarify dissatisfactions in a partnership in communicative ways before they consolidate into a resigned attitude. In this way, parents can hand on a positive model of relations to the following generation.

4. The complexity of possible effects is illustrated by one specific finding: The degree of repression perceived by daughters is influenced by the resigned dissatisfaction of mothers at both the first and second waves. However, these relations contradict each other at each wave. A high maternal dissatisfaction in 1976 predicts a low level of repression in the daughters' partnerships, whereas the situation is completely reversed in 1992. The more dissatisfied the mothers are with their current marriage situation, the more the daughters feel repressed in their partnership. Therefore, it is particularly the change in the mothers' perceptions of dissatisfaction that has a strong impact on the daughters' feelings of repression.

The long-term process through which parents impart a model of marital relations to their children has, as confirmed earlier, considerable impact on the children's partner relations. What is important is that the situation as reported 16 years ago is still effective today and reveals a complex interaction with the current situation.

As a result of parental influences, the children develop their own image of their parents' marital relations over time. However, this image cannot be traced back exclusively to the parents' descriptions of their own marriages. The children's personality and learning biography also provide a major contribution to these cognitive concepts. To clarify this issue, we now study whether the impact of the children's perception of their parents' marital relations on their own partner relations is just as strong as the impact of the parents' perspective.

The children used a different instrument to describe their parents' marital relations than the one used by the parents. It is based on the four dimensions "Closeness," "Communication," "Control," and "Conflict," and has already been presented in detail in chapter 5—for the assessment of current parent–child relations.[9] The results are presented in the same way as in Table 6.4. Once again, multiple correlations were computed for each scale measuring the filial generation's own partner relations. However, this time, the descriptions of parental relations from the children's perspective were used to predict the quality of the children's current partnerships. The results are reported in Table 6.5. We focus on comparing these results with the findings presented in the last section.

For the sons, there is only one significant relation. The degree of conflict in their own relations is higher when they perceive more conflict in their

TABLE 6.5
Relations Between Children's Self-Perceived Partner Relations and
Their Perception of Parental Marital Relations

Marital (partner) relations scales	SONS (n = 60)		DAUGHTERS (n = 73)	
Affection	/		Communication	.22
			$R^2 = .04$	
Conflict	Conflict	.29	Communication	-.26
	$R^2 = 7$		$R^2 = .06$	
Resigned Dissatisfaction	/		Communication	-.25
			$R^2 = .05$	
Repression	/		Communication	-.39
			$R^2 = .14$	

parents' relations. Thus, the sons' perceptions of their parents' marital relations have much less impact on their own relations than their parents' perceptions. Among daughters, the relation between their perceptions of their parents' marital relations and their own partner relations is more revealing. The perceived quality of communication in parental marital relations plays a major role here. The better the communication between parents from the daughters' perspective, the greater the degree of affection in their own partnerships and, at the same time, the lower the conflict, resigned dissatisfaction, and repression. What is notable here, in contrast to the findings on the parents' perceptions, is that a positive aspect of relations is effective. In contrast, perceived parental control or conflict are insignificant.

In comparison with the findings reported in the previous section, relations are generally much weaker. When considering why this is so, two aspects—apart from the use of different concepts of relations—should be taken into account. First, most children no longer live at home. This makes it harder for them to describe their parents' marital relations. Perhaps this leads to ideas about the parents' marital relations that are just as divorced from the parents' subjective view on the reality of their relations as the children's ideas about their parents' relations were when they were still living in their families of origin. Second, the influence of parental perceptions is a process that starts long before children can consciously construct their own independent opinions of their parents' marriage. It may be that this process starting in early childhood already lays down foundations that shape the children's own partnerships, and that these can no longer be abandoned so easily in favor of a developmentally determined, autonomous understanding of parents' marital relations.

The Impact of Current Parent–Child Relations on Partner Relations in the Filial Generation. With regard to the complex interplay between diverse intrafamilial relations that may all have a more or less strong impact on the children's partnerships, we have already mentioned children's current relationship with their parents. We now look at this aspect in more detail. In particular, we return to the question of whether any relations can be ascertained between parent–child relations from the children's perspective and the children's own partner relations.[10] The instrument used to assess current parent–child relations has already been described in detail in chapter 5. Here, we only repeat that it uses the four relationship scales "Closeness," "Communication," "Control," and "Conflict."

The analysis is similar to that reported in the previous sections. The main difference is that we now relate various aspects of the children's partner relations to current parent–child relations. The differentiation between sons and daughters is retained. However, there is also a further refinement. The children's relations are broken down into relations to the father and relations to the mother, and ascertained separately for these two relationship constellations. An additional analysis includes relations to both parents. This should reveal, above all, whether the influence of one parent can overshadow the influence of the other. Some provisional hypotheses were formulated regarding the expected results.

1. Up to now, we have studied the impact of marital relations on marital or partner relations (i.e., we have addressed the same type of relations), whereas now we are interested in the impact of parent–child relations on marital or partner relations. It is necessary to consider that even when these parent–child relations concern relations between parents and their adult children, they are basically of a different type than the relations within a partnership. Thus, if significant relations are found, it can hardly be expected that the proportion of variance explained will be higher than in the previous sections.

2. Because of the basic difference between these two types of relationships, the impact of the quality of parent–child relations on marital or partner relations should be due particularly to general aspects of relations that can be viewed as a basic precondition for successfully shaping any relations, be they between parents and children or between spouses. Among the relationship concepts used here, this should particularly concern the scale "Communication." Communication as the ability to talk to each other and enable the reciprocal expression of thoughts and feelings represents, in some ways, a basic precondition for all other aspects of a relationship. Therefore, we anticipate that the quality of parent–child communication will have a strong impact on the children's partnerships.

We now turn to the results of our analyses, as reported in Table 6.6. The upper half of the table presents results for sons; the lower half, for daughters. Apart from three cases dealing with different-gender constellations (mother–son and daughter–father relations), significant results are found. Basically, this allows us to regard current parent–child relations as a further variable impacting on partner relations. As anticipated, the amount of variance explained is lower than before. In general, the effects of the parents' marital relations and those of parent–child relations on the children's partner relations seem to balance each other out.

Another question is whether gender-specific constellations can be found. Measured in terms of variance explained, there are, apart from the scale "Affection," no conspicuous discrepancies between sons and daughters. Although the variance explained focuses on different scales for each gender, the total relation seems to be equally strong for both.

With regard to the parents, it can be seen that the relation to the mother is more dominant here, and this is also stronger in daughters than in sons. For daughters, this is revealed particularly in the analyses that combine relations to both father and mother to predict partner relations. The results clearly confirm that the relation to the mother plays a more important role here.

Furthermore, the network of relations is more complex in daughters. For sons, only one aspect of parent–child relations is significant per partner relations scale, whereas the scale "Affection" clearly shows another picture for daughters. The perceived closeness to mother, but also the extent of conflict in the mother–daughter relation, together with positive communication with the father, prove to be central aspects of parent–child relations that are accompanied by a high level of affection in the daughters' partnerships. It is notable here that when conflicts are embedded within a basically positive relationship, they have a favorable impact in terms of an emotionally more intensive partnership.

Finally, the expectation that the quality of communication between parents and children is particularly important for the children's partnerships is confirmed. The relationship concept "Communication" is involved in almost one half of all significant relations. Thus, the ability to communicate adequately actually proves to be a basic relationship skill that is equally important in various relationship contexts.

PERCEPTION OF PARTNER RELATIONS IN THE OTHER GENERATION

The second part of this chapter focuses on findings on the intergenerational perception of marital or partner relations (i.e., the description of the parental marriage by the children, as well as the description of the children's partner relations by their parents).

TABLE 6.6
Relations Between Children's Self-Perceived Partner Relations and Their Current Relation to Their Parents

Children:	SONS					
Own partnership	Relation to father (n = 62)		Relation to mother (n = 60)		Relation to father and mother (n = 60)	
Affection	Comm.	.34	Comm.	.32	Comm.-F	.34
	R^2 = .10		R^2 = .09		R^2 = .10	
Conflict	Comm.	-.27	Conflict	.34	Conflict-M	.34
	R^2 = .06		R^2 = .10		R^2 = .10	
Resigned Dissatisfaction	Comm.	-.32	Comm.	-.39	Comm.-M	-.39
	R^2 = .09		R^2 = .14		R^2 = .14	
Repression	Closeness	-.30	/		Closeness-F	-.30
	R^2 = .07				R^2 = .07	
Children:	DAUGHTERS					
Own partnership	Relation to father (n = 73)		Relation to mother (n = 74)		Relation to father and mother (n = 71)	
Affection	Conflict	.32	Closeness	.74	Closeness-M	.69
	Comm.	.56	Conflict	.32	Conflict-M	.35
	R^2 = .10		R^2 = .25		Comm.-F	.23
					R^2 = .33	
Conflict	/		Control	.33	Control-M	.33
			R^2 = .09		R^2 = .09	
Resigned Dissatisfaction	Closeness	-.24	Comm.	-.36	Comm.-M	-.36
	R^2 = .05		R^2 = .12		R^2 = .12	
Repression	/		Comm.	-.25	Comm.-M	-.25
			R^2 = 5		R^2 = .05	

Note. F = Relation to father. M = Relation to mother. Comm. = Communication.

210

Assessment of Partner Relations
in the Other Generation

The data referring to this issue are based on a procedure used to describe the current relations between parents and children (see chap. 5). The same four relationship scales—"Closeness," "Communication," "Control," and "Conflict"—are used here. However, for economic reasons, the number of items per scale was reduced from six to four. A further change in the scale was also necessary. Because this question did not address a relationship in which the respondent was personally involved, we had to drop the separate estimation of one's own and the other's contribution, which had been used in the assessment of current parent–child relations. In the present case, each item was presented only once, with the instruction that the respondent should estimate the relationship in question as a whole. We also added one further item that permitted a global quality judgment on the relationship to be described, using a scale ranging from *very good* (1) to *very bad* (4).

First, it has to be ascertained whether the four scales continue to deliver statistically reliable scores after introducing these modifications. Table 6.7 reports the reliability coefficients of the modified questionnaire for the total sample and various subsamples. All scales and all sampling groups produce coefficients that agree almost exactly with those obtained with the original questionnaire for assessing current parent–child relations. Although values on the scales "Control" and "Conflict" are slightly lower than the others, in general the values can be viewed as very satisfactory. Now that the statistical reliability of the scales has been documented sufficiently, we turn to the actual questions in this section. We begin with how the parents perceive their children's partner relations.

Parents' Perception of Their
Children's Partner Relations

Once more, we start with a look at the means on the individual relationship scales. These convey the best impression of how the parent generation generally rates its children's partnerships. The values are presented in Fig. 6.7 following the usual pattern. Alongside the mean scores for the total group of parents, the figure also gives corresponding scores for fathers and mothers separately. It can be seen that parents give a thoroughly positive estimation of partnerships in the filial generation. This is revealed, first, by the mean for the global rating of the relationship that, at 4.35, is close to the maximum score of 5.0. Second, the scores on the other four scales confirm this positive picture: affection and communication, two functionally related concepts that both support the high scores for a good partnership that can be ascertained here; and control and conflict, which round off this positive picture with low means.

TABLE 6.7
Reliabilities of the Scales on Externally Perceived Intergenerational Relations

Intergenerational marital (partner) relations scales	Total (n = 321)	Parents (n = 162)	Father (Son) (n = 75)	Father (Daughter) (n = 87)	Mother (Son) (n = 70)	Mother (Daughter) (n = 89)	Children (n = 180)	Son (n = 89)	Daughter (n = 91)
Closeness	.90	.84	.83	.85	.84	.85	.91	.90	.92
Communication	.89	.85	.83	.86	.85	.87	.88	.86	.90
Control	.77	.69	.75	.61	.72	.67	.77	.76	.79
Conflict	.85	.81	.82	.79	.77	.70	.89	.81	.93

Note. All coefficients: $p < .001$.

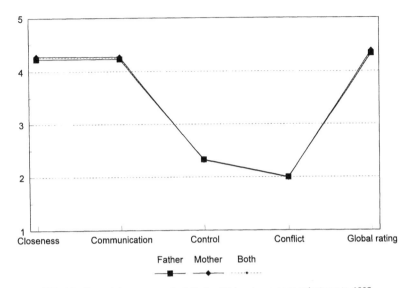

FIG. 6.7. Parents' assessment of their children's partner relations in 1992.

The results portrayed in Fig. 6.7 arouse the suspicion that parents may overestimate the quality of their children's partnerships. This can be checked by comparing the children's own perceptions with the external perceptions of their parents. However, this approach cannot be accessed directly with the given data because self-perceptions and perceptions by others are assessed with two different instruments. Nonetheless, we attempt this in a way that permits an approximate answer to this question.

First of all, some further explanations of the parents' reports are necessary. Figure 6.7, which gives separate profiles for men and women, shows that parents clearly exhibit no gender differences in their perceptions of children's partnerships. Perhaps it is less the gender of the rater and more the gender of the child whose partnership is being described that is decisive here. For this reason, we performed mean comparisons that took account of both the parents' and children's gender. Four groups of parent–child constellations can be formed in this way: mother–son, mother–daughter, father–son, and father–daughter. This produces the following results.

If groups are formed only according to the parents' gender (i.e., the gender of the persons performing the ratings), then, as anticipated, no differences can be ascertained in the rating of the children's partnerships. Generally, mothers and fathers produce similar ratings. However, if groups are based on the child's gender—that is, the son being rated or the daughter being rated—this leads to a statistically significant difference for one of the four relationship dimensions. Parents perceive far more conflict in the sons' partnerships than in the daughters' partnerships.

The most conspicuous results refer to the interactions between the parents' gender and the gender of the children being rated. These are significant for the scale "Communication" and for the score on the global rating of the partnership. This somewhat complex finding is illustrated in Fig. 6.8. The figure displays the means for the four groups on these two scales. Only the upper section is presented on the ordinate so that the effects stand out more clearly. In both scales, the interaction takes the following form. Both parents assign a higher score to the child of the opposite gender. For example, the global score that the fathers assign to the partnerships of their daughters is higher than the corresponding score that they assign to their sons, whereas the situation is inverted completely in the mothers, for whom the sons' partnerships have higher scores than those for their daughters. It is difficult to interpret this finding, particularly because the differences, although significant, tend to have low effect sizes. It is conceivable that parents anticipate that their own child of opposite gender is able to be more successful in a partnership because they attribute their own, less successful experiences to their own gender, and this anticipation also enters into the perception of actual partnerships.

We still have to tackle the question on the agreement between partners. As in the assessment of own marital relations, coefficients were computed for the level of agreement on the rating of the partnership of the shared child. These coefficients reveal the degree of similarity between fathers' and mothers' perceptions of their children's partnerships. Because this concerns

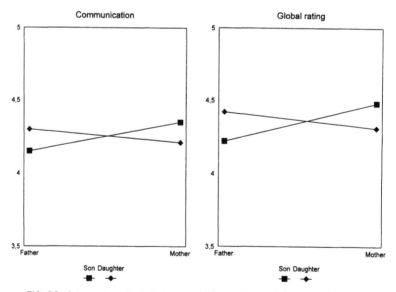

FIG. 6.8. Interaction effects between child's gender and the parent's perception on the relationship scales "Communication" and "Global rating."

the partnership of their own child, one can anticipate at least a moderate level of agreement in the parents' perceptions on all scales, although this should not be higher than the level of agreement on their own marital relations. Table 6.8 reports these coefficients. Once again, a separate analysis was carried out for the parents of sons and the parents of daughters.

The values for the total group are in line with expectations. All scales reveal an intermediate level of agreement between the paternal and maternal descriptions of children's partnerships. In these data, it has to be taken into account that we do not have any information on what proportion of the parents' reports are based on the fact that the relationship they are judging is part of the social network of their everyday lives or which proportion of this judgment is perhaps based only on the child's reports about his or her relationship. The latter case, which applies to a large part of our sample (only 12% of the children still live with their parents), would certainly lead to a reduction in the level of agreement between parents. This would be the case, for example, when children talk about their relationship problems predominantly with one parent and not with the other.

There is a surprising result when pairs of parents who were asked to rate their sons' partnerships are compared with those who commented on their daughters' partnerships. The level of agreement among parents of sons is much higher on all scales; it even attains the levels of agreement found in the ratings of own marital relations.

How can this be explained? The level of agreement between parents is based on the extent to which both parents possess the same information on their children's relationships. One basis for this is the reciprocal exchange of information between parents. It can be assumed that this exchange of information is more intensive in some couples than in others. The present findings could then be explained by saying that the parents exchange more information on their sons' partnerships than on their daugh-

TABLE 6.8
Parental Agreement on Perceptions of Children's Partnerships

Parental perception of children´s partnerships	All parents (n = 144)	Parents of sons (n = 65)	Parents of daughters (n = 79)
Closeness	.46	.65	.34
Communication	.48	.59	.42
Control	.34	.42	.25
Conflict	.47	.65	.33[1]
Total	.44	.59	.38

1: $p < .05$. All other coefficients: $p < .001$.

ters'—an explanation for which there is little indication. Against the background of previous research findings, it is more likely that it is not the exchange of information between parents, but the exchange of information between parents and children that could explain this finding, if it is assumed that sons and daughters differ in this aspect.[11]

Accordingly, the high intrapair agreement on the partnerships of sons would be due to the fact that sons do not engage in a comprehensive exchange of ideas on their partnerships with either their fathers or mothers. Thus, fathers and mothers are equally lacking in orientation and develop a joint picture of sons' partnerships. Particularly when this shared picture of the sons' partnerships is based on their own marital relations, the result is a high level of agreement between parents. The lower levels of agreement in parents' ratings on daughters could be due to the daughters communicating predominantly with only one parent about their own partnerships. The imbalance of information that this engenders between parents also cannot be compensated completely through interparent communication. Here as well, a low level of agreement between parents is facilitated when the daughters' partnerships differ in essential points from the model given by the parents' relationship. Thus, conceivable explanations for this finding can be found, but they require further empirical support.

Children's Perception of Their Parents' Marital Relations

In the analysis of the parents' perception of their children's partnerships, the most lasting impression was that the descriptions were suspiciously positive. Figure 6.9 shows the results on the opposite case: parental marital relations from the perspective of the children. If the parents' view seems to be an idealistic description, the children's perspective could be labeled *realistic*. The global ratings tend to describe the parents' marriages as good. Closeness and satisfactory communication dominate over control and conflict. However, the different profiles for sons and daughters also included in the figure reveal several clear gender differences. These all show that daughters present a less favorable estimation of their parents marital relations than sons do. They assign their parents less closeness, a less positive global rating, but more control and conflict. Does this mean that the daughters' perspective is more realistic than that of the sons? Or is this a rather pessimistic perspective that deviates more strongly from reality than the clearer perception of the sons? We return to this issue later.

First, we want to perform a direct comparison of the intergenerational perceptions of partnerships. Figure 6.10 contrasts the two profiles for parents and children. Differences are clearly visible. Although both profiles take the same direction, the children rate their parents' marital relations more nega-

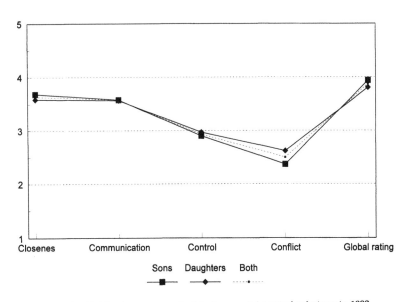

FIG. 6.9. Children's assessment of their parents' marital relations in 1992.

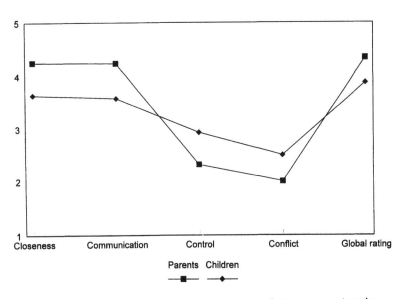

FIG. 6.10. Intergenerationally perceived partner relations: comparison between parents and children.

tively on all scales, compared with the parents' estimations of their children's partnerships. However, this should not be understood as implying that the children's descriptions reflect poor marital relations among their parents. In terms of the scale ranges, both profiles depict functional marital relations.

Comparison of Self- and Other Perceptions in Parents and Children

In this puzzling interplay of contrasting intergenerational perceptions of various dyadic relations, one inevitable question is whether there are also agreements between one's own perception of a partnership and the other person's perception of the same partnership. The level of agreement between two different descriptions of the same relationship provides information on how far, for example, parents and children possess the same information on the child's partnership. At the same time, this also provides an indirect measure of intergenerational communication.

Some of the questions raised earlier could also be answered through a comparison of self- and other perceptions of the partnerships studied (e.g., whether the parents' view of their children's partnerships is an overestimation, whereas, in contrast, the children describe their parents' marital relations more realistically).

However, the fact that we assessed own partner relations and the partner relations of the other family generation with different instruments means that we cannot make a direct comparison by computing correlations. Therefore, we can apply only the following approximate procedure here: The external perception of a partnership consisted of the four scales "Closeness," "Control," "Conflict," and "Communication," as well as a global rating of the quality of the relationship. This externally rated global score of relationship quality is the basis for the following assumptions.

1. Externally rated relationship quality correlates with the four scales on the self-perception of a relationship.

2. If it is assumed that persons giving an external rating also possess sufficient information about this relationship, the following correlations can be anticipated between the global rating and the four relationship scales: a positive correlation with affection, and high negative correlations with conflict, resigned dissatisfaction, and repression.

3. The higher these correlations are, the closer the relationship between self- and other perception.

The next two tables report these correlations between the four self-perception scales and the externally rated global rating. Table 6.9 contains the correlations between the children's self-perception and their parents' global

TABLE 6.9
Correlations Between Children's Self-Perceived Partner Relations
and Parents' Global Rating

Children:	Global rating					
Own	By mother			By father		
partnership	Total (n = 109)	Son (n = 40)	Daughter (n = 70)	Total (n = 110)	Son (n = 43)	Daughter (n = 67)
Affection	.37***	.53***	.27**	.26**	.41**	.17
Conflict	-.31***	-.52***	-.20*	-.23**	-.44*	-.15
Resigned Dissatisfaction	-.39***	-.54***	-.32*	-.23**	-.44**	-.10
Repression	-.17*	-.17	-.17	-.18	-.18	-.09

*p < .05. ** p < .01. *** p < .001.

rating. Global ratings are presented separately for fathers and mothers, and they are also split according to the children's gender. Likewise, Table 6.10 reports the correlations among the four parental self-rating scales and the children's global rating. Here as well, findings are split according to the children's and parents' gender.

First of all, we want to check whether the empirical correlations take the same direction as our theoretical predictions. Values in both tables confirm this. There is a continuously positive correlation between the global rating and affection, whereas the correlations among the global rating and conflict, resigned dissatisfaction, and repression are all negative. These two tables can answer some of the questions raised earlier, particularly by comparing the vertical columns in one table with those in the other. These each address the same group of persons, although the perspectives alternate between self- and other perceptions.

First, are the children's external perceptions more realistic than those of their parents? The data in the tables confirm that this is obviously the case. The correlations between the parents' external perceptions and the self-perceptions of the children (Table 6.9, first column for mothers, fourth column for fathers) are all lower than the correlations between the children's external perceptions and the self-perceptions of the parents (Table 6.10, first column for correlation between child and mother perspective, fourth column for correlation between child and father perspective). Thus, it seems that the children's external perception is much closer to the self-perspective of the parents, compared with the relation between the parents' external perspective and the self-perspective of their children. This supports the hypothesis that the children's intergenerational perceptions are more "realistic," in that they show a comparatively higher level of agreement with the subjective self-ratings of marital relations by the parents.

TABLE 6.10
Correlations Between Parents' Self-Perceived Partner Relations
and Children's Global Rating

Parents´ratings on marital (partner) relations scales	Global rating by children					
	Total (n = 161)	M-S (n = 79)	M-D (n = 82)	Father (n = 163)	F-S (n = 82)	F-D (n = 81)
Affection	.43***	.36***	.48***	.43***	.30**	.52***
Conflict	-.44***	-.42***	-.46***	-.35***	-.34***	-.35***
Resigned dissatisfaction	-.47***	-.32**	-.55***	-.40***	-.25*	-.25***
Repression	-.29***	-.28**	-.31**	-.29***	-.18	-.18***

Note. M-S = Rating of mother by son. M-D = Rating of mother by daughter.
F-S = Rating of father by son. F-D = Rating of father by daughter.
*p < .05. **p < .01. ***p < .001.

The external perception of daughters is—as Fig. 6.9 shows—generally much more negative than that of the sons. Here as well, we can ask which perception is closer to the self-perception of the parents. A comparison of the columns "M-S" versus "M-D" and "F-S" versus "F-D" reveals that the daughters' perceptions show closer links to the parents' self-perceptions than that of the sons, particularly on the relationship scales "Affection" and "Resigned dissatisfaction." This discrepancy between sons and daughters is particularly conspicuous in relation to maternal self-perceptions. Therefore, this can be interpreted as support for a stronger exchange of information on relationship issues among mothers and daughters, which leads to a higher level of agreement.[12]

Table 6.9 also shows that mothers seem to be better than fathers at coordinating their descriptions of the children's partnerships with the children's own self-perceptions. Comparisons of Columns 1 versus 4, 2 versus 5, and 3 versus 6 show markedly higher correlations for the mothers' ratings. Is this an indication that children are more likely to confide in their mothers when they have partnership problems? If this is the case, then mothers should have to rely far less than fathers on other possible relationship information when describing their children's partnerships. The importance of personal relationship to the child becomes particularly clear when it can be confirmed that the child's perception of the partnership is determined, to a certain extent, by the estimation of one's own relationship to this child. However, the more direct information one has about the child's partnership, the less one is forced to draw on one's own relationship to the child as a source of information. This raises the question of whether our data are able to confirm that when mothers describe the partnerships of their children, they draw less on the perception of their own relationship to the children than the fathers do.

Table 6.11 reports the relevant findings here (see p. 222). This is an attempt to predict the external perception of the children's partnerships from the parent's own current relationship to the children. In parents of sons and parents of daughters, the comparison between mothers and fathers reveals that the current relationship to the children explains less variance in the perception of the children's partnerships in the mothers than in the fathers. If a further discrimination is made according to the children's gender, it becomes clear that, when estimating the sons' partnerships, both parents exhibit a much stronger orientation toward their own relationships with sons than is the case in parents of daughters.

A more detailed examination of these findings reveals an almost complete transfer of own relationship with the child to the picture that is painted of the child's partnership. Those columns in Table 6.11 that summarize the values for fathers and mothers combined clearly reveals that each scale on the own relationship to the child functions as a powerful predictor for the corresponding scale on the perceived children's partnerships. A high level of affection in the own relationship to the child leads to the perception of much affection in the children's partnerships; a high conflict potential in the parent–child relationship leads parents to describe the children's partnerships as full of conflict as well. Thus, there is some support for the idea that parents "project" their view of their current relationship to their children when assessing the latter's partnerships.

This information on the diverse influences to which the perception of one's own partnerships and those of other family members are subjected raises a few general points to be repeated here. The empirical description of relationships cannot provide a report on an objective "relationship reality," but only different descriptions taken from various perspectives given by persons who possess a more or less comprehensive information base because of their shared history of relationships. The perception of intrafamilial relationships represents the outcome of a complex interaction process. For example, one's own marital relations influence the perception of the current relationship to the child and vice versa. These interaction processes express themselves in different ways for each gender-specific constellation of persons, and this in terms of both the strength of these relations as well as their specific content. Thus, they represent a special aspect of gender-specific socialization that, across the generations, is also reflected in current partner relations.

A BRIEF SUMMARY OF THE MOST IMPORTANT POINTS

- Parents generally describe their own marital relations as very positive. This is expressed in high values for affection and comparatively low values for conflict, resigned dissatisfaction, and repression.

TABLE 6.11
Relations Between Parents' Perceptions of Their Children's Partner Relations and Parents' Perceptions of Their Current Relation to Their Child

Own relation to child	Parents of sons					
	Father of son $(n = 64)$		Mother of son $(n = 66)$		Both $(n = 130)$	
Closeness	Conflict	-.27	Conflict	-.40	Closeness	.28
	Comm.	.36	$R^2 = .14$		Conflict	-.25
	$R^2 = .30$				$R^2 = .23$	
Control	Closeness	-.35	Control	.44	Closeness	-.26
	Control	.23	$R^2 = .18$		Control	.32
	$R^2 = .23$				$R^2 = .22$	
Conflict	Closeness	-.45	Conflict	.34	Conflict	.38
	$R^2 = .19$		$R^2 = .10$		$R^2 = .13$	
Communication	Comm.	.62	Closeness	.40	Closeness	.26
	$R^2 = .37$		$R^2 = .15$		Comm.	.32
					$R^2 = .29$	

Own relation to child	Parents of daughters					
	Father of daughter $(n = 67)$		Mother of daughter $(n = 70)$		Both $(n = 137)$	
Closeness	Closeness	.47	Conflict	-.32	Closeness	.27
	$R^2 = .21$		$R^2 = .09$		Conflict	-.22
					$R^2 = .17$	
Control	Control	.42	Control	-.35	Closeness	-.17
	$R^2 = .17$		$R^2 = .11$		Control	.33
					$R^2 = .16$	
Conflict	Closeness	-.23	Conflict	.35	Conflict	.43
	Conflict	.39	$R^2 = .11$		$R^2 = .18$	
	$R^2 = .27$					
Communication	Conflict	-.24	Conflict	-.33	Conflict	-.28
	Comm.	.43	$R^2 = .10$		Comm.	.27
	$R^2 = .31$				$R^2 = .19$	

- Although this positive global picture is retained across the two waves of measurement, it became weaker at the follow-up in 1992. The mean for affection dropped, and the mean for resigned dissatisfaction increased.
- In 1976, gender differences are revealed in a much stronger perception of repression among women. Sixteen years later, the women also perceive a higher level of resigned dissatisfaction.
- The relative stability of the parents' marital relations that can be observed across the 16-year interval is only moderate, and thus suggests changes between the two waves for the majority of the parent generation. A detailed inspection reveals that these changes generally shift toward less favorable estimations of marital relations across time, in which women, in particular, exhibit a strong sensitivity for "repression."
- The comparison between the parent and filial generations at the second wave in 1992 shows a markedly lower level of resigned dissatisfaction in the younger generation. In addition, the younger generation seems to practice a "more functional" model of relations than the parents. This is formed by the interaction of two, at first glance, rather incompatible aspects of relations—namely, affection and willingness to face conflict—and forms a basis that should enable young couples to cope constructively with potential crises in their relationships.
- The parents' marital relations prove to have a strong impact on the children's partnerships, and this holds for the quality of the parents' marriage in both 1976 and 1992. The impact on the daughters' partner relations is stronger. For example, the degree of repression that young women perceive in their partnerships is strongly determined by the resigned dissatisfaction expressed by their mothers in their own marital relations 16 years before. In general, it holds that it is mostly the negative aspects of parental marital relations that show a relation to the also unfavorably rated partnerships of the children.
- Current parent–child relations as perceived by the children show similarly strong relations to children's partnerships. Relations to the mother prove to be more significant than those to the father. It is particularly the perceived quality of parent–child communication that is associated with positive partnerships in the filial generation.
- When perceptions of the partner relations of the other generation are compared, one central finding is that the children seem to be better at seeing their parents' marriage through their parents' eyes than their parents with regard to the children's partnerships. Parents tend to idealize their children's partner relations (i.e., their reports are more positive than those of the children themselves).
- Daughters are most successful at describing their parents' marital relations in the way that the parents do, particularly when the precision of

their reports on their mothers' perspective is inspected. It is therefore, above all, the mother–daughter constellation in which the most intensive exchange of information about relationships seems to occur. This is additionally confirmed by the fact that mothers are much less influenced by their own relationship to their children than fathers are when describing the children's partnerships.

END NOTES

1. The role of various subsystems within a family system, and the increased focus on this in empirical research on families are documented in Gable, Belsky, and Crnic (1992) and Luster and Okagaki (1993).
2. Overviews of various ways of assessing marital or partner relations are given in Bradbury (1995), Grotevant and Carlson (1989), O'Leary (1987), and Touliatos, Perlmutter, and Straus (1990).
3. See Schneewind (1988a) and Schneewind, Beckmann, and Hecht-Jackl (1985).
4. However, the results of factor analysis deviate from the findings on the parents' marital relations documented so far in one aspect: For the women, items in the scale "Repression" loaded on two factors and had to be distributed across two scales. This resulted in one scale that continued to be labeled "Repression" and also assesses this aspect in the way described earlier, whereas the second scale assesses the amount of jealousy in the relationship. This takes account of both the personal contribution and the contribution of the other partner (sample item: "In our marriage, it is my spouse who is jealous"). However, to provide better comparisons between different generations and perspectives, the scale "Jealousy" is dropped in the following.
5. Glenn (1990) pointed to the need for such longitudinal approaches to research on marital quality in his overview of research on marital relations in the 1980s (see also Fincham & Bradbury, 1990).
6. Instead of focusing on the impact of an individual person or his or her characteristics on a relationship, research on relationships is increasingly shifting toward a study of the "impact of relationships on relationships" (see Dunn, 1988; Hinde & Stevenson-Hinde, 1988).
7. Basic texts on social learning theory are Bandura (1986) and Rotter (1972).
8. For an explanation of the beta coefficients, see the section on the relation between critical life events and physical health in chapter 3.
9. For a detailed explanation of how this instrument for assessing current parent–child relations was modified for this changed question, see the later section in this chapter on the assessment of partner relations in the other generation.
10. Compare the work oriented toward attachment theory in Cohn et al. (1992) and Steele and Steele (1994) for a discussion on the potential cross-generational transfer of certain qualities of parent–child relations to the children's partner relations.
11. Support for these hypothesized differences in the information exchanged between parents and their sons or daughters can be found in Grotevant and Cooper (1986) and Youniss and Smollar (1985).
12. This is in line with the findings reported in chapter 5—that, on the one hand, closeness and communication are stronger in mother–daughter relations than in all other parent–child constellations, and, on the other hand, the discrepancies between the parent and child perspectives are clearly lower for the various aspects of current parent–child relations.

7

CHANGES IN FAMILY CLIMATE

Chapter 1 mentioned that one central concern of this study is to look at "families in context" and "families as a context of individual development." As a consequence, we had to take account of various levels of access when transforming our theoretical concept into empirical research—namely, the individual level, the relations level, the family level, and the ecological level. This chapter takes a closer look at information on the family level.

THE CONCEPT OF FAMILY CLIMATE

The instrument used on the family level is called the "Family Climate Scales." This a German-language adaptation of the American "Family Environment Scale."[1] The name reveals that this scale was developed against a theoretical background that tried to shift the overemphasis of research on personalities toward a greater integration of the environment. Put in brief, the concern was to introduce an ecological perspective into psychological research—an approach to which our study is committed.

In the various areas of everyday life that interest psychologists (e.g., school, work and career, or family), this represents an attempt to pay more attention to specific environmental features when describing and explaining human perception and behavior. A theoretically rich and differentiated explanation becomes possible only when the impact of the environment and the interaction between properties of the environment and personality characteristics are included.

One first step in transforming such a theoretical goal into research practice has to be to develop methods for describing various living environments that can then be used to plot the impact of various environmental features on behavior and vice versa. These attempts to develop descriptive inventories for various living environments stem from the Family Environment Scale. Hence, the goal is to describe the living environment of the "family." However, why is the German adaptation of this instrument called Family Climate Scales rather than Family Environment Scales? This is because the German word for environment (*Umwelt*) is a broad term that can be described from a variety of perspectives. The Family Climate Scales cover only a narrowly defined area of the family environment.

Generally, a discrimination is made between the physical and social environments.[2] The physical environment includes geographical and climatic conditions, housing conditions, infrastructure, and so forth. Although these environmental conditions can, in principle, be described objectively, they may nonetheless have a considerable impact on subjective, personal well-being, and thus also on behavior. One single example is the size of accommodation: It is easy to understand that this can impact on the shaping of family life, and sufficient data are now available to confirm this.[3]

The concept of the social environment is discriminated theoretically from these aspects of the environment. As a social being, an individual is confronted with other persons in all areas of life, and these other persons' characteristics and behaviors constitute an individual's social environment. Unlike the physical environment, which can be described objectively, this concept focuses on a person's subjective perceptions. Although certain aspects of the social environment are accessible to objective description, such as the number of persons present at a family gathering, characteristics and behaviors of individuals or groups of persons are subject to the evaluation and judgment processes of the individual, and it is these processes that regulate their significance as a social environment. The concept of social climate refers precisely to this subjective perception of the totality of persons and the relationships between them that constitutes a specific area of social life. Hence, alongside family climate, one can also talk about social climate in other areas (e.g., school or teaching climate, or company or working climate).[4] The concept of "climate" provides a fitting description of which aspect of the social environment is concerned. Even everyday language has adopted an expanding "meteorological jargon" to describe social relations. For example, we say that there was an "atmosphere" at the party or that "a storm was brewing."

ASSESSMENT OF FAMILY CLIMATE

The Family Climate Scales are designed to assess precisely these "atmospheric" qualities in family relations. It has to be noted that the explicit concern is to describe the family as a whole. The focus is not on characteristics of individual persons or the description of certain relationships within the family (such as the relation between father and son), but on the relational or interactional climate of the family as a total system. We assess family climate with a questionnaire containing 42 items that refer to the respondents' complete family. This focus is emphasized with phrases such as, "In our family, . . ." or "In our home, . . ." This leads to a general emphasis on a "we" perspective.[5]

Questions for Parents and Children

In the 1992 follow-up, the Family Climate Scales were presented with different instructions for parents and children. The starting point was the data collected in 1976. At that time, father, mother, and child were asked about their current family climate. Although it would seem meaningful to ask the same question 16 years later, we only have to think about which phase of life the respondents are going through at the second wave to see that this approach cannot be adopted without modifications.

We could still present the question on family climate to the parents in 1992. However, it can certainly be assumed that the subjective perception of family togetherness has also changed for parents as a result of personal and familial developments over the past 16 years. This applies particularly to the question of who is still living with the parents or how many children have already left home. Nonetheless, it can be assumed that the parents possess an internal model of their "own family," which they had, after all, founded themselves, despite these development-related changes in the composition of households. Regardless of all changes, this "own family" remains the reference point for parents when talking about family, as we confirm in detail further later (see the section on what does "own family" mean to parents in 1992).

For the representatives of the children's generation, who are now ages 25–30, it is not possible to ask about current family climate. It can be anticipated that the reference point for the concept of "own family" has changed in at least some of these respondents. Many of the children are living with partners or are married, and some of them have started their own families. Therefore, they tend to associate the concept of "own family" or questions on current family climate with their newly founded families, rather than the family of origin.

Even if this could be circumvented through the use of precisely formulated instructions, a large part of the children's sample—whether with or without their own new families—no longer lives in the parental home at Wave 2. Although one could certainly ask this group about the current family climate in their family of origin, in line with the prior discussion on the concept of family climate, it has to be assumed that the subjective perception of family climate is based mostly on a long period of living together. Thus, if we were to ask persons who no longer live in their families of origin about the family climate, we would obtain information that is shaped strongly by memories of the times when they still lived in their families of origin. If such reports are to be analyzed meaningfully, we have to know something about whether and how reports on currently perceived family climate and reports from memory differ. This is hard to present for the perceived family climate of an adult child in our sample.

However, because the children in our sample assessed current perceived family climate at the first wave, we can compare the difference between data given from current experience in 1976 and data from memory. We did this by asking the children (and their parents) in 1992 to think back 16 years and answer the questions on family climate in a way that would reflect the relations within the family at that time. This permits a comparison of current and retrospective data on one and the same topic—namely, "current family climate in 1976."

Primary and Secondary Scales

Family climate can be broken down into 10 concepts or primary scales:

Scale A: Conflict versus harmony. This scale assesses the extent of conflict and friction within the family, contrasted with a more harmonious, peaceful, and understanding way of dealing with each other. This means that there are high scores for harmony when scores for conflict are low (Sample item: "In our family, things are harmonious and peaceful").

Scale C: Cultural orientation. The topic of this scale is the extent to which the family engages in cultural and intellectual pursuits, or how far existing cultural infrastructures are used (Sample item: "In our home, hardly anybody ever goes to see an exhibition or visit a museum").

Scale D: Flexible versus rigid rules. This concept refers to how strongly family life is determined by set rules, and how far these rules are viewed either as irrefutable family law or tend to be applied flexibly depending on the situation, so that change becomes possible (Sample item: "Punctuality is an absolute rule in our family").

Scale E: Openness. This scale assesses the extent to which family communication is characterized by open dealings among members. One important aspect of this concept is the possibility or impossibility of expressing emotions overtly—in particular, negative emotions (Sample item: "When a member of our family has got something to say, he or she comes right out with it").

Scale F: Independence. This dimension assesses the dilemmas resulting from contradictions between individual and family priorities. It particularly concerns how far individuals are allowed to pursue their own needs, goals, and desires independently from the family without having to anticipate being sanctioned (Sample item: "In our family, nobody needs to feel that they can't do what they want during their leisure time").

Scale G: Achievement motivation. This scale assesses the status of achievement orientation, pride, and striving for success within the family. It addresses one's own achievement motivation, as well as the spurring on of other members of the family to higher achievement (Sample item: "In our home, we often talk about how well we are doing at school or work").

Scale H: Order versus chaos. This concerns the degree of planning and coordination within the family. The pole "chaos" depicts a family life in which there is a lot of muddle; the pole "order" depicts careful planning, coordination, and predictability of behavior. High scores stand for chaos and low scores for order (Sample item: "In our family, everything always gets done at the last minute").

Scale I: External contacts. This scale describes how far the family has contacts with the outside world, or how far it blocks itself off and is self-sufficient. This places particular emphasis on social contacts with friends and acquaintances (Sample item: "Friends often come to visit us or join us for dinner").

Scale J: Active leisure-time planning. An active design of leisure time in the sense of spontaneity and adventurousness is contrasted with a more passive, restful use of leisure time (Sample item: "We often go to the movies, sports events, or on trips").

Scale K: Joint versus authoritarian decision making. This concerns whether all members of the family have equal rights or at least a voice in making important decisions. Authoritarian decisions lead to a strong intergenerational power gap (Sample item: "Everyone in our family has the same rights when a decision has to be made").

This structuring of family climate into 10 comparatively independent concepts was tested and confirmed for both waves as well as for each research question (current and retrospective family climate). Therefore, we can assume that family climate assessed in this way possesses structural stability. The precision of measurement of the 10 family climate scales also proved to be satisfactory, making it possible to make sound statements on the individual aspects of family climate presented later.

By analyzing the relations between the primary scales, it is possible to transpose the primary-scale structure of family climate into a less complex and clearer second-order structure consisting of three scales. Table 7.1 presents these second-order scales, as well as the primary scales underlying them.[6] We now present a short sketch of the content of these three higher

TABLE 7.1
Distribution of Primary Family Climate Scales on the Second-Order Factor

Primary Family Scales	Secondary factor I positive emotional climate	Secondary factor II stimulating climate	Secondary factor III normative-authoritarian climate
Conflict vs. harmony	$+^1$		
Cultural orientation		+	
Flexible vs. rigid rules			+
Openness	+		
Independence	+		
Achievement orientation	-		
Order vs. chaos			-
External contacts		+	
Active leisure-time planning		+	
Joint vs. authoritarian decision making	-		

Note. The plus and minus signs stand for significant loadings found in several independent studies.

dimensions of family climate on the basis of the primary scales charac-
terizing each second-order factor.

Factor I: Positive emotional climate. As the table shows, this factor is composed primarily of high scores on harmony, openness in family communication, and independence for the individual member of the family. A lower
score on familial achievement motivation and a tendency toward joint decision making also contribute to this factor. High scores on this factor characterize a family climate in which there is a dominant atmosphere of communicative openness and mutual understanding, and in which sufficient
consideration is also given to the needs of each individual. In contrast, low
scores characterize a more conflictual and less open family atmosphere that
restricts individual autonomy. This is further accentuated by a strong emphasis on achievement.

Factor II: Stimulating climate. The stimulation factor unites the three primary scales "Cultural orientation," "External contacts," and "Active leisure-time planning." High scores indicate an atmosphere dominated by outward-looking spontaneity, activity, and social openness. In contrast, low scores characterize a family life with a low range of shared activities, a lack of energy, and little pleasure in outside contacts.

Factor III: Normative, authoritarian climate. A strongly normative and authoritarian family climate is characterized by a rigid attitude toward rules and a strong tendency toward order. Correspondingly, high scores on this scale represent families that strive to orient themselves toward existing rules to maintain order in family life at whatever cost. In contrast, low scores characterize families in which less value is placed on planning, predictability, and structure in living together. In the extreme case, these are families in which nearly everything is left to chance, which often means that they are ruled by "chaos."

This second-order scale structure of family climate has been confirmed repeatedly in many studies. It has also been tested and confirmed on the basis of all our data from both waves.[7] The structure is also retained across various subsamples (parents, children, fathers, mothers, sons, daughters). Therefore, here as well, we can talk about a structural stability of family climate at different waves and in different subsamples. This confirmation of structural stability is a basic precondition for the following reports on relative and absolute stability, as well as the comparisons of perceived family climate in different groups.

CURRENT FAMILY CLIMATE FROM THE PARENTS' PERSPECTIVE

As mentioned earlier, we obtained parents' reports on current perceived family climate at both waves. Thus, the analyses of change and stability in family climate over the past 16 years are also based exclusively on this subsample.

Relative Stability of Current Family Climate

When comparing data from the two waves, we first look at relative stabilities. In the form of correlation coefficients, these provide information on how far the relative position of the individual person within the group of all respondents has remained stable. Table 7.2 reports the stability coefficients of the 10 primary scales and the 3 secondary dimensions for the total sample of parents, as well as the subsamples of fathers and mothers.[8] The mean stability

TABLE 7.2
Relative Stabilities of Family Climate Scales in Parents

Family Climate Scales	Fathers (n = 205)	Mothers (n = 209)	Both (n = 414)
Conflict vs. harmony	.34	.43	.39
Cultural orientation	.57	.64	.61
Flexible vs. rigid rules	.43	.35	.39
Openness	.26	.35	.31
Independence	.26	.38	.33
Achievement orientation	.37	.37	.37
Order vs. chaos	.44	.35	.39
External contacts	.48	.50	.49
Active leisure-time planning	.36	.34	.35
Joint vs. authoritarian decision making	.22	.13[1]	.18
Mean stability	.38	.39	.39
I Positive emotional climate	.39	.45	.42
II Stimulating climate	.55	.59	.57
III Normative-authoritarian climate	.49	.43	.45
Mean stability	.48	.50	.49

1: $p < .05$. All other correlations: $p < .01$.

(computed on the basis of the stabilities of the primary sales) for the total group is $r = .39$. Although this coefficient is statistically significant, comparisons with, for example, the stabilities of personality traits (see chap. 2) show that family climate has generally been subject to greater variation. A conspicuously large proportion of parents have shifted their relative positions within the sample. When it is considered that most families have had to cope with a wealth of different family developmental tasks in the interval between the two waves, one can hardly expect data that refer explicitly to family interaction to be as stable as, for example, personality traits.

A differentiated inspection of the individual scales also indicates a rather moderate stability of family climate, although a few marked differences can be seen. These can provide indications on which aspects of family climate are influenced particularly strongly by family development processes and which remain comparatively unaffected. The lowest value of $r = .18$ is found in the scale "Joint versus authoritarian decision making." The tense relationship between authoritarian and joint decision making in 1976 probably results, above all, from the parents' relationship with their young children. If the authoritarian decision-making style is dominant in a family in 1976, one can assume that this has more to do with the parents than the children. When the same question is posed in 1992, this premise can no longer simply be taken for granted because of the changes in the age structure and composition of the families. A strongly authoritarian decision-making style could now be expressed in, for example, a husband who dominates his partner. These qualitative differences in authoritarian decision-making behavior at the two waves could explain the low stability coefficients. If the stabilities of the other scales are analyzed against this background, three groups can be discriminated:

1. Scales that focus particularly on parent–child interactions tend to show low stabilities because of the processes of family development during the intervening years ("Joint vs. authoritarian decision making," " Independence," "Openness").

2. Scales that tend to be independent of parent–child interactions, and on which scores were already dominated by parental behavior in 1976, show the highest stabilities ("Cultural orientation," "External contacts").

3. Scales that refer to interaction processes that concern both parent–child and marital relations to approximately the same extent show intermediate stabilities ("Conflict vs. harmony," "Flexible vs. rigid rules," "Achievement motivation," "Order vs. chaos," "Active leisure-time planning").

A comparison between mothers and fathers in terms of their stabilities on the individual scales first reveals that all differences tend to be slight.

Fathers have higher scores than mothers on the second-order scale "Norm orientation." Thus, the aspects of order, planning, and structure show less change in the fathers' perception of family life compared with the mothers'. The situation is inverted in the scales that form the second-order factor "Positive emotional climate": Most of these scales show higher stabilities in the mothers. Finally, the coefficients of the scales forming the stimulation factor do not reveal any gender-specific differences.

Mean Changes in Parents' Perceptions of Current Family Climate

As already mentioned in chapter 2, statements on the relative or differential stability of a concept do not allow us to say anything about whether there have been changes in the strength of this concept over time. Such statements require comparisons of the means at the two waves. Figure 7.1 presents the profiles of the means on all 10 primary scales at the first and second waves for the parent generation.

A first glance at the mean profile at the two waves reveals slight differences on some scales. However, compared with the potential range of 1.0–2.0, we can state that perceptions of family climate remain similar. Therefore, it seems appropriate to start with a description of this obviously stable general family climate, and then to analyze the changes in means that arise and what they may mean.

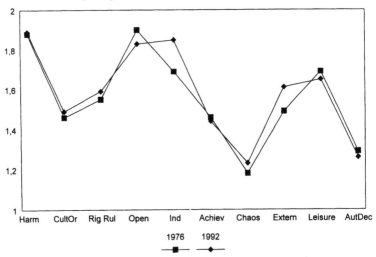

Harm = Harmony vs. conflict; CultOr = Cultural orientation; Rig Rul = Rigid vs. flexible rules; Open = Openness; Ind = Independence; Achiev = Achievement orientation; Chaos = Chaos vs. order; Extern = High vs. low external contacts; Leisure = Active vs. passive leisure-time planning; AutDec = Authoritarian vs. joint decision making.

FIG. 7.1. Current family climate: Profile of parents' means at both waves.

The description is based on the three second-order dimensions of family climate:

1. Positive Emotional Climate. A strong positive emotional climate should be characterized by a high level of harmony, accompanied by high openness and a strong degree of autonomy for the individual member of the family. The figure shows the highest values on precisely these scales compared with all others. In addition, a positive emotional climate is characterized by lower achievement motivation and less authoritarian decision making. This is also reflected in the figure. Thus, from the parents' perspective, we are dealing with families that clearly meet the criteria for a strongly positive emotional family climate.

2. Stimulating Climate. Scores are moderate for cultural orientation and external contacts, whereas for active leisure-time planning values are even higher than the scale median. Thus, our families generally exhibit an intermediate level on the stimulation dimension, suggesting a balance between activity and relaxation in family life.

3. Norm Orientation. The extent of rule orientation oscillates in the middle between rigidity and flexibility, whereas the tendency toward order is clearly dominant on the scale "Order versus chaos." Thus, it seems that a certain degree of predictability in family life is possible without impairing adaptability and flexibility.

In summary, the general picture is one of families that are predominantly emotionally positive and exhibit a high degree of balance between structure and reliability on the one hand and openness and flexibility on the other.

This general picture does not take account of differences between the two waves. These are dealt with later. Figure 7.1 shows that marked changes in means across the 16-year period have occurred on only a few scales. However, when these differences are tested for statistical significance, we find that the only nonsignificant scales are "Conflict versus harmony," "Cultural orientation," "Achievement motivation," and "Joint versus authoritarian decision making." On the remaining scales, even slight differences between means are significant in statistical terms, and thus interpretable. Here, as in other findings from our study, we are confronted with the fact that even small differences attain significance as a result of relatively large sample size—but because they are so slight, they can only be interpreted with caution. To some extent, a rather conservative approach would seem advisable in such cases, and it should be assumed that the stability hypothesis tends to be retained despite significant differences. As a result, only the three most conspicuous changes between 1976 and 1992 are discussed here.

In comparison with 1976, there is a decline in openness, an increase in independence, and an increased number of external contacts in 1992. These three relatively strong changes can all be interpreted against the background of the familial development processes to which the parents have been subject during this 16-year period. These extend from the phase of intensive parenthood to the so-called "empty nest" phase. The structure of relations and the communication processes within the family have shifted from a concentration on the children and their upbringing to a stronger emphasis on parental partnership. This provides a plausible explanation of higher values for independence in the respondents, as well as increased external contacts. As far as the reduction in openness is concerned, it has to be noted that this value is still clearly in the upper range of the scale. Although one can talk about a slight reduction in openness over the years, one cannot say that the level is generally low. In all, it seems possible that reduced claims on the parents by their children have led parents to pay more attention to their own interests. This is also in line with the predictions of family development theory.[9]

Agreement Between Fathers and Mothers

Our next research question concerns the comparison between mothers and fathers. The mean comparisons presented previously were based on the total sample of parents. However, what do things look like if fathers and mothers are inspected separately in 1976 and 1992? Are there recognizable gender differences? Can we ascertain a change in these differences across time? Figures 7.2 and 7.3 present the mean comparisons for fathers and mothers at the two waves.

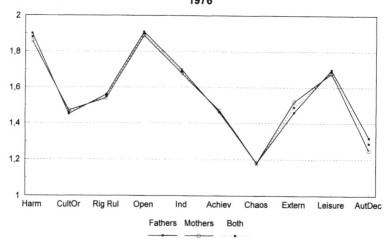

Harm = Harmony vs. conflict; CultOr = Cultural orientation; Rig Rul = Rigid vs. flexible rules; Open = Openness; Ind = Independence; Achiev = Achievement orientation; Chaos = Chaos vs. order; Extern = High vs. low external contacts; Leisure = Active vs. passive leisure-time planning; AutDec = Authoritarian vs. joint decision making.

FIG. 7.2. Current family climate: Profile of mothers' and fathers' means in 1976.

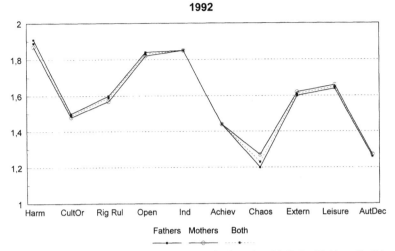

Harm = Harmony vs. conflict; CultOr = Cultural orientation; Rig Rul = Rigid vs. flexible rules; Open = Openness; Ind = Independence; Achiev = Achievement orientation; Chaos = Chaos vs. order; Extern = High vs. low external contacts; Leisure = Active vs. passive leisure-time planning; AutDec = Authoritarian vs. joint decision making.

FIG. 7.3. Current family climate: Profile of mothers' and fathers' means in 1992.

Without reporting statistical tests in more detail, these figures already reveal that no mentionable gender differences in family climate scores can be ascertained on any of the family climate scales in either 1976 or 1992. It is clearly recognizable that the deviations in the two gender-specific curves from the mean curve of the total group are minimal at both waves, and thus unequivocally fail to confirm gender-specific differences in the perception of family climate. This finding also remains stable across time, as a comparison of the two figures reveals.

However, the comparison of fathers and mothers on the level of means fails to take account of one important aspect: These are not two independent samples of mothers and fathers, but reports from fathers and mothers within the same family. How far do mothers and fathers agree in their assessments of family climate within their own families? Has the level of this agreement changed or remained stable over time? The statistical measure that provides information on this is the correlation coefficient that, in this case, represents the intrapair correlation at the two waves. These intrapair correlations are reported for both waves in Table 7.3.

It is clear that the strong similarity between men and women depicted in the group comparison has to be qualified when the analysis is shifted to the husband and wife level. The mean coefficients computed on the basis of the primary scales are $r = .42$ for Wave 1 and $r = .48$ for Wave 2. This indicates a moderate level of agreement between spouses. In other words,

238

CHAPTER 7

TABLE 7.3
Parents' Level of Agreement of Family Climate Scales Between
1976 and 1992

Family Climate Scales	Current 1976 (*n* = 199)	Current 1992 (*n* = 198)
Conflict vs. harmony	.53	.60
Cultural orientation	.62	.60
Flexible vs. rigid rules	.32	.33
Openness	.31	.40
Independence	.23	.33
Achievement orientation	.32	.21[1]
Order vs. chaos	.38	.50
External contacts	.52	.57
Active leisure-time planning	.41	.55
Joint vs. authoritarian decision making	.25	.28
Mean correlation	.42	.48
I Positive emotional climate	.41	.45
II Stimulating climate	.53	.63
III Normative-authoritarian climate	.38	.49
Mean correlation	.48	.59

1: $p < .01$. All other correlations: $p < .001$.

in a thoroughly notable proportion of the parent generation, one can assume clear differences between the paternal and maternal views of family climate. Although a predictable drawing together of paternal and maternal perceptions of family climate across time is shown by the higher mean correlations at the second wave, and this is found to the same extent on the basis of the primary and second-order dimensions, this increase does not attain statistical significance.

A closer look at the internal aspects of family climate should provide more information on this. Two aspects deserve particular mention.

1. All individual dimensions of family climate reveal a trend toward a higher intrapair correlation over the observed period of 16 years. Thus, that which has been mentioned already on the level of mean correlations is also confirmed in a more detailed inspection. However, these are moderate increases on all scales. In light of the comprehensive changes that these spouses have experienced over the last 16 years, particularly in the domain of their families, one could also have anticipated a greater convergence in the perception of family climate, particularly against the background that the intrapair correlations in 1976 are relatively low for most scales. Apparently, a shift in family life from adolescent children to postparental companionship does not necessarily lead to a mutual adjustment of perceptions of family climate. The finding that this also holds for the absolute levels of family climate is discussed once more later.

In two subscales, the general trend toward a slight increase in intrapair correlations cannot be confirmed. For the scale "Cultural orientation," the correlation sinks from $r = .62$ to $r = .60$. In view of the low difference, as well as the fact that these are the two highest values, this drop can be viewed as being random.[10] The same applies for the scale "Achievement motivation," although the low initial correlation of $r = .32$ in 1976 drops to $r = .21$ in 1992.

2. There are recognizable differences between the scales that form each of the three second-order dimensions. The clearest agreements are those of $r = .41$ to $r = .62$ for the primary scales C, I, and J, which combine to form the second-order factor "Stimulation." This addresses aspects of family life that are more accessible to objective description. The phrasing of the items is close to behavior. It is obviously easier to agree on how often one goes to the theater compared with whether one cultivates an open style of communication within the family.

The second-order factor "Norm orientation" shows the strongest increase—from $r = .38$ to $r = .49$. The role of order and planning in daily family life shows clear differences in ratings between parents, and this is stronger in 1976 than 16 years later. The fact that one subaspect of family life that can lead to controversial perspectives in this domain—namely, childrearing—now has less or even no importance may be one reason for a higher level of agreement between parents in 1992.

The second-order factor "Positive emotional climate" shows only a slight increase in intrapair correlations—from $r = .45$ to $r = .49$. These values do not justify talking about a confirmed increase in the correlation between spouses at Wave 2. In addition, correlation coefficients found on the level of the primary scales underlying this factor are also the lowest. These address areas of family life that are more subject to personal evaluation and judgment processes than those tapped in the stimulation scales. There are fewer concrete reference points on the behavioral level that could contribute to a higher level of agreement in the parental perspective. In addition, this domain addresses aspects of family life that, independent of the presence of children, also involve major aspects of relationship patterns even in a marital couple that is now living alone. These continue to offer sufficient opportunity for having different opinions on family climate.

What Does "Own Family" Mean for Parents in 1992?

When considering the instructions under which we asked parents and children to answer the Family Climate Scales, we wondered which reference point the respondents draw on for the concept of "own family." We assumed that parents would retain their internal model or idea of what is meant by the "own family," even when there have been major changes in family structure, reflected, among others, in which members of the family still live with their parents at the second wave. However, we also argued that the concept of family climate calls for a longer period of cohabitation for the persons summed together as the family. Thus, at Wave 2, there are two factors that could have an antagonistic impact on the parents' answers to the questions on current family climate in 1992: the idea of which people make up the family that has grown and consolidated across time, regardless of whom is living with whom, and a clear decimation of the circle of persons who currently share the home with the parents. The latter is confirmed by the data in Fig. 7.4, which displays which members of the family are living together with the parents surveyed at the second wave.

It can be seen that 127 pairs of parents live with no other members of the family (i.e., more than 50% of all pairs of parents). A further 64 couples live only with their own children, whereas those couples who live together with members of several other family generations (their own parents, children, grandchildren) play hardly any role. The question is now whether this changed living situation has a strong impact on the perception of family climate, or whether the internal concept of family climate continues to dominate. If the latter applies, then those parents who live as a couple in a two-person household should not differ, or differ only slightly, from those who still live together with other family members. We tested this question by forming two groups of parents: couples living alone and couples living together with one or more family member. These two groups were then compared in terms of their mean scores on the primary scales of family

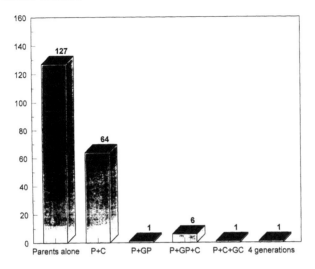

P=Parents; C=Children; GP=Grandparents; GC=Grandchildren

FIG. 7.4. Housing situation from parents' perspective at Wave 2 (absolute frequencies).

climate. The results, which are not presented in more detail here, clearly show that the living situation has no serious impact on the perception of family climate. Significant differences are found on only three scales: Parents who live alone report less conflict, less chaos, and fewer authoritarian decisions. However, despite their statistical significance, these differences tend to be minimal. It seems as if the personal idea of who belongs to one's own family has more impact on the description of family climate than the actual current living constellation.

FAMILY CLIMATE IN RETROSPECTIVE

We mentioned earlier that "retrospective family climate" was assessed in both parents and children at Wave 2. More precisely, in 1992, we asked respondents to report what they thought their family climate had been like in 1976. Therefore, we were asking them to place themselves once more in a life state that they had experienced 16 years before. This makes it possible to compare the family climate actually perceived in 1976 with the memory of this family climate 16 years later. One particular advantage of such a comparison is that it can provide information on how personal family history is perceived. Is the past idealized? Is it judged to be worse in retrospect than it actually was? Or is it possible to form a precise reconstruction of the past in memory in a kind of rational perception of history? The following analyses offer some approaches to an explanation of these questions.

The Parents' Perspective

We first look at the parents' perspective, focusing initially on the mean weights on the 10 primary dimensions of family climate. Then we turn to a closer inspection of the correlations among the various reports on family climate.

Comparison Among Means. For the parents, our data set permits the comparison mentioned earlier, as well as the possibility of referring to the data on current family climate at the second wave in 1992. However, because a simultaneous presentation of results from these three perspectives would be rather confusing, we start with the simplest question: Do the parents' mean scores on family climate differ between the current assessment of family climate in 1976 and the retrospective assessment in 1992? Figure 7.5 presents the profiles for these two descriptions.

When it is assumed that something that has to be rated retrospectively—in this case, the family climate 16 years ago—can be reproduced well, there should be few differences between means across the 10 scales of family climate, and any differences that do occur should be small. An initial glance at the corresponding profiles in Fig. 7.5 shows that this does not seem to be the case. Statistical tests of the means reveal that the only scales that do not differ significantly are Scales C ("Cultural orientation") and H ("Order vs.

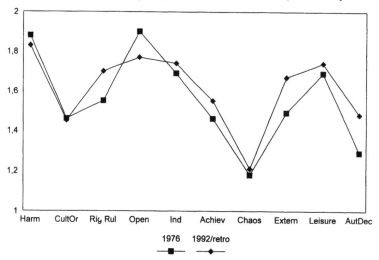

Harm = Harmony vs. conflict; CultOr = Cultural orientation; Rig Rul = Rigid vs. flexible rules; Open = Openness; Ind = Independence; Achiev = Achievement orientation; Chaos = Chaos vs. order; Extern = High vs. low external contacts; Leisure = Active vs. passive leisure-time planning; AutDec = Authoritarian vs. joint decision making.

FIG. 7.5. Profile of parents' means for current family climate assessed in 1976 and retrospective family climate assessed in 1992.

chaos"). In addition, many scales reveal much higher differences than those found previously in the comparison between current family climate in 1976 and current family climate in 1992 (see the section on the relative stability of current family climate). This is a first indication that retrospectively assessed data do not seem to provide an adequate reproduction of this topic.

What type of differences are they? Once again, the following description is based on the three second-order dimensions of family climate.

1. *Positive Emotional Climate.* In retrospective, parents report more conflict, independence, achievement motivation, and authoritarian decision making, as well as less openness. Thus, there seems to be a much weaker perception of a family climate with positive emotional overtones in retrospective than in the reports made at the time.

2. *Stimulation.* The score for cultural orientation is reproduced accurately, whereas the level of active leisure-time planning and, in particular, frequency of external contacts is clearly overestimated in retrospective. Hence, parents believe that they used to live in a more stimulating family climate than that reported in their 1976 ratings.

3. *Norm Orientation.* The low score for chaos in 1976 (which can be equated with high order) is reproduced well, whereas the preference for strict rules is overestimated strongly in retrospective. In all, greater importance is assigned to the factor "Norm orientation" in retrospective.

If this view is related to general values favoring a family climate with a strongly positive emotional atmosphere, a high level of stimulation, and an intermediate norm orientation, an interpretation of these differences leads to the impression that parents judge their family history more negatively in retrospective than they actually experienced at the time. It may be easier to understand how this negative bias has arisen when the data on actual family climate in 1992 are also included. It could be anticipated that the differences between "current 1976" and "current 1992" would be larger, particularly in light of the long interval of time between the two waves and the more or less decisive changes in all areas of life that most families have gone through over this period. In contrast, differences between "current 1976" and "retrospective 1976" could also be expected to be weaker because both reports refer to the same "reality"—namely, family climate in 1976.

As Fig. 7.6 shows, neither of these predictions can be confirmed. It is conspicuous that, in many scales, the difference between "current 1976" and "retrospective 1976" is much higher than the difference between "current 1976" and "current 1992." The following train of thought seems to provide a plausible explanation for these findings: The respondents also proceed from the assumption that past and present family climate differ considerably. When making their retrospective description, they take the perceived

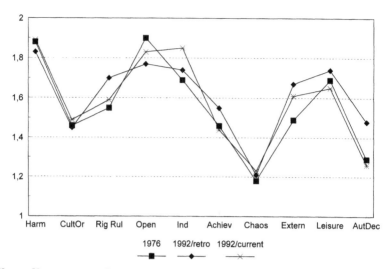

Harm = Harmony vs. conflict; CultOr = Cultural orientation; Rig Rul = Rigid vs. flexible
rules; Open = Openness; Ind = Independence; Achiev = Achievement orientation;
Chaos = Chaos vs. order; Extern = High vs. low external contacts; Leisure = Active vs.
passive leisure-time planning; AutDec = Authoritarian vs. joint decision making.

FIG. 7.6. Profile of parents' means for current family climate assessed in 1976
and 1992, as well as retrospective family climate assessed in 1992.

current situation as an anchor, and the description of the past has to differ
clearly from this anchor—to some extent, according to the motto, "things
must have been different then compared with now." Therefore, although
one believes that one comes closer to the real description of 1976 by distancing oneself from the current perception of 1992, the opposite occurs.
By drawing on the present as a reference point for describing the past, the
description of the past becomes more inaccurate because the aspect of
reality being described is more stable across time than one assumes.

However, this attempt at an explanation has to consider that the starting
point—"the present day as a reference point for describing the past"—is
entered here only as an unconfirmed presumption. Information on whether
this presumption is correct can be gained from the following correlative
analysis.

Correlations in Parental Family Climate Across Time. A comparison of
the means for various aspects of family climate only provides information
on the mean weight of the individual aspects for the sample as a whole.
However, it is just as important to ascertain the relative position of the
individual respondents within the sample on each of the three descriptive
aspects of family climate.

The importance of these different perspectives has already been revealed
in the reports on stability. The fact that the means for current family climate

do not differ between 1976 and 1992 on, for example, the scale "Conflict versus harmony" does not permit the conclusion that there have been no changes within the parent generation on this scale. For example, it is conceivable that some respondents who perceived a high level of mutual understanding in 1976 now perceive a more conflictual family climate in 1992, whereas others attain roughly the same scores at both waves. This would generally lead to highly similar means, but only a moderate correlation, and would then have to be interpreted as implying that the parent generation shows only a moderate differential stability on this scale. In line with these arguments, which were discussed previously, we now investigate the retrospective family climate and its correlations with the two questions on current family climate. Three patterns of intercorrelations result, and are described briefly, together with hypotheses on the strength of the anticipated relationship, and then tested against the data.

1. Current 1976 and Current 1992. This concerns the relative or differential stabilities across the two waves mentioned earlier. In view of the long period of time between the two waves, which represents a period of numerous decisive changes that could impact on the climate in many families according to the perspective of family development theory, we anticipate that correlations will tend to be moderate. This would also be in line with previously reported findings on the mean stability across the 10 primary dimensions ($r = .39$; see the section on the relative stability of current family climate).

2. Current 1976 and Retrospective 1992. These correlations refer to reports on family climate that should describe the same reality. The decisive difference is the 16 years between the two reports. If it is assumed that the earlier family climate can be rated correctly in retrospective, despite this time interval, these correlations should be notably higher than the stability correlations.

3. Current 1992 and Retrospective 1992. This concerns correlations between data that describe two different "realities": the current family climate in 1992 and the family climate in 1976 viewed retrospectively from 1992. Because the description focuses on different sections of reality, correlations are anticipated to be rather moderate to low. If it is also assumed that the retrospective assessment permits a close approximation to the current family climate of the time, the resulting correlations should be at least as high as the stability correlations.

Table 7.4 reports the pattern of correlations. We initially compare the first three columns. The mean correlations computed across the 10 primary scales already reveal that our hypotheses cannot be confirmed. The mean correlation between "current 1976" and "retrospective 1992" is $r = .41$, which is only slightly higher than the mean stability of $r = .39$. This suggests that

TABLE 7.4
Correlations Across Time for Family Climate Scales in Parents

Family Climate Scales	Current 1976 Current 1992 (n = 414)	Current 1976 Retro 1992 (n = 421)	Current 1992 Retro 1992 (n = 412)	Difference Column 3 - Column 2
Conflict vs. Harmony	.39	.41	.58	.19
Cultural orientation	.61	.62	.72	.10
Flexible vs. rigid rules	.39	.37	.66	.29
Openness	.31	.27	.64	.37
Independence	.33	.33	.60	.27
Achievement orientation	.37	.41	.74	.33
Order vs. Chaos	.39	.40	.74	.34
External contacts	.49	.49	.56	.07
Active leisure-time planning	.35	.40	.49	.09
Joint vs. authoritarian decision making	.18	.31	.48	.17
Mean correlation	.39	.41	.63	.22
I Positive emotional climate	.42	.40	.68	.28
II Stimulating climate	.55	.55	64	.09
III Normative-authoritarian climate	.49	.44	.75	.21
Mean correlation	.49	.47	.78	.19

All correlations: $p < .001$.

most parents are not capable of reproducing their perception of current family climate in 1976 with any great precision. Thus, the time factor impacts on the actual levels of family climate, as confirmed by the moderate stabilities, as well as the image one has of the past.

We anticipated that the correlations between "current 1992" and "retrospective 1992" would be slightly lower than the stability correlations. This was based on the assumption that there would be a close relation between "current 1976" and "retrospective 1992." However, as can be seen, this assumption is not confirmed. If we wanted to retain our assumption on "current 1976" and "retrospective 1992," despite this finding, this would mean that the retrospective description of family climate in 1976 would be related to neither earlier nor current reality. It would therefore be influenced more strongly by some other factor that has not been taken into account here. However, a glance at the table shows that this is not the case. The mean correlation for "current 1976" and "retrospective 1992" of $r = .63$ is clearly higher than the other two correlations. This finding indicates that the retrospective description of the family climate, as it was in 1976, depends strongly on the current situation in which this description is being given. The correlations for the individual primary scales also provide impressive support for this trend: They vary between $r = .48$ and $r = .74$. This provides further empirical support for our hypothesis that the description of the past takes the current situation as its anchor point.

What causes this strong orientation toward the present? The available data do not provide a satisfactory answer to this question. However, plausible hypotheses can be derived. Apart from the fact that there is a general trend across all domains of family climate to draw on the present when describing the past, it is conceivable that this is particularly the case when one is uncertain about whether "it was really like that then." The difference between the correlations of "current 1992" and "retrospective 1992" and "current 1976" and "retrospective 1992" can be viewed as an indicator for such a potential uncertainty: The higher the latter in comparison with the former, the more likely it is that reliance on the present is strengthened by perceived uncertainty.

We can gain an impression on whether this assumption is plausible by comparing the content of the scales with the highest and lowest differences and determining whether those with low differences tend to indicate a more certain judgment of the past, whereas those with high differences indicate that describing the past is more of a difficult task. A further criterion in this comparison is also how closely the phrasing of the items concerned relates to actual behavior.

The lowest differences are found in the scales in the stimulation dimension and for the scale "Authoritarian decision making." These are also aspects that can be viewed as easier to remember, and their items are phrased in concrete terms that are close to behavior. In contrast, the highest differences are exhibited by the scales "Openness," "Order versus chaos," and "Achievement motivation." It is conceivable that these concepts are harder to recall because of their high level of abstraction, or that recalling them elicits uncertainty. In addition, the meaning associated with these concepts may well have changed for the respondents over the past 16 years. In 1976, openness may have meant something completely different for an individual compared with openness in 1992, which could also lead to strong uncertainty in retrospective descriptions. Such plausible considerations suggest that uncertainty in retrospective judgment may be one reason for the strong reliance on the present. Although such considerations are no substitute for an empirical test of this hypothesis, we cannot test them with the present data.

The Children's Perspective

Results on the children are presented in somewhat less detail because we cannot compare three different descriptions of family climate in the children's sample for reasons already mentioned. Figure 7.7 presents a comparison of the means of current family climate in 1976, with the means of the data assessed retrospectively 16 years later.

Here as well, we cannot say that the retrospective data agree with the current description made in the past. Except for Scales C ("Cultural orientation"), H ("Order vs. chaos"), I ("External contacts"), and J ("Active leisure-time planning"), all differences between means are statistically significant. On some scales, the sizes of these differences are also notable. For a more detailed description of these differences, we orient ourselves once more toward the three second-order factors of family climate.

1. Positive Emotional Climate. Similar to the parents, the children also show the strongest differences between their past and present views on the scales representing this factor. More conflict, achievement motivation, and authoritarian decision making, combined with less openness and independence, clearly confirm that earlier family climate is perceived more negatively in retrospective.

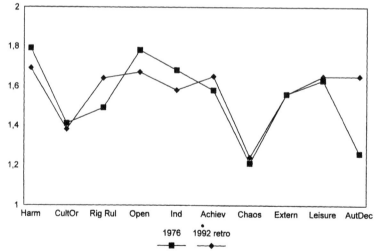

Harm = Harmony vs. conflict; CultOr = Cultural orientation; Rig Rul = Rigid vs. flexible rules; Open = Openness; Ind = Independence; Achiev = Achievement orientation; Chaos = Chaos vs. order; Extern = High vs. low external contacts; Leisure = Active vs. passive leisure-time planning; AutDec = Authoritarian vs. joint decision making.

FIG. 7.7. Profile of children's means for current family climate assessed in 1976 and retrospective family climate assessed in 1992.

2. *Stimulation.* The means for the three scales in the stimulation dimension exhibit no significant differences. Therefore, it seems as if this aspect of family climate is easy to reproduce.

3. *Norm Orientation.* A generally stronger orientation toward norms from the retrospective viewpoint can be ascertained, particularly in the overestimation of the factor "Rigid rules."

Thus, in general, children also show a negative bias in their retrospective judgments on earlier family climate. However, as in the parents, it is necessary to point out that the former family climate is generally still rated as being thoroughly flexible and generally emotionally satisfying, despite these markedly negative overtones in retrospective perception.

Regarding correlations, it is not possible to perform such a differentiated analysis for the children's sample as that carried out on the parents. Here, the only correlations available are those between current family climate in 1976 and its retrospective description carried out in 1992. To provide some sort of basis for comparing these scores, Table 7.5 also includes the corresponding data on the parent sample. First of all, we see whether the hypothesis formulated (but not confirmed) for the parents—that there would be a stronger relation between perceived family climate in 1976 and its retrospective description in 1992—also holds for the children. The children's data contradict this hypothesis even more clearly. The mean correlation of $r = .31$ suggests that the children are also not capable of reconstructing the earlier family climate 16 years later with sufficient precision. As could be anticipated, the highest correlations are found, as in the parents, on the stimulation dimension. However, here as well, values of $r = .51$, $r = .34$, and $r = .38$ reveal that the retrospective view presents a distorted image of the past.

When interpreting these findings, it is necessary to take account of the particular features of the children's sample. These are persons ages 25–30 who have to recall a period during which they were ages 9–14. One can assume that developmental processes interfere with memory to an even stronger extent in this group than in the parents. The correlations are correspondingly weaker.

With the available data, we cannot test whether the children's retrospective view is eclipsed by the current situation to the same extent as in the parents. However, if we had been able to test this, we might well have found an even stronger misjudgment of the former situation. Many of the children now have steady partners, and some have started their own families. The own family, which now forms an alternative model to the family of origin, would then form the anchor point for the description of the past. Under such conditions, a sufficiently precise reproduction of the former family climate becomes even less probable.

TABLE 7.5
Correlations Between Current and Retrospective
Family Climate Scales: Comparison Between
Children and Parents

Family Climate Scales	Parents current 1976 retro 1992 (*n* = 421)	Children current 1976 retro 1992 (*n* = 191)
Conflict vs. harmony	.41***	.36***
Cultural orientation	.62***	.51***
Flexible vs. rigid rules	.37***	.39***
Openness	.27***	.31***
Independence	.33***	.11
Achievement orientation	.41***	.24***
Order vs. chaos	.40***	.24***
External contacts	.49***	.34***
Active leisure-time planning	.40***	.38***
Joint vs. authoritarian decision making	.31***	.20**
Mean stability	.41***	.31***
I Positive emotional climate	.40***	.33***
II Stimulating climate	.55***	.46***
III Normative-authoritarian climate	.44***	.41***
Mean stability	.47***	.40***

** $p < .01.$ *** $p < .001.$

Parents and Children Compared

After presenting relatively independent descriptions of perceived family climate from the perspectives of the parent and children's generations, we turn to a comparison between the two. First, we analyze the means for the individual family climate scales. We concentrate on comparing parents and children in terms of current family climate in 1976 and the retrospective ratings given in 1992. A further step takes account of the fact that we possess reports on family climate from the perspectives of the mother, father, and one child in each family. This enables us to ascertain which intrafamilial relations are present, or whether and how these have changed over time.

Mean Comparisons Between Parents and Children. We start by comparing parents and children at Wave 1. The question here is whether parents and children, who were then ages 9–14, differ in their estimation of family climate. In view of the phase of the family life cycle that the respondents were going through at the time, differences between the generations can be anticipated on at least some of the Family Climate Scales. Figure 7.8 depicts the mean profiles of parents and children at Wave 1. Generally speaking, the profiles are similar for both generations. They are also similar to the other mean profiles reported so far, independent of research question and sample. To some extent, we can even summarize these results in advance, and state that the family climate generally proves to be remarkably stable in terms of means and individual aspects, regardless of the group of persons involved, the time point, and the research question examined. The similarity between the various profiles is much more conspicuous than those differences found on closer inspection. This is also the case for the generation differences at Wave 1, depicted in Fig. 7.8. Statistical tests on the difference between means produce the following findings in terms of the three second-order dimensions.

1. Positive Emotional Climate. On this dimension, the parents report more harmony and openness and less achievement motivation compared with their children. However, it should be noted that the children's means on the

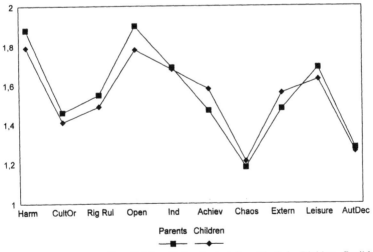

Harm = Harmony vs. conflict; CultOr = Cultural orientation; Rig Rul = Rigid vs. flexible rules; Open = Openness; Ind = Independence; Achiev = Achievement orientation; Chaos = Chaos vs. order; Extern = High vs. low external contacts; Leisure = Active vs. passive leisure-time planning; AutDec = Authoritarian vs. joint decision making.

FIG. 7.8. Profile of parents' and children's means for current family climate assessed in 1976.

scales "Harmony" and "Openness" also lie within a range that indicates a positive perception of earlier family life. The scale "Authoritarian decision making" should also be emphasized. It was specifically designed to tap family interactions referring to the exercise of authority in childrearing behavior. Contrary to our expectations, no intergenerational differences can be found.

2. *Stimulation.* Parents report a significantly higher level of active leisure-time planning and less external contacts than children, which can be interpreted as a more family-centered perspective among parents. However, in general, it seems that both parents and children experienced a moderate level of stimulation.

3. *Norm Orientation.* There are no generation differences on either of the norm orientation scales. A high level of order, which is reflected in low scores for chaos, coupled with a balance between rigid rules and flexibility, contribute to a family climate representing a generally high level of norm orientation.

At the first wave, this results in a mean profile in which the description presented earlier provides a good illustration of the situation of the families surveyed in 1976. These were families that mostly had one or even more children of various ages at the time, and that had adjusted their family interaction to the given situation in line with this family constellation. Despite being statistically significant, the generation differences that occur tend to be slight, particularly when they are "translated" into percentages of explained variance. It becomes clear that only a small proportion of the variation in perceived family climate can be explained by generation membership. We return to this finding later.

This background raises the question of whether the generally high level of agreement between the perspective of the parent and children's generations is maintained when they have to describe the same content retrospectively 16 years later. We have already shown that the former family climate cannot be reproduced exactly in retrospective. If both parents and children are considered to be subject to the same processes that are responsible for this, we are still left with the question of whether the perspectives of parents and children have drifted further apart or closer together over time.

There are plausible justifications for either assumption. For example, on the one hand, increasing differences between parents and children could open up a generation gap that can only develop when the children are able to discuss their joint past with their parents from an egalitarian position. On the other hand, a drawing together of the two perspectives could be the outcome of a retrospective description in both partners based on greater distance and less personal involvement. The fact that both groups describe their family past from the distance of 16 years could make these descriptions more objective than they were at a time when they were both "caught in the middle of things." Such a mutual increase in objectivity should result in a closer agreement on the family climate that was actually present at the time, as well as a mutual drawing together of the perspectives of both generations.

Figure 7.9 puts an end to these speculations, and depicts the mean profile of the retrospective depictions of family climate from the perspective of the parent and children's generations in 1992. Both profiles are already familiar from the separate descriptions of retrospective data from parents and children (see Figs. 7.5 and 7.7). Therefore, we do not say anything more about the quality and levels of the retrospective view. We are far more concerned with comparing parents and children. The figure supports the hypothesis that generation differences have become stronger in comparison with Wave 1. Thus, a drawing together of the generations has not occurred, but more of an accentuation of generation-specific viewpoints. There are not only more significant differences between means across the various scales, but also larger differences between means, indicating that larger proportions of the variance in retrospective family climate data can be explained by generation membership in 1992. Table 7.6 illustrates this trend in more detail.

The table reports the significant generation effects for both 1976 and 1992, as well as the proportions of the total variation in the various Family Climate Scales explained by generation membership. The arrows in the table refer to the perspectives of the parents. For example, the upward pointing arrow for

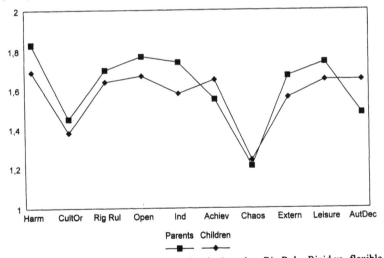

Harm = Harmony vs. conflict; CultOr = Cultural orientation; Rig Rul = Rigid vs. flexible rules; Open = Openness; Ind = Independence; Achiev = Achievement orientation; Chaos = Chaos vs. order; Extern = High vs. low external contacts; Leisure = Active vs. passive leisure-time planning; AutDec = Authoritarian vs. joint decision making.

FIG. 7.9. Profile of parents' and children's means for retrospective family climate assessed in 1992.

TABLE 7.6
Generation Effects in Family Climate Scales at Both Waves

Family Climate Scales	1976		1992	
	Significant generation effect	Variance explained (%)	Significant generation effect	Variance explained (%)
Conflict vs. harmony	↑[1]	2,25	↑	4,84
Cultural orientation		0,49	↑	1,44
Flexible vs. rigid rules		0,49		0,36
Openness	↑	6,25	↑	2,25
Independence		0,01	↑	5,29
Achievement orientation	↑	2,56	↑	3,24
Order vs. chaos		0,25		0,09
External contacts	↓	0,81	↑	2,25
Active leisure-time planning	↑	1,21	↑	1,44
Joint vs. authoritarian decision making		0,81	↓	7,84
I Positive emotional climate	↑	2,89	↑	8,41
II Stimulating climate		0,09	↑	2,89
III Normative-authoritarian climate		0,64		0,25

Note. Direction of arrow = perspective of parental generation.

the scale "Conflict versus harmony" means that the parents report significantly higher harmony values than their children in 1976, and the same in 1992 in the retrospective ratings. However, just determining statistical significance tells us little about the extent of the differences. For example, if the values for explained variance for 1976 and 1992 are compared for the harmony scale, it can be seen that only 2.25% of variance can be explained by generation membership in 1976, whereas 4.84% is explained in 1992. In other words, the impact of generation membership is almost twice as strong in retrospectively assessed family climate than it was for the current perspective in 1976. In summary, we can read off the following trends in the results:

1. There are more significant generation effects in 1992 compared with 1976. These involve the scales "Cultural orientation," "Independence," and "Authoritarian decision making," as well as the second-order "Stimulation" dimension. In all cases, it is the parent generation that makes the more "favorable" estimation.

2. The aspects of family climate that already showed significant generation differences in 1976 remain significant. However, the proportion of variance explained by these stable effects increases markedly across all scales (with the exception of "Openness"). It is particularly this finding that illustrates how much more the parent and children's generations differ in their retrospective judgments than they do in the comparison of actual family climate in 1976. For example, 8.41% of the total variance on the second-order factor "Positive emotional climate" is explained by generation membership alone in 1992. In view of the many possible variables to which such retrospective judgments can be exposed, this finding should not be underestimated.

3. Another finding should be mentioned that is not to be found in either the figure or the table. At both waves, we also tested whether men and women differed in their judgments. For 1976, there are fewer external contacts and more authoritarian decision making from the women's perspective. In 1992, they perceive more harmony and independence. However, none of these effects explains more than 2% of variance. Thus, compared with the clear generation effects, gender effects are negligible.

After ascertaining that the generation differences are larger in 1992 than in 1976, we now have to describe the content of these effects. We start with the mean profile of the parents' retrospective data. This was described earlier (see the section on the comparison between means from the parents' perspective) as showing that the positive emotional climate is underestimated, whereas stimulation and norm orientation are overestimated. We now compare the children's means with those of their parents:

1. Positive Emotional Climate. The children give a clearly less favorable retrospective estimation of this aspect than the parents do. Lower values for harmony, openness, and independence, coupled with higher values for achievement motivation and authoritarian decision making, speak out clearly. The view that a young adult has on his or her family past seems to be subject to a negative shift, and this is stronger than the shift in parents when they look back on a phase of life in which they were already adults.

2. Stimulation. The stimulation scales show the same result (i.e., a stronger shift toward less stimulation compared with the parents). However, it should not be forgotten here that the children's sample did well at reproducing the means of 1976 on this scale.

3. Norm Orientation. No significant generation differences are found for this factor in either the primary scales or the second-order level.

In summary, the first second-order factor, "Positive emotional climate," reveals a clear polarization between the parent and children's samples in the retrospective description of former family climate collected in 1992.

Intrafamilial Correlations in 1976 and 1992. One aspect of our study has not been mentioned so far in the reports on family climate—that we have data from the father, mother, and one child within the same family. The comparisons so far have paid no attention to the intrafamilial relations between parents and children. We turn to this now. The correlations between father and mother, father and child, and mother and child are used to ascertain the dominant level of agreement in perceptions within dyads of family members at specified points in time for the three second-factor Family Climate Scales. Figure 7.10 depicts the pattern of intrafamilial correlations in the three second-order factors for the current family climate in 1976, and for the retrospective description of family climate carried out in 1992.[11]

A first trend that can be ascertained across all three scales, as well as across both waves, is that the correlations between father and mother are

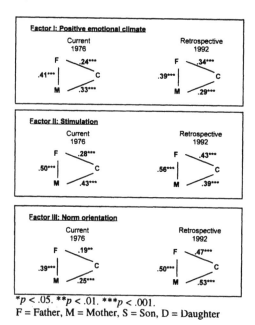

*p < .05. **p < .01. ***p < .001.
F = Father, M = Mother, S = Son, D = Daughter

FIG. 7.10. Intrafamily correlations of second-order factors for current family climate assessed in 1976 and retrospective family climate assessed in 1992 (*n* = 164).

nearly always much higher than the correlations between father and child or mother and child. The origins or the size of these correlations, which, in the given context, can be interpreted as a measure of the agreement between the perspectives on the corresponding aspect of family climate, is explained, to a large extent, through the intensity of their reciprocal exchange of opinions. In 1976, this should have been greater between parents than between parent and child. For the parents, their 9- to 14-year-old children were certainly less likely to be partners with whom they exchanged opinions on family concerns than their spouses.

If this is true, we can anticipate similarly high values for the correlations between parents at the second wave, whereas the correlations between parents and children should be higher than at the first wave. This assumption is based on the expectation that the type of relations between parents and children has changed by 1992, in that parents now view their adult children as competent interaction partners. The results presented in the figure support this hypothesis. In addition, the correlations between parents have also increased in size. It would seem that an increasingly mutual picture of the own family past has developed through the many years of living together.

If the agreement between mother and child and father and child is compared across the two waves, the results indicate that the agreement between mother and child is somewhat higher at Wave 1 than that between father and child—a difference that can no longer be found at Wave 2. This may indicate that children had more contact with their mothers than their fathers at Wave 1, which would increase the probability of agreement on estimations of family climate. These specific inner-family contact frequencies can no longer be anticipated at the second wave. In line with this, mother–child and father–child correlations are almost equally high.

The next question addresses potential differences between the three second-order scales and the inner-family agreement in rating them. Results on this can be summarized as follows.

1. Positive Emotional Climate. It is conspicuous that the moderate level of agreement on this domain at the first wave does not increase over the years. Particularly between parents and children, differences are maintained up until the children are young adults, and cannot be reduced at this time by, for example, a process of shared construction of the past. Correlations are generally lower for this factor than for the two others. This indicates that the socioemotional climate is subject to personal evaluation and judgment processes, and these seem to be difficult to influence even for the closest members of the family.

2. Stimulation. This factor shows higher interpersonal agreements for all constellations of persons in comparison with the first factor. In general, a slight drawing together of perspectives can be ascertained across time.

3. Norm Orientation. A different pattern is clear in this domain of family climate. At the first wave, the parent–child correlations have by far the lowest values. This is understandable because this factor taps areas of family life in which the family is guided into ordered and regulated paths through the authority of the parents. In this situation, the children have to tolerate their parents' measures more or less passively. The low correlations result particularly from the fact that the parents tend to report moderate scores from their perspective, whereas the children give mostly higher scores.

The result of the comparison between the two waves is astonishing. The parent–child correlations are the lowest in Wave 1, whereas in Wave 2 parent–child agreements are now higher than those on the two other scales. The following idea offers one possible explanation for this remarkable increase in agreement between parents and children. At the time, the children were too young to be actively involved in forming their own and their family's norm orientation. However, this has changed during the intervening period. Earlier, the parents' norms had to be tolerated more or less passively. However, during the course of personality development, the children have developed their own points of view on this issue. This, in turn, is embedded, to a large extent, in discussions with their own parents, and finally leads to higher parent–child agreement in the retrospective assessment of earlier family climate under the conditions at Wave 2. However, this in no way means a complete adaptation of childhood beliefs to those of the parents because the actual correlations of $r = .47$ for the father–child constellation and $r = .53$ for the mother–child constellation indicate that a notable measure of disagreement continues.

The results so far refer to the entire group of families. No separation has been made between families with a daughter and families with a son. This may cover up potential gender-specific features. Therefore, we performed a separate analysis of these two types of family and compared the outcomes. These results are displayed in Fig. 7.11.

A widespread assumption based primarily on psychoanalytical thought is that children tend to orient themselves toward their same-gender parent when perceiving their environment.[12] Our first test of this assumption is restricted to data from 1976. It is clear that this hypothesis cannot be confirmed. In other words, there is no indication that sons agree more with their fathers than with their mothers, whereas the opposite holds for daughters. With one exception, the mother–child correlation, independent of the child's gender, is always higher than the father–child correlation at the first wave. It would seem that the higher frequency of contact between mother and child also plays an important role here. However, the differences between mother–child and father–child correlations tend to be moderate, so that one has to recognize a degree of paternal influence at Wave 1.

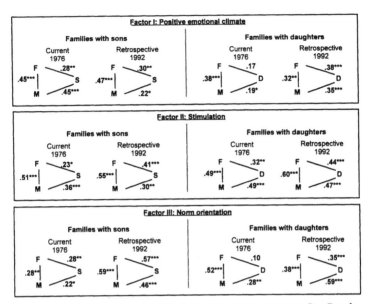

*p < .05. **p < .01. ***p < .001.   F = Father, M = Mother, S = Son, D = Daughter

FIG. 7.11. Intrafamily correlations of second-order factors for current family climate assessed in 1976 and retrospective family climate assessed in 1992—split for families with sons (n = 82) and families with daughters (n = 82).

Against this background, the next question is this: What do these correlations look like 16 years later? Is it possible to ascertain an increasing similarity between children and their same-gender parents? Or is the opposite true—that there is a stronger dependence on the parent of the opposite gender? The results indicate a differentiated picture. Among sons, it becomes clear that agreement with the father has grown remarkably during this time, compared with agreement with the mother. It seems that the fathers also become increasingly important for their sons as they grow older. Whereas the mother was still dominant between the ages of 9 and 14, the relationship has now inverted.

In contrast, changes among daughters reveal a different picture. Whereas a higher level of agreement with the father can still be clearly recognized among sons, relations are more balanced among daughters. Correlations between mother and daughter and father and daughter are about equal in size. The previously close relationship to the mother has now developed into a balanced relationship to both parents.

One exception, which is also documented in the figure, should not be ignored. This concerns the factor "Norm orientation." Here, the agreement between daughter and mother is clearly dominant at r = .59. A glance at the sons reveals an agreement with the father of r = .57 on this factor. These two correlations are by far the highest values at the second wave, whereas the corresponding correlations with the opposite-gender parent are much lower. It would seem as if, specifically in the domain of norm orientation, a gender-specific formation of perception can be traced in the children's generation.

Further support for this assumption can be found when the analysis shifts from the rather abstract second-order dimensions to the more detailed level of the primary dimensions. Once again, Fig. 7.12 depicts, split according to gender, the correlation pattern for the scale "Chaos versus order" that forms a component of the "Norm orientation" factor.

The trend toward a same-gender orientation among children, as far as the orientation toward family norms is concerned, becomes even more apparent on this less abstract level of analysis. The orientation of girls toward their mothers and of boys toward their fathers, which is revealed in the retrospective rating on family climate at the second wave only on the level of second-order factors, can also be ascertained here at Wave 1. This suggests that if observation is differentiated sufficiently, such gender-specific orientations are not just to be found when children become adults, but are already present at an earlier age.

We discuss one more interesting finding on internal family relations. This no longer focuses on differences between girls and boys, but once more on clear differences in results between two waves. Figure 7.13 displays the results for the scale "Openness." A quick glance at the figure reveals what the concern is here. At the first wave, there are no mentionable correlations with father or mother for either boys or girls. Correlations between $r = .06$ and $r = .07$ suggest that there is not the slightest relationship between parental and filial perceptions of internal family openness in 1976—not even a negative relationship, although one could anticipate that a lack of agreement on high or low openness would lead parents and children to perceive this aspect contradictorily. This could express itself in parents reporting a

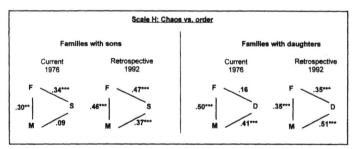

$*p < .05.$ $**p < .01.$ $***p < .001.$ F = Father, M = Mother, S = Son, D = Daughter

FIG. 7.12. Intrafamily correlations on the primary scale "Chaos vs. order"—split for families with sons ($n = 82$) and families with daughters ($n = 82$).

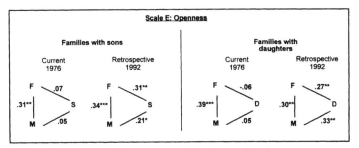

*p < .05. **p < .01. ***p < .001.   F = Father, M = Mother, S = Son, D = Daughter

FIG. 7.13. Intrafamily correlations on the primary scale "Openness"—split for families with sons (n = 82) and families with daughters (n = 82).

high level of openness in family relations, and children perceiving a low level. The consequence would then be high negative correlations. However, as mentioned earlier, this is not the case.

There is a remarkable development over the next 16 years: There are suddenly substantial parent–child correlations on all constellations. Although values between r = .21 and r = .33 are still not particularly high, they nonetheless indicate a degree of retrospective parent–child agreement. We seem to be confronted here with a phenomenon that is found frequently in studies applying the same measurement instrument with an interval of many years. The children's understanding of the concept of "openness" has changed over the course of the years.[13] They seem to associate it with other realities in 1976 compared with 1992. No doubt, also due to discussions with parents, there has been a change in the breadth of meaning of the concept, as well as a shift toward the parents' perspective in the retrospective estimation of the quantitative strength of this concept.

Findings on the domain of internal family correlations can be summarized by stating that, on a more abstract level, correlations between parents rise, and that parent–child correlations show some gender-specific patterns. In addition, it proves to be thoroughly worthwhile to also analyze individual content areas more precisely on the level of the primary scales.

Retrospective Error in Rating Earlier Family Climate

The previous sections have shown that the retrospective description of family climate reveals clear differences compared with the way family climate was actually perceived at the time. These differences were ascertained on the level of comparisons between means. For example, the statement that parents and children retrospectively report less openness in their family relations than they actually perceived in 1976 is based on the group as a whole. However, this does not rule out the possibility that there are differences within the group regarding how well their retrospective perspective reproduces the earlier perspective. Some individuals may show a high level of agreement between their past and retrospective views. However, others may overestimate the degree of openness in the past, or even underestimate it—a possibility that also applies to all other areas of family climate. The following inspects the phenomenon of under- or overestimating earlier family climate in more detail to see whether such phenomena can be related to current relations between parents and their children.

Under- and Overestimation of Family Climate: A Comparison Between Parents and Their Children. The first step is to form values that provide information on whether, and to what extent, a respondent under- or over-estimates earlier family climate. For each respondent, we subtracted the past estimation from the retrospective estimation. This computation was carried out for all primary and second-order scales, and produced differential values ranging between −1.0 and +1.0. All persons with a negative score underestimate earlier family climate on the scale concerned because the earlier value is higher than the retrospective value, leading to a negative differential score. Vice versa, positive values represent an overestimation from the retrospective position.

We are initially interested in how overestimation, underestimation, and—as a third possibility—exact reproduction are distributed across the different aspects of family climate in terms of the second-order dimensions. This raises one difficulty that has to be dealt with in advance. It is still necessary to define which differential scores should be labeled *overestimation, underestimation*, or a *direct hit*. The latter category seems to be particularly problematic. On the basis of differential scores, a hit can be assigned only to those persons who score exactly zero. However, such an absolutely exact reproduction of the earlier value is highly improbable. Therefore, we defined *hits* as those differential scores that lie between −0.25 and +0.25 (i.e., values that do not go beyond a set deviation from the earlier score on current family climate). As a result, persons with values below −0.25 are "underestimators" and those with values above +0.25 are "overestimators." Figure 7.14 displays the distributions of these differences split for the three second-order dimensions and for parents and children.

It is clear that the hit category has the strongest representation across all three scales. A comparison of the two extreme groups of "underestimators" and "overestimators" reveals the following picture: The factor "Positive emotional climate" tends to be underestimated, whereas "Stimulation" and "Norm orientation" tend to be overestimated. One possible explanation for this is that memory reconstructs a family climate that is believed to provide the best fit with families that are in the middle of their life cycle. Thus, families with several children of varying ages are assigned a family

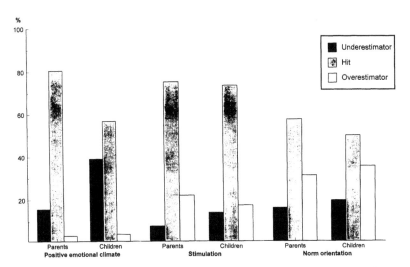

FIG. 7.14. Retrospective error in assessing family climate in parents and children.

climate that tends to be stimulating, that places value on fixed rules and orderly patterns, and in which, as a result, the positive aspects of the social climate may tend to suffer.

A comparison of the patterns of error in parents and children on the three second-order dimensions produces the following findings.

1. Positive Emotional Climate. This is where we find the strongest generation differences. Whereas both groups contain few overestimators (4%), there are clear differences in the distribution of hits and underestimators. Compared with the parents, there are far more underestimators among the children (39% vs. 16%) at the expense of hits (57% vs. 81%). Hence, compared with their parents, children exhibit a strong tendency to overestimate the emotional climate that can also be confirmed statistically.

2. Stimulation. Whereas both generations show the same frequency of hits, the parents show a minimally higher tendency to overestimate, and the children exhibit a slight trend toward underestimation. However, this is not statistically significant.

3. Norm Orientation. There are far fewer hits here compared with the other two second-order scales. Differences between parents and children are slight and not statistically significant.

In summary, in those aspects of family climate that tap major components of social relations, such as harmony, openness, and independence, differences in the frequency of underestimation and hits can be found between the parent and children's generations. Retrospectively, the children's generation reveals a clearly less favorable outlook on this important aspect of relations.

We now examine whether membership of the group of under- or overestimators relates to the current quality of parent–child relations, particularly in terms of the factor "Positive emotional climate." We are also interested in whether such relations reveal differences between parents and their children.

Under- and Overestimation of Family Climate and Current Parent–Child Relations. Chapter 4 gave a detailed description of the instrument used in Wave 2 to assess the current quality of relations between parents and children in 1992. To recap, we again list the corresponding four relation dimensions, with the first pole in each case representing a high scale score: (a) "Emotional proximity versus distance," (b) "High versus low communication," (c) "Control versus acknowledged autonomy," and (d) "High versus low conflict."

Scale (d) provides a quantitative measure of the conflict in the relationship, whereas Scale (b) taps quantitative aspects of communication, as well as qualitative features such as openness, amount of stimulation, and so forth. Both the questionnaire format and the instructions made it possible for both parents to describe their relationship to the child, and for children to give information on their relationships with their fathers and mothers. This gives two scores on each scale for the children: one for the relationship with the father and a second one for the relationship with the mother.

We now test whether persons who differ in the retrospective estimation of family climate in terms of over- or underestimation also reveal differences in their weightings on the relations scales. If such differences actually can be found, one possible interpretation would be that the quality of current parent–child relations may have an impact on the way in which earlier family climate is rated incorrectly in retrospective. The acceptability of these types of interpretation will depend, among others, on which scales reveal which differences.

This question is tested separately for child–father relations, child–mother relations, and the particular parent–child relationship. In addition, gender was controlled as a further possible variable. Table 7.7 reports the results of these computations for the retrospective assessment of positive emotional climate.

This only reports results for the children. The upper half of the table presents results on the children's relations with their fathers, the lower half with their mothers. A glance at the column labeled *Error effects* reveals clear relations to all four scales. The effects for the factor "Error" are entered from the perspective of underestimators here. Put more precisely, an upward

TABLE 7.7
Children: Relations Between Retrospective Under- or Overestimation
of Positive Emotional Family Climate and Current Relation to Parents

Child's relation with father ($n = 196$)	Gender effects[1]	Error effects[2]	Variance explained by gender (%)	Variance explained by error (%)
Closeness vs. distance	/	↓	1,69	12,96
Communication	/	↓	0,04	16,00
Control vs. autonomy	/	↑	0,01	9,00
Conflict	/	↑	0,01	10,24
Child's relation with mother ($n = 198$)	Gender effects	Error effects	Variance explained by gender (%)	Variance explained by error (%)
Closeness vs. distance	↑	↓	4,41	17,64
Communication	↑	↓	8,41	17,64
Control vs. autonomy	/	↑	1,21	9,61
Conflict	/	↑	0,09	10,24

Note. 1: direction of arrow = female perspective. 2: direction of arrow = perspective of persons who underestimate positive emotional climate.

pointing arrow in the scale "Conflict" should be interpreted as indicating that a person who underestimates positive emotional climate exhibits higher scores on current conflict with father and mother. In contrast, young adults who overestimate the positive emotional climate report less conflict in their current relationships with either their fathers or mothers. Gender effects are entered in the table from the female perspective. An upward pointing arrow indicates higher scores for women on the corresponding scale.

Both the current relationship with the father and the current relationship with the mother show significantly different ratings on all four scales as a function of the type of retrospective estimation of positive emotional family climate. The effects for both types of relation take the same direction: Children who underestimate the positive emotional family climate perceive current relations with father and mother as (a) more distanced, (b) shaped more by control than by acknowledged autonomy, (c) more conflictual, and (d) less communicative.

This pattern of findings supports the previously mentioned causal inter-pretation that the children's current relations with their parents are a pos-sible cause of their error in estimating earlier family climate. On the basis of this interpretation, more negative relations with the father or mother today lead to a negative bias in retrospective ratings of positive emotional family climate. It has to be recalled here that this aspect of family climate covers areas of similar content on the family level that were collected for current relations on a dyadic level using the four relations scales.

Particular mention should also be made of the proportions of common variance in current relations and incorrect ratings of family climate reported in the last column of the table. The scales "Closeness versus distance" and "Communication" prove to be particularly significant for relations with fa-thers, as well as for relations with mothers. This provides adequate confir-mation that the way in which the children's generation perceives relations with fathers and mothers at Wave 2 is strongly associated with the error in their retrospective rating of positive emotional family climate.

The next question is whether this is also the case for parents. Is the perception of the relationship with their child associated with errors in estimating positive emotional family climate? The corresponding results for the parent sample are reported in Table 7.8. Compared with the results reported in Table 7.7, the relationship is evidently less clear-cut in the parents. Only one significant effect is found for the scale "Control versus acknowledged autonomy." Parents who underestimate positive emotional family climate in retrospective perceive their current relations with their children far more in terms of mutual control. However, the proportion of common variance is only 2.25%. Compared with the proportions of variance explained in the children, this effect has to be viewed as being rather small.

TABLE 7.8
Parents: Relations Between Retrospective Under- or Overestimation
of Positive Emotional Family Climate and Current Relation to Child

Parents´relation with child (n = 408)	Gender effects[1]	Error effects[2]	Variance explained by gender (%)	Variance explained by error (%)
Closeness vs. Distance	↑	/	1,21	0,49
Communication	↑	/	1,69	1,21
Control vs. Autonomy	/	↑	0,09	2,25
Conflict	/	/	0,25	0,64

Note. 1: direction of arrow = female perspective. 2: direction of arrow = perspective of persons who underestimate positive emotional climate.

Thus, among parents, in contrast to their children, perceptions of current relations with their child seem to play hardly any role in the retrospective assessment of positive emotional family climate.

How can this be explained? If it is assumed that current relations with the members of the older or younger generation in the family are used as a reference for the retrospective description of one's own family, the children in our survey will refer to their two parents. However, parents may not only refer to the child who is participating in the survey, but also to all the other children in the family. Thus, it may have been possible to detect associations for the parent group similar to those found for the children's group if we had possessed information on the state of current relations with all their children, instead of being limited to information on just one child.

The associations described so far address only one second-order factor of retrospectively assessed family climate. The computations described earlier were also carried out for the two remaining second-order factors "Stimulation" and "Norm orientation." The mere fact that we do not need to provide a table here indicates that the results of these analyses did not produce any substantial relations. No associations to current parent–child relations could be found for either the retrospective error in rating stimulation or the corresponding value for norm orientation. This applies equally to parents' and children's perspectives. However, this simultaneously confirms the conjecture formulated earlier—that the greatest number of similarities in content exist particularly between the socioemotional climate of family relations and the dyadic relationship aspects of parent–child interaction.

A BRIEF SUMMARY OF THE MOST IMPORTANT POINTS

• The current family climate reports of parents reveal a picture of families with a highly positive emotional climate and a moderate level of stimulation at both waves. In addition, there is a balance between flexibility and adherence to rules in the degree of familial norm orientation.

• Hardly any changes can be ascertained in the mean perception of family climate across the 16-year interval. A minimal increase in independence and external contacts, as well as an equally small decrease in openness, are hardly worth mentioning in comparison with otherwise stable means.

• However, when the relative temporal stability of the various aspects of family climate is examined for each individual person, results clearly indicate that many respondents have changed their perception of family climate over the course of 16 years. There are conspicuous gender differences in that the perception of a positive emotional family climate has remained more stable across time among mothers than fathers, whereas fathers exhibit less change than mothers in the extent of norm orientation.

• The levels of agreement on current family climate between spouses document major differences between paternal and maternal perceptions. This can be ascertained already at the first wave in 1976, and has also changed only slightly over the next 16 years. Neither the long interval of 16 years nor the fact that most spouses have reached the developmental phase of postparental companionship during this interval lead to a marked drawing together of these two points of view.

• Examinations of the retrospective description of the family climate in 1976 by the parents particularly investigated whether such a description could reproduce the earlier rating of family climate, or whether the retrospective judgment would be influenced more by current family climate. The analyses confirm the hypothesis that the parents draw predominantly on the present when describing the past.

• On average, parents and children retrospectively judge the family climate in 1976 to have been more negative than they had experienced it at the time. Both generations report lower values for positive emotional climate and higher values for norm orientation.

• Only very low generation differences can be found for the current rating on family climate carried out in 1976. In contrast, the retrospective description of the same content 16 years later shows that a generation-specific view of family history has developed. In particular, children's retrospective rating of emotionally positive family relations is far lower than that of the parent generation.

• To ascertain how similarly or dissimilarly the members of one family judge the type and form of family life, we computed so-called "intrafamilial correlations." At the first wave, there were markedly higher correlations between the two parents than between either father or mother and child. Sixteen years later, not least because of the changed quality of relations between parents and children, higher intergenerational correlations are found. In other words, young adults and their parents have drawn closer together over the years in their judgments on the quality of their family life.

• At both waves, gender-specific effects can be confirmed, showing that girls—particularly with regard to the degree of norm orientation in the family—orient themselves more toward their mothers, and boys orient themselves more toward their fathers.

• Children reveal clear associations between errors in retrospective ratings of family climate (i.e., the discrepancy between the family climate experienced in 1976 and the retrospective estimation of earlier family climate carried out in 1992) and the current relations with their parents in 1992. However, such associations are found almost exclusively for the aspect of a positive emotional relationship climate in the family. Individually, they mean the following: The more stressed current parent-child relations are, the stronger the negative bias in the retrospective description of family climate. In contrast, for parents, only slight associations can be confirmed. Thus, the young generation depends more strongly on the quality of current relations with their mothers and fathers when assessing the way the family used to live together in the past than their parents do.

END NOTES

1. See Moos and Moos (1986), Schneewind (1988b), and Schneewind, Beckmann, and Hecht-Jackl (1985).
2. Overviews of the major concepts in environmental or ecological psychology can be found in Moos and P. M. Insel (1974), Sundstrom, Bell, Busby, and Asmus (1996) and Stokols and Altmann (1987).
3. Two sources of empirical support for this are the report of the Scientific Advisory Board for Family Issues to the Federal Ministry of Youth, Family, and Health (Wissenschaftlichen Beirat für Familienfragen, 1975) and Vaskovics (1988).
4. The concept of social climate developed by Moos (1979) has been used to develop assessment instruments for other domains in addition to family climate (see Moos & E. J. Insel, 1974; Moos & Trickett, 1974).
5. The type of Family Climate Scales used in this study is based on the Family-Perceived Family Climate Scales (F-FKS) developed by Schmidt-Rinke (1982). The scale structure underlying this version was determined on the basis of means computed on the item level across the father, mother, and child in one family. This results in a slightly modified structure (see Schneewind & Ruppert, 1992) compared with the FKS (see Schneewind, 1988b). Scale b ("Orientation toward religious norms") was dropped at the second wave.
6. This table contains no precise reports in the form of factor-loading coefficients. Plus and minus signs report the factor pattern repeatedly found in studies on the FKS (see Schneewind, 1988b, 1993).
7. Nonetheless, our second-order scale structure differs in one aspect from the findings of previous studies: These indicate that high achievement orientation is an indicator for a strong norm orientation (i.e., it is located in the third second-order factor and not, as described previously, in the factor "Positive emotional climate"). This may be an effect of sample selection at Wave 2. As mentioned already, nearly all families participating at Wave 2 are characterized by a higher education level in both generations, more highly qualified jobs, and higher incomes. In a sample with such a structure, it is conceivable that family members take achievement for granted, and do not have to strive toward it through strict compliance with rules and norms. Correspondingly, the usual relation to Scales D ("Flexible vs. rigid rules") and H ("Order vs. chaos") was also weaker.
8. See chapter 2 for an explanation of the different aspects of stability.
9. See the references on family development theory in Note 5, chapter 3.
10. See Steiger (1980).
11. Sample sizes are smaller here because these intrafamilial correlations are computed on the basis of those families in which all three members participated in the survey at both waves.
12. Freud (1938) has had a decisive impact on the scientific discussion on this topic, with his concept of the Oedipus complex and his theory of defense mechanisms (in this case,

particularly regarding "identification with the aggressor"). For a review of gender-specific childrearing and socialization, see Eagly (1987), Huston (1983), and Maccoby and Jacklin (1974).

13. On the topic of the "functional equivalence" of development-related constructs, see Wohlwill (1973).

8

PERCEPTION OF CHANGES
IN SOCIETY

Previous chapters have been oriented toward the various systemic levels given by the ecopsychological approach of our study. Beginning at the individual level, which used multidimensional personality questionnaires and personality rating scales to focus on the "system of the individual," the next higher level addressed dyadic relations within the families surveyed. Both the marital and partner relations of the representatives of the two generations, as well as intergenerational relations within the families, can be assigned to this level. Extending this level of dyadic relations led to a perspective on the family as a holistic network of relations. The findings on family climate reported in the previous chapter correspond to this step from the relational dyad to the family system.

Shifting the focus of analysis from the individual to the family reveals that a broadening perspective is accompanied by an increasing complexity in the concepts and issues studied. This becomes particularly clear with the next step, which is made in this chapter—namely, the step from the family to its ecological surroundings.

Defining *ecological surroundings* as all context conditions that potentially exist beyond the borders of the family confronts us with an absolutely incalculable number of social, material, and natural phenomena that would seem appropriate for inclusion in our study. For example, there can be no doubt that a detailed survey of the quality, structure, and estimation of respondents' jobs would deliver important information that would also help to understand processes within the family. Likewise, it would seem appropriate to link together a comprehensive analysis of the families' social networks with data on internal family relations. Thus, ecological surroundings defined in this way require further systematic structuring if they are to serve as an action-guiding concept within the framework of psychological research. In recent years, it has become customary to talk about "meso-systems" or "macrosystems" to describe these contents, and this means aspects of the individual and familial environment that go beyond mere family relations.[1] The variety given by such a definition of ecological surroundings is confronted with the limits of what can be performed in practice. Therefore, the complexity of the ecological surroundings has to be reduced in such a way that the data collection covers only a set, clearly defined segment in line with the goals of the particular study.

Because one of the goals of the first survey in 1976 was to confirm an interdependence between internal family relations and numerous different ecological contexts, it focused on detailed assessments of parental working life, the planning of vacations and leisure time, as well as the social network.[2] In contrast, the follow-up in 1992 focused more strongly on actual or perceived change and stability across the 16-year interval.

Chapter 1 presented a summary of important social and political events in the years when the two surveys were carried out in order to provide an anchor for readers' memories. Another reason for this was to document the great potential for change on a social level that can be assigned to the time factor alone when the interval involved is sufficiently large.[3]

This becomes even clearer when the two cornerstones of this 16-year interval, as well as the major events that have occurred between them, are taken into account. Examples include the political collapse of the Eastern bloc countries and the unification of the two Germanies that this allowed. Such occurrences are objective events. These objective events and the public interest they arouse also make a strong contribution to determining an individual's perspective on the society in which he or she lives. However, this individual perspective is, in turn, exposed, to a great extent, to subjective evaluation processes. All this can be assigned to the ecological context of our respondents in the sense of the prior definition. The treatment of ecological context at the second wave focuses on the individual subjective perception of societal framing and living conditions. This particularly allows us to examine whether persons who are exposed to the same objective processes of societal change more or less agree on their perception of this societal context, or whether the differences are greater.

ASSESSMENT OF PROCESSES OF SOCIETAL CHANGE

First, we sketch how we have assessed this aspect of the ecological surroundings. Two considerations were decisive here. First, as mentioned already, we were not searching for objective measures for the societal level of the socioecological surroundings. We were far more interested in the subjective perception of this context level. An example may illustrate how this involves widely differing aspects. At the time of writing this chapter—August 1994—Germany has just experienced the hottest summer since the beginning of systematic weather records. An objective fact associated with this is a drastic increase in ozone levels, often beyond maximum official limits. In the state of Hesse, the Minister of the Environment imposed a speed limit to lower ozone levels, whereas others viewed this as a vote-catching trick or a useless measure. Hence, the same objective event led to widely differing, subjective estimations expressed, in turn, in clearly discriminable actions. This example provides another argument in favor of our focus on subjective perceptions: It is less the objective facts, but far more the subjective evaluation and estimation of these facts that guides and determines an individual's behavior. Therefore, if one wants to understand people's behavior, one should not just view the environment "as it is" separately from the persons in it, but far more in the way it is expressed in the views of the individuals.

Second, we were less interested in diagnosing the actual state of societal context conditions, but more in the developmental processes to which these events between 1976 and 1992 were subject from the perspective of the parent and children's generations in our survey. Because we had collected no information on this abstract context level in 1976 that could be used as a basis for present-day comparisons, questions in 1992 had to refer explicitly to the perceived change or stability in societal conditions. For a series of different content domains, our respondents had to use 5-point scales to rate whether the importance of the domain in question (e.g., general prosperity) had *decreased strongly* or *to some extent* (1 or 2), had *remained unchanged* (3), or had *increased slightly* or *strongly* (4 or 5). On the one hand, this type of scaling makes it possible to find out whether any change has occurred at all; on the other hand, it reveals the direction of any potential change by differentiating between increase and decrease. Respondents were specifically instructed not to describe their perceptions of their own personal situation, but—as so-to-speak "external observers"—the society in which they live in terms of any changes that may have occurred.

After these initial comments, we turn to the content of this assessment instrument. Because no relevant questionnaire assessing such processes of change on a societal level was available at the time, we had to construct a new instrument for this purpose. The greatest difficulty was to develop a provisional structure for the diversity of societally and socially relevant areas of change. The rough structure that was finally chosen surveyed changes in the following four domains: (a) "General living conditions," (b) "Life areas," (c) "Fields of influence," and (d) "Threats."

Internal aspects of each of these domains were formulated in different ways. Although our goal was to assess subjective perceptions, actual objective changes could be taken into account in the formulation of items, particularly in the domain of "Threats." Some of the items for "General living conditions" and "Life areas" could be derived from the results of recent psychological and sociological research.[4] Finally, other potentially relevant items were gathered from our own everyday experiences, or by comparing our own experiences with those of others. The final compilation of items, whose relevance for the assessment of perceived change first has to be estimated on the basis of empirical data, is reported in Tables 8.1–8.4.

These items permit an assessment of the subjective perceptions of change across a broad range of societal context conditions. Usually, psychological tests are constructed by trying out a preliminary form of the test, and then selecting only those items that comply with certain psychometric criteria.

TABLE 8.1
Items for Rating Changes in General Living Conditions in Society

General living conditions
1) People's general prosperity
2) People's degree of anxiety about the future
3) The importance of consumption, money, property, and other material values
4) The feeling that people have no influence on the really important things
5) The willingness to commit oneself fully to something
6) Work ethics
7) The degree of personal freedom
8) People's loneliness
9) The degree of joie de vivre and light-heartedness
10) The degree of egotism
11) Tolerance for different opinions and other life styles
12) Interpersonal coldness and indifference
13) The degree of optimism
14) The degree of conflict between young and old
15) The gap between poor and rich
16) The degree of conflict between the genders (between men and women)
17) The degree of hassle and stress
18) The importance of cultural life (involvement in art, music, literature, etc.)
19) The feeling of living in a complicated world
20) The feeling that one does not really know what one should orient oneself toward anymore
21) The feeling that things are somehow inflexible and bogged down in our society
22) The feeling that there is too much talk and not enough action in our society
23) The feeling that important decisions are simply postponed in our society
24) General satisfaction

TABLE 8.2
Items for Rating Changes in Important Life Areas

Life areas
1) Family life
2) Living in a partnership
3) Living with children
4) Social gatherings and friendships
5) The priority of private life
6) Looking after one's own body (healthy nutrition, exercise, relaxation)
7) Work and career
8) Education (school, training, and further training)
9) Leisure time
10) Vacations and journeys
11) Eroticism and sex

This procedure could not be applied here. We had to achieve a comparably economic, while nonetheless sufficiently exhaustive, compilation of items merely on the basis of considerations of content.

STRUCTURING OF AREAS OF SOCIETAL CHANGE

The assessment of changes in society were roughly separated into four domains: "General living conditions," "Life areas," "Fields of influence," and "Threats." As mentioned earlier, this separation was based on purely theoretical considerations, just like the formulation of the corresponding items.[5] These considerations were not directed, as is usually the case, to formulating items in such a way that they would each assess a set number of different aspects of a higher level concept that could then be summarized to form a

TABLE 8.3
Items for Rating Changes in Important Fields of Societal Influence

Fields of societal influence
1) Politics
2) Business
3) Mass media
4) Advertising
5) Church and religion
6) Administration and bureaucracy

CHAPTER 8

TABLE 8.4
Items for Rating Changes in Societal
Threat Factors

Threat
1) Through noise
2) Through environmental pollution
3) Through traffic conditions
4) Through climate catastrophes
5) Through nuclear power stations
6) Through military confrontations
7) Through incurable diseases
8) Through incompetent politicians
9) Through the potentials of genetic technology
10) Through violence, aggression, and criminality
11) Through poverty
12) Through refugees
13) Through immigrant workers
14) Through unemployment

scale. Although in our case such considerations did not play any role in the compilation of the items in the four domains of perceived change, it nonetheless seems meaningful to compute factor analyses on the items in the domains covered as a first step of analysis. There are two reasons for this. First, this produces a reduction of the high number of items to a smaller number of factors with interpretable content that can then be entered into the further analysis. Second, the factors obtained can provide information on which aspects of the perception of change are perceived as belonging together or being independent of each other.[6]

The following sections report the results of factor analyses on three domains of change. A factor analysis was not performed on the domain of fields of influence because it contained only six items. It generally holds that the reports of all persons participating in the second wave are included (i.e., both parents and children) so that the factor analyses are based on a sample of 613 respondents.

General Living Conditions

With one important exception, all items on change in "General living conditions" were entered into the factor analysis. The exception was the change in general satisfaction because, according to our understanding, this concept is already on the same theoretical level of abstraction as the factors that should be formed from the remaining items. We address the relations between perceived change in general satisfaction and the change concepts formed through factor analysis later. Initially, we present the results of the factor analyses in terms of the highest loadings for each item (see Table 8.5).

The 23 items can be reduced to eight factors that can be viewed as independent areas of the perception of change. Internal consistency coefficients for each of these eight factors were obtained through a reliability analysis. These values lie between alpha = .70 and alpha = .31. When it is considered that item selection was not concerned with constructing internally consistent scales, but more with covering the broad area of change-relevant life conditions as comprehensively as possible, the empirical consistency coefficients are surprisingly high. This is also an indication that it is thoroughly acceptable to limit the following analyses to the eight extracted factors.

We use the findings of factor analysis to present a short sketch of the various concepts of perceived change for the domain "General living conditions." The items on Factor 1 all express a degree of inflexibility on the level of social and political action, therefore we label it "Social immobility." Factor 2 groups together positive loadings on the willingness to commit oneself and work ethics with negative loadings on egotism and coldness/indifference; this reveals a concept labeled "Self-centeredness." Factor 3 particularly reflects changes with a strong emotional background, and can be summarized under the label "Emotional insecurity." Factor 4 shows a mixed pattern of loadings with negative loadings on optimism and *joie de vivre* and positive loadings on the feeling of living in a complicated world and no longer knowing what orientations to follow—"Lack of orientation" characterizes this constellation of features. Factor 5 subsumes changes regarding the degree of "Conflict," particularly between the genders and the generations. Factor 6 joins together the role of personal freedom and tolerance for other opinions and lifestyles into one concept labeled "Societal openness." Factor 7 addresses different aspects of "Prosperity" in society, whereas Factor 8 is labeled as representing perceived "Lack of influence."

Finally, two particular features of this constellation of factors should be mentioned. First, the question on the role of cultural life was not entered into any of the factors because it had a complex distribution of loadings. Second, the item on the role and importance of consumption, money, and possessions was entered to an equal extent into the computation of three scales—namely, "Emotional insecurity," "Prosperity," and "Lack of influence" for both statistical and content-related reasons. This reveals the first important finding. The close relation of the importance of consumption and possessions to emotionally negative life circumstances, such as egotism, fear of the future, and stress, indicates that our respondents have a somewhat ambivalent evaluation of material prosperity. This is supported by the equally significant relation with the items on the scale "Lack of influence." Our respondents clearly associate an overemphasis on material value orientations with a more negative rating of societal living conditions.

TABLE 8.5
Factor Structure of General Living Conditions

FACTORS	Item	Loading	Reliability
1	Things are inflexible and bogged down	.61	
	Too much talk, not enough action	.85	.70
	Postponed decisions	.82	
2	Willingness to commit oneself	.62	
	Work ethics	.66	
	Egotism	-.47	.53
	Coldness and indifference	-.49	
3	Anxieties about the future	.73	
	Consumption, money, property	.49	.55
	Loneliness	.46	
	Hassle and stress	.64	
4	Joie de vivre, light-heartedness	-.39	
	Optimism	-.50	.57
	Complicated world	.74	
	Search for orientation	.67	
5	Generation conflict	.75	.41
	Gender conflict	.59	
6	Personal freedom	.63	.36
	Tolerance	.73	
7	General prosperity	.71	.31
	Consumption, money, property	.41	
8	No influence on really important things	.42	
	Consumption, money, property	.71	.42
	Poor versus rich	.38	

Important Life Areas

The domain "General living conditions" continues to provide an extremely heterogeneous picture even after reduction through factor analysis, whereas the domain "Life areas" reveals a clearer structure. The 11 items are distributed across three factors whose internal consistency scores of alpha = .51, alpha = .65, and alpha = .67, respectively, are highly satisfactory, especially in light of the procedure used for selecting items (see Table 8.6).

Factor 1 combines items that all address areas of life that can be viewed as pleasant, hence it is labeled "Hedonistic orientation." Factor 2 also seems easy to interpret, this time as a pattern predominantly addressing "Personal relations." Finally, Factor 3 covers the remaining important area of life—the aspect of "Work and career."

Threats

The domain "Threats," consisting of 14 items, can also be reduced successfully to three dimensions through factor analysis. Consistency analyses provide values of alpha = .61, alpha = .73, and alpha = .75, and thus also indicate a thoroughly satisfactory precision of measurement on the scale level (see Table 8.7). The contents of the resulting scales are easy to interpret and differentiate. Factor 1 contains aspects that can be labeled "Threats resulting

TABLE 8.6
Factor Structure of Important Life Areas

FACTORS	Item	Loading	Reliability
1	Private life	.45	.65
	Looking after one's body	.54	
	Leisure time	.83	
	Vacations, journeys	.80	
	Eroticism, sex	.58	
2	Family life	.78	.67
	Partnership	.74	
	Children	.76	
	Friendship, social gatherings	.46	
3	Work and career	.81	.51
	Education	.61	

TABLE 8.7
Factor Structure of Perceived Threat

FACTORS	Item	Loading	Reliability
1	Noise	.67	.75
	Environmental pollution	.80	
	Traffic conditions	.73	
	Climate catastrophe	.58	
	Nuclear power stations	.55	
	Genetic technology	.45	
2	Violence, aggression, criminality	.44	.61
	Refugees	.85	
	Immigrant workers	.89	
	Unemployment	.54	
3	Military confrontations	.67	.73
	Incurable diseases	.73	
	Incompetent politicians	.57	
	Poverty	.56	

from technology." Factor 2 is compiled from the greatest variety of "Threats through societal influences." The items on Factor 3, which initially appears to be rather heterogeneous, can be seen to have the common denominator of "Threats through fatelike influences." The high consistency coefficient of alpha = .73 also indicates that these superficially different items nonetheless assess something in common. The fact that the respondents place poverty and incapable politicians in the same area of meaning as military conflicts and incurable diseases gives pause for thought. It is particularly remarkable that the first two threats mentioned, which are principally open to change through appropriate action, appear here in a perceptual context that tends to indicate more of a subjection to fate or a low openness to influence by the individual.

PERSONAL SATISFACTION AND THE PERCEPTION OF CHANGE

The attempt to group items with factor analysis, which we applied to various content areas for the assessment of societal change, has revealed that meaningful domains of societal change can be formulated, and that their contents can be interpreted. This indicates that the selection of items for this instrument is able to reflect a sufficiently broad spectrum of aspects of change. However, one potential problem with this instrument is that the respondents were asked to abstract themselves from their personal situation and to base their judgments on the total societal environment. For example, when asked about the role of prosperity, we were not interested in whether the aspect of "prosperity" had become more or less important to the respondents in recent years, but in their estimation of change in the importance of prosperity over the last 16 years in society as a whole.

Before we can feel reasonably confident in interpreting the replies, it is necessary to find a way to test whether the respondents actually managed to achieve this abstraction from the personal to the societal level when working on the questionnaire. One possible way to test this would be given if ratings on the personal situation and the more comprehensive societal level were available for the items used. A comparison of these two response perspectives should produce clear differences on at least some items. For example, it is conceivable that the level of hassle and stress has declined in a person's personal surroundings, whereas the same aspect is increasing on the societal level.

It was not possible to control this for all items. However, we could examine this issue in one content area for which both perspectives were surveyed. If it can be shown that this one question was answered in line with the instructions, there is some justification for concluding that the remaining items have also been answered correctly.

This question addresses the change in general satisfaction. In addition to rating this aspect with reference to society as a whole, all respondents were asked about their personal life satisfaction, as well as their satisfaction with their housing and careers, which also, in turn, contribute to general life satisfaction. In addition, these three scores are also available from the first wave for the parent generation. Therefore, the following results refer only to this subsample. In this sense, the test on whether the instructions for the change questionnaire were understood in the way intended is also linked simultaneously to an overview of change in personal satisfaction among the parents.

Measures of Satisfaction in the Parents for the Years 1976 and 1992

We first look at the distribution of the three measures of satisfaction in the parent generation at the first wave. Figure 8.1 presents a comparison of these data. Results are very clear: On all three measures of satisfaction, only a negligibly small percentage of parents was completely or rather dissatisfied in 1976. Even the highest score in the intermediate category of "things are just about alright" is only 13.3% (for job satisfaction), whereas on all three

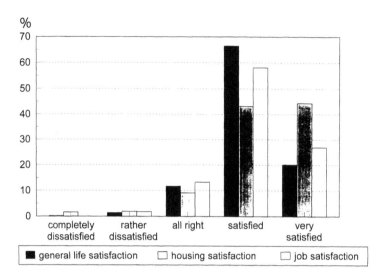

FIG. 8.1. Distribution of parental satisfaction scores at Wave 1 in 1976.

measures, the majority of the parent generation report that they are satisfied or even very satisfied. Thus, we can ascertain a generally very high level of life satisfaction, which is also reflected in the distributions of the somewhat more objective measures of job satisfaction and satisfaction with housing. As Fig. 8.2 shows, the picture is similar 16 years later.

The proportion of completely or rather dissatisfied persons remains equally small, just like the percentage of persons who rate themselves in

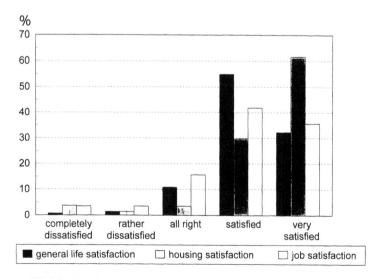

FIG. 8.2. Distribution of parental satisfaction scores at Wave 2 in 1992.

the intermediate category. As in 1976, the majority of the sample is distributed across the two categories *satisfied* and *very satisfied*. Satisfaction with housing increased, whereas job satisfaction and general satisfaction remained stable. In summary, the parents attain high scores on all three measures of satisfaction at both waves. These results indicate a notable measure of stability on the level of means.

However, if we look at the differential stabilities in the three satisfaction scores by computing correlations between the corresponding ratings at the first and second waves, as in the previous chapters, the picture changes: Values of $r = .34$, $r = .24$, and $r = .18$ for general, job, and accommodation satisfaction, respectively, indicate that there have certainly been major intraindividual changes in personal satisfaction.

Changes in Personal and Societal Satisfaction

This is the point at which we can build a bridge to the question that we are actually interested in—namely, the comparison between change in personal satisfaction and perceived change in satisfaction in society as a whole. The measures of personal satisfaction at Waves 1 and 2 can be used to construct a differential score providing information on how personal satisfaction has changed over the past 16 years. Figure 8.3 depicts the distribution of these differential scores for the three measures of satisfaction. These differential scores are based on the same scaling as the items from the change questionnaire.

The clear majority reveals no change in either general satisfaction or satisfaction with job and housing. The corresponding values lie between

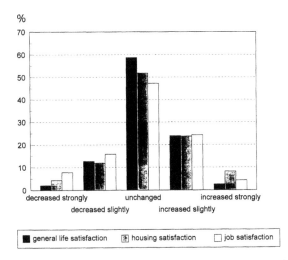

FIG. 8.3. Changes in satisfaction scores between 1976 and 1992.

47% and 59%. In contrast, a change in satisfaction is found in a much smaller proportion of parents. In general, this reveals a slight trend toward more parents reporting an increase in satisfaction. Thus, formulated in cautious terms, one can state a slight increase in personal satisfaction in the parent generation.

How does this finding correspond to the perceived change in general satisfaction in society? If respondents based their answers to this question on their personal situation, there should be a clear agreement between the distributions. Figure 8.4 compares the change in general societal satisfaction with the change in personal satisfaction.

It would be hard to find a clearer confirmation of the fact that two different concepts are being tapped here. As already mentioned, the personal satisfaction of the parents in our survey has remained the same or has increased slightly over the last 16 years, whereas the judgment on the same content in relation to society as a whole shows a completely reversed trend. Clearly, societal satisfaction has declined strongly from the parents' perspective. More than 70% of respondents see a more or less strong decline in general satisfaction over the last 16 years.

This is also confirmed by correlations between measures of change in personal satisfaction and the perceived change in satisfaction in society. With values of $r = .00$, $r = .00$, and $r = .04$, it is impossible to find the slightest connection between general as well as job and housing satisfaction on the one side and the estimation of the level of satisfaction in society on the other. Therefore, we can state finally that our respondents definitely seem to be

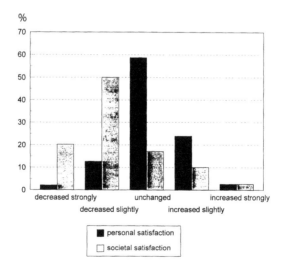

FIG. 8.4. Distribution of perceived societal and personal satisfaction in parents.

capable of discriminating between the personal and societal levels. In addition, we find clear differences in the reports on the different levels, indicating a much more critical judgment on the level of satisfaction in society.

A COMPARISON OF THE PERCEPTION OF CHANGE IN SOCIETY ACROSS THE GENERATIONS

The prior summation of the individual aspects for judging societal change into factors provides information on which content-related aspects of domains of change are perceived as being related. These findings alone already produce some results that give pause for thought. One only has to consider which aspects respondents associate closely with (e.g., the importance of consumption and money, or the threat through poverty or incompetent politicians). However, we still have no information on the respondents' perception of how these aspects have changed. This is addressed in the following sections, once more separated into the four domains presented at the beginning of the chapter. Apart from the domain "Areas of influence," the presentation is based on the concepts derived from factor analysis. Furthermore, we look for potential generation differences by comparing scores between the parent and children's generations.

General Living Conditions

Figure 8.5 displays the results for the eight content areas into which "General living conditions" can be categorized. The top of the figure gives the scale extending from *decreased strongly* across *unchanged* to *increased strongly*. For each content area, both the mean and standard deviation are entered; each upper line refers to the parent generation, and each lower line refers to the children's generation.

We start with the value 3.0 on the scale at the top of the figure, which marks the point at which each living condition is stable. It is immediately evident that there has been an increase for all concepts apart from general satisfaction, as discussed earlier. The level of "Emotional insecurity" has increased particularly strongly. This includes, in particular, hassle and stress, fears about the future, loneliness, and orientation toward material values. The second-largest increase is in "General prosperity"—a notable finding. It seems as if increasing prosperity is not necessarily accompanied by a positive rating on the general emotional state, but rather its opposite.

This negative trend is supported by further findings. "Societal immobility," a concept composed of items addressing society's inability to act and make decisions, is also located in the area of stronger increase, closely

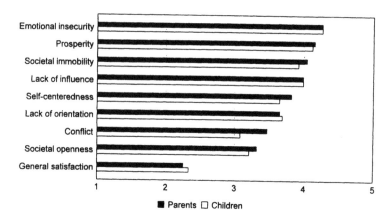

(1 = decreased strongly; 2 = decreased slightly; 3 = unchanged; 4 = increased slightly; 5 = increased strongly)

FIG. 8.5. General living conditions: Means of the eight factors split for parent and children's generations.

followed by "Lack of influence." Thus, we gain a general picture of a social life characterized by negative emotions accompanied by feelings of powerlessness. The estimated increase in "Self-centeredness" also fits into this picture. Self-centeredness is characterized by a preponderance of egotism, coldness, and indifference, as well as a decrease in commitment and work ethics. It seems as if in the areas in which one has the feeling that one cannot change things, even if one wants to, the only remaining option is to assert one's own needs. The simultaneous increases in "Lack of orientation" and "Conflict" complete the picture of a society that, at least from the perspective of our respondents, offers few opportunities and starting points for exerting a personal influence. There is a recognizable tendency toward individualization that, as witnessed by the high increase in emotional insecurity, does not necessarily lead to an increase in well-being in such a societal context.

The slight increase in "Societal openness" also does not seem to compensate for this. It seems as if, in the minds of the respondents, recent trends in general living conditions characteristically reveal a somewhat negative picture. This interpretation is confirmed when we also see how these perceived changes relate to general satisfaction. The multiple correlations between the various aspects on which the eight concepts are based and the index of change in satisfaction (see Table 8.8) show clearly that these perceptions of change are not value-free, but that there are clear relations to general satisfaction within this societal environment.

Another conspicuous aspect of the size of these correlations is that the highest values are found in those scales whose items provide the best

TABLE 8.8
Living Conditions: Multiple Correlations Between the Variables
Underlying Each Factor and Perceived Change in Satisfaction in Society

General living conditions	R
Emotional insecurity	.25
Prosperity	.21
Societal immobility	.24
Lack of influence	.22
Self-centeredness	.32
Lack of orientation	.38
Conflict	.14
Societal openness	.21

Note. All correlations: $p < .001$.

characterization of the well-being of an individual in a society shaped in this way—namely, "Lack of orientation" and "Self-centeredness." In comparison, the correlations for "Increased prosperity" and the generally stable level of "Conflict" tend to be low.

Up to now, we have not compared perceptions in the two generations. A glance at the means and standard deviations in Fig. 8.5 reveals an astonishing level of agreement between the parental and the filial generations on nearly all scales. Potential expectations, such as that the younger generation would deliver more negative ratings because of a more critical perspective on their societal living conditions, or that the parent generation, which is now well established and settled in its surroundings, would tend to give euphemistic ratings on their life context that cannot be confirmed. Although a few generation differences on "Self-centeredness" and "Conflict" attain marginal statistical significance, the dominant picture is of a high level of agreement between parents and their children.

Important Life Areas

The description of the results on "General living conditions" reveals a tendency toward increasing individualization. The findings on the change in the importance of certain life areas illustrated in Fig. 8.6 provide further support for this assumption. The factor "Hedonistic orientation" proves to be the one life area with the strongest increase over the past years. Even "Work, career, and education," which has also gained in importance, has not increased so much. The picture of a society in which, stated pointedly, everyone has to look out for themselves is complemented by the finding that

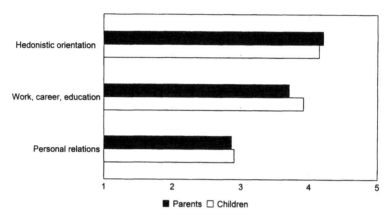

(1 = decreased strongly; 2 = decreased slightly; 3 = unchanged, 4 = increased slightly; 5 = increased strongly)

FIG. 8.6. Life areas: Means of the three factors split for parent and children's generations.

the importance of "Personal relations" has tended to remain unchanged over time, and, in any case, cannot compete with the increase in importance of "hedonistic" life areas, such as the private sphere, leisure time, or vacations. It is notable here that the importance of friendships has increased, whereas the status of "families" has decreased, indicating a shift in personal relations away from the family. Here as well, the parental and filial generations have similar perceptions of societal realities. The strongest difference, found for "Work, career, and education," is largely explained through the different life phases of the two generations. Whereas the filial generation is currently confronted with the important task of finding a place in occupational life and constructing their own career identity, many parents are already retired or facing retirement in the near future. We suspect that a mixing together of personal and societal evaluation perspectives has occurred here.

Fields of Influence

The strong increase in the feeling of having no influence was discussed previously as a characteristic of current societal reality. It remains to be seen where the respondents locate the powers of influence that enable society to function. Figure 8.7 illustrates the results for some of our rating variables. These results provide empirical confirmation of an impression formulated by many persons who have followed the political and economic events of recent years. The mass media, business, and advertising have made marked gains in influence, whereas those who probably make decisions—who are located in politics—have hardly gained any influence. These

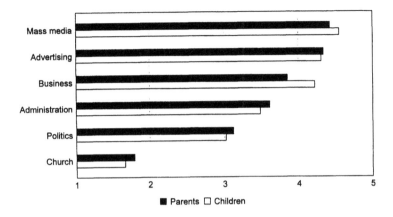

(1 = decreased strongly; 2 = decreased slightly; 3 = unchanged; 4 = increased slightly; 5 = increased strongly)

FIG. 8.7. Fields of societal influence: Means of the items split for parent and children's generations.

results also contribute to an understanding of the changes in general living conditions toward an increased lack of influence and societal immobility reported earlier. The influence of the average individual citizen on the economy tends to be slight, whereas in the area of politics, a certain illusion of control is maintained through the possibility of voting. Less surprising, although supported by a clear database here, is the clear loss of influence of the church as a societal institution.[7]

Threats

The previous analysis of the perceived changes in the societal life context leads us to anticipate a similarly negative picture of change in the results on threat factors. One reason for this is that the threat factors given to our respondents, and the estimation of their increase or decrease in importance, are more objective than the items in the domains of change addressed so far. For example, it is an objective fact that the stress of noise has become an increasingly chronic problem in recent years. Nonetheless, we still have to ask how these objective facts are represented in the subjective experience of our respondents. Figure 8.8 depicts these results. Not unexpectedly, al-though in no way reducing the cause for concern, the results depict a society whose exposure to threats from a series of different factors has increased enormously in recent years. The total threat scores confirm this clearly.

On a differentiated level, it can be seen that threats resulting from tech-nology have the strongest impact, closely followed by threats through so-cietal influences. It is easiest to find differences between the generations in the latter area, although these are minimal in size. Their main cause is the

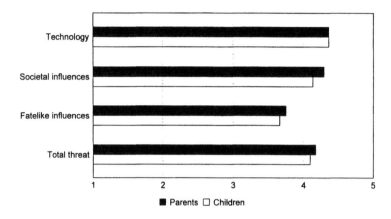

(1 = decreased strongly; 2 = decreased slightly; 3 = unchanged; 4 = increased slightly; 5 = increased strongly)

FIG. 8.8. Threats: Means of the factors split for parent and children's generations.

stronger perception of the threat of refugees and immigrant workers among the parental generation. Both generations perceive an equally strong threat from technology. This summarizes, among others, a series of aspects that threaten the environment. The present data do not confirm the frequent claims that the younger generation has a higher environmental awareness than the older one.

Threats through fatelike influences also show a clear increase. On the one hand, this indicates that our label for this scale is possibly not particularly appropriate because, if something like fate exists, it should actually be equally threatening or beneficial at all times. On the other hand, a glance at the individual scale items reveals that the perception of societal realities in this domain is characterized by a high degree of skepticism, if not pessimism, among respondents. An example is the finding that the threat through military confrontations has increased slightly in the perceptions of respondents (the corresponding mean is 3.22), although one could have anticipated a decrease in recent years due to the defusing of the East–West conflict that dominated this aspect for decades.

It is worth looking at how these data relate to the perceived change in satisfaction in society as a whole. Table 8.9 reports the multiple correlations between each indicator of the three threat factors and perceived change in societal satisfaction, as well as the corresponding relations with personal life satisfaction at the second wave.

None of the correlations between personal satisfaction at Wave 2 and the changes in threats to society is significant. This is a further confirmation that parents and children have followed the instructions correctly and made

TABLE 8.9
Threats: Multiple Correlations of the Variables Underlying Each Factor
With Perceived Change in Satisfaction in Society and Personal
Satisfaction at Wave 2

Threat through...	Change in satisfaction in society	Personal satisfaction at wave 2
Technology	.22***	.14
Societal influences	.27***	.09
Fate like influences	.18***	.13
Threat (total)	.30***	.22

Note. N = 406. *** p < .001.

their judgments from the perspective of society. In contrast, when one remains on the level of the societal context, all relations clearly attain a high level of significance. On a general level, then, the respondents see a clear connection between the increase in threats and the change in general satisfaction, although their own personal satisfaction is scarcely affected by the threats they perceive on a societal level.

RELATIONS AMONG THE DOMAINS OF SOCIETAL CHANGE

Up to now, we have subjected the individual domains of societal change to separate analyses. However, one can also ask whether there are relations among the different domains. For example, how do perceptions of changed societal living conditions relate to perceptions of changed threat factors? Although it is not possible to make causal interpretations here, any correlations that arise could provide initial indications for causal hypotheses. Table 8.10 presents these correlations for the domains "General living conditions" and "Threats." Because a detailed description of all these correlations would take up too much space, the following only discusses the most conspicuous findings.

We initially focus on the values in the table's last column, which report the correlations between the perception of changed living conditions and the total threat score. Here, we can state that an increase in emotional insecurity, lack of influence, societal immobility, and lack of orientation shows a clearly confirmed relation to a perceived increase in threat. Thus, an increased threat potential is viewed as strongly related to living conditions that address reduced action potentials, as well as feelings of uncertainty in the face of increasingly complex life contexts. The impression arises of a society in which one sees oneself as almost paralyzed by one's own

TABLE 8.10
Intercorrelations Among General Living Conditions and Threats

General living conditions	Technology	Societal influences	Fate like influences	Total threat
Societal immobility	.18***	.31***	.29***	.32***
Self-centeredness	.10**	.21***	.14***	.18***
Emotional insecurity	.39***	.28***	.22***	.38***
Lack of orientation	.28***	.22***	.21***	.31***
Conflict	.17***	.20***	.22***	.25***
Societal openness	.05	-.00	-.03	.01
Prosperity	.15***	.02	-.09*	.04
Lack of influence	.33***	.19***	.24***	.33***

Note. $N = 612$. * $p < .05$. ** $p < .01$. *** $p < .001$.

restricted possibilities and the great lack of transparency, and exposed more or less helplessly to increasing feelings of threat.

However, these results also indicate that an environment that is assigned less immobility, lack of influence, and lack of orientation is perceived to be correspondingly less threatening, or that it is possible to counter the occurrence of certain threats through preventive action. In line with this, those living conditions that have little to do with the aspect of helplessness and overwhelming complexity have no or much lower correlations with the perception of threat. These include, above all, societal openness and prosperity, as well as self-centeredness.

Finally, in the context of prosperity, one finding should be pointed out that cannot be found in Table 8.10. The threat resulting from technology correlates positively with increased prosperity (i.e., the more general prosperity increases, the greater the estimated threat resulting from technology). If this correlation is computed separately for the parental and filial generations, the following result is obtained: The rather low correlation of $r = .15$ for the total group drops to $r = .09$ for the parental generation, whereas it rises to $r = .33$ for the filial generation. This is one of the few findings that reveals differences between the generations. We interpret this as a possible indication that—at least from the perspective of the younger generation—a greater level of material prosperity, which should actually be an important precondition for avoiding and reducing the threat of damage to the environment, actually contributes to its opposite.

The clear shift in importance in the three most important life areas also reveals interesting patterns of correlations with changed living conditions, as Table 8.11 shows. The clearest increase, as mentioned previously, is for

TABLE 8.11
Intercorrelations Among General Living Conditions and Life Areas

General living conditions	Hedonism	Personal relations	Work and career
Societal immobility	.06	-.04	.03
Self-centeredness	.23***	-.16***	.01
Emotional insecurity	.30***	-.11**	.25***
Lack of orientation	.13***	-.15***	.06
Conflict	.08*	-.15***	.08*
Societal openness	.09**	.14***	-.04
Prosperity	.31***	.00	.11**
Lack of influence	.22***	-.00	.16***

Note. $N = 613$. * $p < .05$. ** $p < .01$. *** $p < .001$.

a hedonistic life orientation. This is accompanied on the side of living conditions with increased self-centeredness, emotional insecurity, lack of influence, and prosperity. These are the living conditions that, as already shown in the context of threat, tend to make it more difficult to commit oneself on a societal level. However, it is precisely these living conditions that show clear relations to a life orientation that, to some extent, signalizes a turning away from societal life and, instead, a turning toward a lifestyle that seeks satisfaction within the private sphere.

For the area of "Personal relations," which has been subject to stagnation or even a loss in importance in recent years, the changes in important living conditions tend to be generally unfavorable. The negative correlations with self-centeredness, emotional insecurity, lack of orientation, and conflict clearly confirm this, although they are rather low. Against the background of a trend toward deteriorating general living conditions in the eyes of parents and children, it seems as if a hedonistic orientation and the importance of personal relations have, at least in part, an antagonistic relationship to each other.

A final word on "Work, career, and education": The increased importance of this area shows the highest correlation with a general emotional uncertainty on the side of living conditions. Even without the clear proof provided by a more specific, statistical causal analysis, it can be suspected that this reflects a mechanism through which emotional insecurity—expressed particularly through fears about the future, loneliness, and stress—can be compensated by turning increasingly toward one's work, whereas the area of "Personal relations" is simultaneously blended out under such conditions.

Finally, we look at the relations between changed perceptions of life areas and the intensity of perceived threat. These results are reported in Table

TABLE 8.12
Intercorrelations Among Threats and Life Areas

Threat factors	Hedonism	Personal relations	Work and career
Technology	.22***	-.05	.24***
Societal influences	.13***	-.10*	.10**
Fate like influences	.01	.00	.15***
Total threat	.16***	-.06	.22***

*p < .05. ** p < .01. *** p < .001.

8.12. The pattern is difficult to interpret. Against the background of changed living conditions, it seems to be conclusive that an increasing threat through technological and societal influences is accompanied by an increasingly hedonistic orientation. In a situation in which one is exposed to threats that could be thwarted if the necessary conditions for change were available, withdrawal into the private sphere is also an option. In contrast, however, there are comparably high correlations between threat and the area of "Work, career, and education." Is this also a flight from threat, or an attempt to counter threats in this way? This question cannot be answered here. Finally, it can also be seen that the area of "Personal relations" shows no mentionable relations to perceived threats.

How can all these relations be summarized? The impression arises of a complex interplay among the individual areas of societal change. Each relation described in this section can cast light on only one small section of a pattern of relations that is characterized by a variety of connections and possible causal relations. However, it has to be remembered that causal interpretations of single correlations, regardless of how plausible they may be, can have only a hypothetical character at this stage. Further work on these findings should confirm causal patterns through a simultaneous analysis of all relations. For example, it is conceivable that the perception of changed living conditions and changed threat factors will prove to be a simultaneous cause of changes in the importance of various life areas.

GENDER DIFFERENCES IN THE PERCEPTION OF SOCIETAL CHANGES

It has already been pointed out that hardly any of the concepts of societal change show any differences in perception between the parental and filial generations. A further possible source of variation, which has not been mentioned up to now, is gender. Are there any indications that men and women differ in the way they experience changes in societal framing conditions? If this is the case, in which concepts do these differences arise? To answer these questions, we carried out analyses of variance (ANOVAs) for the scales of living conditions and threat factors, in which both gender and generation membership were entered as independent variables. Table 8.13 reports the results of these analyses, which are presented in the same way as in earlier chapters (see e.g., chap. 3). Significant effects are marked with an arrow, taking the female perspective for gender effects and the parental perspective for generation effects. In addition, each significant effect is accompanied by the proportion of variance it explains.[8] The strong agreement between the two generations on the level of means, which has already been mentioned several times before, can be seen clearly. Only three "General living conditions" factors reveal significant main effects. However, with the exception of the scale "Conflict," these explain a negligibly

TABLE 8.13
Gender and Generation Effects in General Living Conditions and Threats

	Gender effects		Generation effect	
General living conditions and threats	Significant effects[1]	% variance explained	Significant effects[2]	% variance explained
Societal immobility	/		↑	0.64
Self-centeredness	/		↑	1.69
Emotional insecurity	↑	2.6	/	
Lack of orientation	↑	1.44	/	
Conflict	↑	1.21	↑	6.25
Societal openness	/		/	
Prosperity	/		/	
Lack of influence	/		/	
Threat through...				
Technology	↑	6.25	/	
Societal influences	/		↑	1.69
Fate-like influences	↑	5.76	/	
Total threat	↑	6.25	/	

Note. 1: direction of arrow=women´s perspective. 2: direction of arrow = perspective of parentalgeneration. n(women) = 311, n(men) = 306, n(parental genereation) = 421, n(filial generation) =196.

small proportion of variance. This suggests that, despite confirmed statistical significance, these differences possess only a minimal status in the explanation of the present data through gender membership.

The same can be said for gender effects. Only on three scales—namely, "Emotional insecurity," "Lack of orientation," and "Conflict"—are any differences to be found at all, and these can also be viewed as rather unimportant because of the small amount of variance they explain. In light of the widespread agreement, it hardly seems possible to interpret the contents of such slight differences. At best, it can be pointed out that the factors indicating a stronger perception of change among women address concepts that are associated predominantly with negative emotional well-being. Content-related aspects, such as fears about the future, loneliness, reduced *joie de vivre* and optimism, and conflicts, can confirm this. This may reflect an increased sensitivity toward the emotional atmosphere in society among women.

Moving to the threats, the picture is somewhat clearer. For both the total threat score and the factors "Technology" and "Fate-like influences," women report a stronger increase than men. Each explains approximately 6% of variance. The present findings do not reveal whether this reveals an increased female sensitivity toward threatening aspects of the life environment, in contrast to male insensitivity or an exaggerated and anxious perspective among women, compared with a more serene and rational outlook among men.

In summary, neither generation membership nor gender really provides any significant contribution to explaining interindividual differences in the perception of changed living conditions and perceived threat. This indicates that, although respondents each report their subjective perspectives, the objective reality of changes in society is so unequivocal that the subjective perspectives in various groups of persons generally show little difference.

INTRAFAMILIAL RELATIONS IN THE PERCEPTION OF CHANGE

The strong evidence of similarity between the parental and filial generations in their judgment of the processes of change in society in recent years raises the question of whether this similarity is being handed down within families. Expressed more precisely, are there inner-family processes of reciprocal, intergenerational influence and adjustment that lead parents and their children to produce an approximately equal assessment of context conditions in society?

In investigating this question, we can take advantage of the circumstance that our sample does not consist of randomly recruited groups belonging to different generations, but of two subgroups linked together by family membership. If the findings discussed actually express intrafamilial and intergenerational processes of mutual influence, this should be reflected in the correlations between the individual members of families. Thus, in this context, the correlation coefficient is interpreted as a measure of similarity between family members.

Table 8.14 summarizes the intrafamilial correlations for the domains "General living conditions" and "Threats." For the changes in "Life areas" and "Fields of influence," only the mean correlation across the scales or items is reported in each case. Fathers and mothers continuously show a weak to moderately strong agreement in their estimation of societal changes. These findings are expected because it can be assumed that living together for many years also results in a certain degree of reciprocal alignment of perceptions of circumstances outside the family. However, we are far more interested in possible intergenerational processes. If these exist, they must be reflected in positive and rather high correlations between parents and their children.

The findings reported in Table 8.14 clearly show that this is not the case. Neither "mother–child" nor "father–child" constellations produce suffi-

TABLE 8.14
Intrafamilial Correlations for All Four Domains of Change

Domains of societal change	Mother/Father ($n=192$)	Mother/Child ($n=169$)	Father/Child ($n=166$)
Societal immobility	.23***	.15*	.20**
Self-centeredness	.33***	.09	.09
Emotional insecurity	.20**	.05	.09
Lack of orientation	.21**	.16*	.02
Conflict	.20**	.20**	.00
Societal openness	.11	.06	.15*
Prosperity	.22**	.06	.11
Lack of influence	.15*	.08	.07
Threat through technology	.35***	.06	.01
Threat through societal influences	.24***	.03	.13*
Threat through fate like influences	.27***	.18*	.05
Life areas Mean correlation	.21**	.03	.06
Fields of influence Mean correlation	.21**	-.01	-.03

*$p < .05$. ** $p < .01$. *** $p < .001$.

ciently high values that would justify assuming such a process of alignment and influence across the intrafamilial generation borders. Although the parental and filial generations reveal few general differences in their assessment of processes of societal change, a differential inspection does not reveal that this similarity is based on inner-family processes.

PERCEPTION OF CHANGE AND PERSONALITY

Our efforts to relate the findings on perceptions of change to factors such as generation and gender or intrafamilial transfer processes have produced few tangible results. Earlier on, we expressed the suspicion that the subjective view on objective context conditions in society is distorted, to a very limited extent, by these or other individual characteristics. Nonetheless, the following attempts to relate perceptions of changes in society to variables on the individual level. We examine whether personality characteristics assessed with the Sixteen Personality Factor Questionnaire (16 PF) have an impact on the perception of change.[9]

We are not interested in tracing back the majority of the perceptions of societal change to the personality of the respondents. Rather, we want to test whether specific personality characteristics favor the perception of specific factors of societal change.[10] The results of these analyses are summarized in Tables 8.15 and 8.16.

Personality and Changes in Living Conditions

First of all, it is necessary to ascertain—independent of more far-reaching interpretations of content—whether there are any relations between these two sets of variables. Information on this is reported in Table 8.15. For fathers and mothers, there is a significant relation for all living condition factors, with the exception of "Prosperity." Among the children, in contrast, there are far fewer relations. In more precise terms, "Emotional insecurity," "Conflict," and "Prosperity"—and among the sons "Lack of orientation"—are evidently areas of societal change whose perception among the children has no relationship to their own personality dispositions. Perhaps this indicates that children's judgments are more independent as far as these factors of change are concerned.

However, the fact that any relations are found at all still does not reveal anything about how close they are. This information is given by the r^2 or R^2 values. The more variance in the target variables explained, the stronger the relationship between the target variables involved and the significant personality variables found. Here, there are clear differences between the four groups. The percentages of explained variance confirm that the closest

TABLE 8.15

Prediction of the Eight Living Conditions Factors Through the 15 Scales of the Personality Questionnaire

LIVING CONDITIONS	Fathers (n = 198)		Mothers (n = 204)		Sons (n = 88)		Daughters (n = 89)	
Societal immobility	Rule-consciousness	.26	Apprehension	.25	Apprehension	.21	Openness to change	.23
	Abstractedness	.18					Perfectionism	.22
	$R^2 = .07$		$r^2 = .06$		$r^2 = .03$		$R^2 = .08$	
Self-centeredness	Openness to change	.14	Sensitivity	.20	Tension (-)	.23	Perfectionsim (-)	.22
			Tension (-)	.15				
	$r^2 = .02$		$R^2 = .06$		$r^2 = .04$		$r^2 = .04$	
Emotional insecurity	Emotional instability	.17	Openness to change (-)	.12	/		/	
	Rule-consciousness	.17	Sensitivity	.14				
	$R^2 = .05$		Emotional stability	.23				
			Apprehension	.20				
			$R^2 = .09$					
Lack of orientation	Sensitivity	.25	Sensitivity	.19			Sensitivity	.27
	Apprehension	.14	Tension	.16			Dominance	.21
	$R^2 = .06$		$R^2 = .06$				$R^2 = .08$	

(table continues)

299

TABLE 8.15
(Continued)

LIVING CONDITIONS	Fathers (n = 198)		Mothers (n = 204)		Sons (n = 88)		Daughters (n_= 89)	
Conflict	Abstractedness	.18	Rule-consciousness	.25	—		—	
	Rule-consciousness	.14	Tension	.18				
	Emot. instability	.14	$R^2 = .09$					
	$R^2 = .05$							
Societal openness	—		Liveliness (-)	.16	Abstractedness	.24	Openness to change	.21
			Vigilance (-)	.14	$r^2 = .05$		$r^2 = .03$	
			$R^2 = .04$					
Prosperity	Perfectionsim	.14	Emotional stability	.20	—		—	
	$r^2 = .02$		Liveliness (-)	.20				
			Self-reliance (-)	.17				
			$R^2 = .08$					
Lack of influence	Emotional instability	.20	Perfectionism	.20	Sensitivity	.26	Openness to change	.32
	$r^2 = .04$		Sensitivity	.16	$r^2 = .06$		$r^2 = .09$	
			$R^2 = .04$					

TABLE 8.16
Prediction of Threat Factors by the 15 Scales of the Personality Questionnaire

THREAT	Fathers (n = 198)		Mothers (n = 204)		Söhne (n = 88)		Töchter (n = 89)	
Total threat	Rule-consciousness	.25	Apprehension	.24	Tension	.21	Vigilance	.24
	Emotional instability	.17	Rule-consciousness	.17				
			Dominance	.14				
	$R^2 = .09$		$R^2 = .11$		$r^2 = .04$		$r^2 = .04$	
Threat resulting from technology	Rule-consciousness	.20	Apprehension	.17	Dominance	.24	Abstractedness (-)	.22
	$r^2 = .03$		Sensitivity	.15				
			$R^2 = .05$		$r^2 = .04$		$r^2 = .04$	
Threat through societal influences	Vigilance	.20	Rule-consciousness	.24	Social boldness (-)	.30	Sensitivity	.21
	Rule-consciousness	.15	Apprehension	.19	Tension	.20		
			Liveliness	.14				
	$R^2 = .06$		$R^2 = .12$		$R^2 = .12$		$r^2 = .04$	
Threat through fate like influences	Rule-consciousness	.25	Apprehension	.28	/		Vigilance	.20
	Self-reliance (-)	.23	Liveliness	.18				
	Sensitivity	.19						
	Emotional instability	.14						
	$R^2 = .11$		$R^2 = .09$				$r^2 = .03$	

301

relations between the perception of changed living conditions and person-ality are found among mothers. This is followed by daughters, in whom not all factors of living conditions produce significant regression equations. Least influenced by personality are the judgments of sons in terms of both the number of significant relations and the proportions of variance ex-plained. Compared with the explanatory power of generation and gender, which—as reported earlier—does not exceed 6%, a few clearer effects can be found here for some relations. For example, in both the mothers' perception of conflict and the daughters' perception of lack of influence, personality factors explain 9% of the variance.

Because this initial overview has managed to convince us that all four groups reveal relations between the perception of changed living conditions and a series of personality characteristics, the next concern is to see what this pattern looks like. The question is, Which factors of living conditions are influenced by which personality factors in which group of persons? In addition, does this pattern of relations show any conspicuous regularities in the sense that specific personality factors repeatedly play a role in each of the groups studied? Or can it be confirmed that certain personality factors have a continuous impact across groups for the perception of specific factors of living conditions? If these questions are used as a basis to ap-proach the results reported in Table 8.15, they tend to convey the impres-sion of a broad heterogeneity from which it is difficult to filter out clear trends. Nonetheless, a few conspicuous results can be mentioned.

1. Among daughters, a stronger perception of negative changes in living conditions is associated with individual features that, taken together, paint a picture of personality suggesting a revolt against these living conditions. Thus, openness to change and sensitivity, paired with a rather self-disci-plined and dominant attitude, make it quite conceivable that constraining social context conditions such as societal immobility and a lack of influence are perceived to be particularly impairing.

2. The situation is different for mothers. Here, personality factors such as apprehension, sensitivity, tension, and restrained attitude particularly encourage a stronger perception of increasingly unfavorable living condi-tions. Unlike the daughters, whose negative image of society seems to result from perceived constraints on their own action impulses, among mothers, it is more features of a passive, patient attitude, with little tendency toward active intervention, that contribute particularly strongly to a negative per-ception of changes in society.

3. Among sons, for whom it was already ascertained had the lowest re-lations between perception of society and personality, it is surprising to see that they show a greater similarity to the mothers rather than the daughters who come from the same generation. For example, for mothers and sons,

the perception of societal immobility arises from an attitude of increased apprehension, whereas the perception of lack of influence can be traced back to a higher sensitivity.

4. Among fathers, two further dominant personality traits prove to relate to negative changes in living conditions—namely, rule-consciousness and emotional instability. Rule-consciousness entails a particularly strong compliance with general norms and values, a love of orderliness, reliability, and a sense of duty, whereas emotional stability entails a higher emotional irritability in various everyday activities. Perhaps fathers experience the changes in society over the last few years as increasingly undermining earlier norms and values to which they feel personally committed, and this intensifies as a function of the strength of their emotional susceptibility. In comparison with daughters, fathers construct their own image of society on the basis of a more defensive and conservative attitude.

This pattern of relations between personality characteristics and the perception of changes in living conditions leads to the following conclusion. Reciprocal relations can be found that, at times, explain more variance than generation membership and gender. However, the patterns are heterogeneous in content so that, at best, differences among the four groups are only a trend that should in no way be overinterpreted.

Personality and Changes in the Perception of Threat

Here as well, the analysis follows that in the previous section on "General living conditions." Hence, we investigate whether there is any relationship between the perception of a continuously increasing threat to society and certain personality characteristics. A glance at Table 8.16 gives a positive answer to this question.

With the exception of the perception of fatelike threats by sons, significant relationship patterns are found in all cases. The R^2 coefficients can be used to make statements on the closeness of the relations found. These coefficients indicate that there is a closer relation between perceived threat and personality among parents, compared with children. Values for fathers and mothers often explain between 9%–12% of variance, whereas—with one exception—they do not exceed 4% among the children. Thus, it can be ascertained that perceived threats relate more strongly to personality than the perception of changed living conditions, and that there seems to be a difference between the parental and filial generations. Among children, it seems as if individual differences in the perception of societal threat factors have less to do with personality-related factors, whereas among parents personality structure shows a stronger relation to judgment formation.

The prior section revealed that a further analysis of these relations on the basis of particular contents led to a rather inconsistent picture. The results were rather unsuitable for making consistent statements that differences in the perception of changed living conditions correlate particularly closely with certain personality factors, or that there is a specific cluster of highly predictable personality traits for each of the four groups studied.

Applying the same question to the perception of threat factors reveals a somewhat clearer pattern that can be used to differentiate the four groups. Particularly for the two subgroups in the parent generation, whose proportions of explained variance were much higher than those of the children's generation, relevant patterns of personality can be found.

1. Fathers. Here we find a similar constellation of personality characteristics to that found for living conditions. However, there is one difference: The relation has become much closer. Increased rule-consciousness and higher emotional instability go hand in hand with a more intensive perception of society-related threats. This finding is thoroughly plausible when it is recalled that high rule-consciousness is a major indicator for a strongly norm-related personality attitude. Global societal threats harbor the risk that normative commitments and the sense of security that they convey may lose their validity. When such a conservative personality disposition links up with a tendency toward emotional instability, the result is a high sensitivity for threatening signals. In our case, this is reflected in the perception of a greater potential for societal threat.

2. Mothers. A similar constellation can also be found among mothers. As in the living conditions, an increased tendency toward apprehension also plays a particularly important role in the perception of threat. Added to this, and here fathers and mothers are similar, is a higher rule-consciousness that can be assigned the same relationship to security as in the fathers. In addition, two analyses reveal a significant impact of liveliness in mothers. At first glance, it is hard to understand how increased liveliness can dispose toward a more intensive perception of threat. However, this becomes easier to understand when it is recalled that the content of this concept refers to aspects such as extraversion or openness to the social world because a certain degree of openness to the social world can be viewed as a basic precondition for focusing perception on what is happening in society.

3. Sons. Among the sons, the perception of stress factors is related to two personality characteristics that are both classified to the second-order concept of anxiety. These are inner tension and shyness. Therefore, the perception of societal threat in sons is not mediated by, for example, goal-directed and action-oriented personality dispositions, but by a passive and patient attitude that is nonetheless coupled with high mental tension.

4. Daughters. The lowest proportions of explained variance among daughters, compared with other groups, are given by the scales "Vigilance," "Abstractedness," and "Sensitivity." This reveals the outlines of a pattern of personality characteristics representing a high sensitivity toward information on threats.

In summary, differences in the perception of threats related to society link up with specific personality characteristics. Although these relations are stronger in the parent generation, compared with the children's generation, they never explain more than 12% of variance. The contents create the dominant impression of a heterogeneous pattern of relations. It becomes clear that information on threats has more weight for the parents when it confronts a personality structure characterized by a fixation on normative commitments that ensure security and by a certain lack of emotional stability. Among the young adults, there are clearer gender-specific differences, with the sons revealing a more defensive and the daughters a more sensitive attitude in their perception of societal threats.

CHANGE IN THREATS AND COPING WITH STRESS

Chapter 3 introduced the scales developed to assess individual ability to cope with stress within the context of critical life events.[11] These were concepts providing information in the sense of personality dispositions on how persons try to cope when confronted with stressful situations. Thus, when stress or threats are perceived, different coping mechanisms are activated in each individual. When it is considered that each person possesses his or her own repertoire of coping mechanisms, by inverting the usual procedure applied to such relations, one can ask whether the available coping mechanisms may also have an influence on which environmental conditions are perceived as a stress or threat in the first place. We test this with the data on perceived changes in threats. However, one must recall that the perception of threat refers to the societal, and not the individual, reality, and it has to be admitted that the perception of threats in society does not necessarily have to impact on the personal life world of the respondents. Table 8.17 presents the corresponding correlations.

The table conveys some interesting findings. We first look at the coping scales that reveal no relation to perceived threats. These are "Rational problem solving," "Information search," and "Redefinition." It is conspicuous that this involves those scales that can be assigned to cognitive modes of coping. Although their correlations with perceived threat generally tend to be rather low, the remaining four scales refer to a varyingly strong extent to emotional well-being when processing stress and threats. It is notable that a coping style that leads to the suppression or banishment from consciousness of the mostly unpleasant feelings associated with the stress

TABLE 8.17
Correlations Between Coping Scales and Perceived Changes in Threat

Coping scales	Threat through...			
	Technology	Societal influences	Fate like influences	Total threat
Rational problem solving	-.07*	.01	-.06	-.05
Affect regulation	-.16***	-.05	-.15***	-.16***
Resigned acceptance	.08*	.06	.09*	.10**
Parents	.13**	.05	.12**	.13**
Children	-.05	-.0 2	-.03	-.04
Avoidance	.09*	.11**	.14***	.14***
Parents	.10*	.13**	.15***	.15***
Children	.05	.08	.13*	.11
Social contact	.12***	.01	.15***	.12***
Information search	-.02	.05	-.04	-.00
Redefinition	-.02	.04	.04	.02

Note. * $p < .05$. ** $p < .01$. *** $p < .001$. $n = 598$, n (parents) = 406, n (children) = 192.

facilitates the perception of threats. The correlations support this assumption: High affect regulation (i.e., little emotional expression) and a strong tendency to distract oneself from problems (and thus also associated negative emotions) are accompanied by the perception of stronger threats. Thus, if it is possible to contain the experience of negative feelings within a limited framework through appropriate coping mechanisms, the perception of threats tends to be allowed. Also, the support experienced in the social network, reflected in the scores on the scale "Social contact," makes it more likely that perceptions of threat can be admitted.

The shaded fields in the table additionally point to two interesting differences between the generations. When the filial and parental generations are analyzed separately, the correlations for the scales "Resigned acceptance" and "Avoidance" can be traced back mostly to the parent generation. In parents, a resigned attitude—which, to some extent, contains powerless subjection—combined with the ability to avoid the emotional consequences of this state seems to reinforce a perception of threat. Finally, although the perception of changed societal framing conditions (here limited to threats) may reveal plausible relations with specific coping styles, their effect sizes, as in the personality factors, have only a relatively modest explanatory power.

A BRIEF SUMMARY OF THE MOST IMPORTANT POINTS

• Personal life satisfaction and perceived social satisfaction develop in opposite directions: Personal satisfaction has increased notably over the last 16 years, whereas the majority of respondents see a clear decline on the societal level.

• Negative aspects of "General living conditions" have increased strongly. This particularly involves the degree of emotional insecurity, societal immobility, lack of influence, self-centeredness, and lack of orientation. The fact that there has been a simultaneous increase in the general prosperity of society indicates that prosperity takes a rather ambivalent role within the context of the other changes in society.

• This equivocal picture of society continues for the perceived changes in various life areas. A predominantly hedonistic life orientation, which is expressed in, among others, the dominance of the private sphere, leisure time, and sexuality, as well as in the life area of work, career, and education, shows a strong increase in importance, whereas the relevance of personal relations has tended to remain unchanged or, as far as the status of the family is concerned, shows a notable decline in importance.

• The three factors of collective threats complete this picture of precarious societal context conditions: Threats resulting from technology (e.g., climate catastrophes, nuclear power stations), societal influences (e.g., criminality, refugees), and fatelike influences (e.g., military confrontations, incurable diseases) have all increased strongly in the eyes of our respondents.

• On the level of societal institutions, there is a marked increase in the importance of the sectors mass media, business, and advertising. In contrast, the perceived influence of politics has remained unchanged over time, whereas the churches have experienced a clear loss in influence.

• It is surprising that, with a few exceptions, few generation differences can be found. Parental and filial generations show an overall similarity in their negative judgment of societal actualities. Also, as far as gender is concerned, no interpretable differences can be ascertained in the perceptions of men and women.

• A test of intrafamilial correlations shows that the generally high agreement between parental and filial generations in the perception of societal changes also does not arise through intrafamilial transfer processes.

• When the personality of the respondents is included as an explanatory factor for differences in the perception of changed societal surroundings, clear relations can be confirmed. The more strongly the members of the parent generation perceive the change in "General living conditions" as negative, the more security oriented and instable they are. Women with an increased emotional sensitivity perceive negatively toned societal changes more intensively. Here, it is particularly women in the younger generation who exhibit the psychological personality prerequisites for making an active contribution to changing this situation.

• The relation between perceived threats and personality mostly reveals similar findings to those for "General living conditions," although they are even stronger.

• Individual differences in coping with stress relate, above all, to the intensity of perceived threat. In concrete terms, when persons who perceive a high threat potential in our society are faced with problem situations, they tend to react with resignation, avoidance, and little emotional control, but they also share their problems with others to a greater extent, and, in this way, probably gain confirmation of their views.

• In general, it holds that the respondents' personality characteristics, combined with their gender and generation membership, have a higher explanatory power for differences in the perception of societal changes than an exclusively separate grouping according to generation membership and gender.

END NOTES

1. According to Bronfenbrenner (1979), a *mesosystem* covers the ". . . linkages between settings, both in which the developing person actually participates and those that he may never enter but in which events occur, that affect what happens in the persons immediate environment" (pp. 7–8). In contrast, a *macrosystem* refers to ". . . the complex of nested, interconnected systems . . . viewed as a manifestation of overarching patterns of ideology and organization of the social institutions common to a particular culture or subculture" (p. 8).
2. See Schneewind et al. (1981) and Schneewind, Beckmann, and Engfer (1983).
3. See Harenberg (1993).
4. See, in particular, the studies on changing values in German society (e.g., Gensicke, 1994; Inglehart, 1979; Klages, Hippler, & Herbert, 1992). Psychoanalytically inspired reflections on the changes in German mentality since 1975 can be found in Brähler and Richter (1990).
5. An overview of the domains that were finally surveyed reveals clear parallels to the concept of quality of life as defined by Glatzer (1990). This comparison is suggested particularly by the criteria of multidimensional assessment and the role of the subjective perspective.
6. In the given context, the technique of factor analysis was used predominantly for exploration rather than confirmation. On the methodological principles of factor analysis, see Cattell (1978) or Gorsuch (1974).

7. See, for example, the findings from the second survey on church membership by the German Evangelical Church reported in Hanselmann, Hild, and Lohse (1984), as well as the review of empirical studies in Keil (1988).

8. Effect sizes were determined with the help of Hays' (1963) omega-square measure.

9. For a description of the 16 PF, see chapter 2, as well as Russell and Karol (1994).

10. Several psychological studies are already available for the opposite causal direction—namely, the impact of perceived changes in society on individuals and their personality or self-definitions. Keupp (1989) referred to the "patchwork identity" in this context, and Gergen (1991) referred to the "saturated self" arising through postmodern society.

11. See chapter 3's description and assessment of coping with stress; see also Peterander, Bailer, and Henrich (1987).

9

FINAL COMMENTS

The purpose of these final comments is not to summarize the most important findings in our longitudinal study. The condensed summaries at the end of each chapter under the heading "A Brief Summary of the Most Important Points" should have fulfilled this purpose. Our intention here is to round off the book with a few more general impressions on this work.

The first question concerns the success of our approach: Was it a worthwhile endeavor to plot the individual and familial course of development in two generations linked together by being members of the same family? We consider that the answer to this question is an emphatic "yes." A look at the broad spectrum of findings reveals marked differences alongside notable stabilities, surprising findings together with expected ones, and reassuring findings next to ones that give us pause for thought. Some examples may clarify this.

We were impressed by the high level of stability in individual differences across the very long period of 16 years. Personality characteristics, parent–child relations, marital and partnership relations, and the quality of family relations all exhibit a notable differential stability. However, we also cannot overlook the time- and generation-linked developmental effects that appear in all these domains to a greater or lesser extent. "Continuity in change" seems to be a general slogan that could be used to describe this dialectic between inertia and change.

The most conspicuous findings are age and generation effects in parental childrearing behavior. Both generations orient their childrearing goals, attitudes, and practices toward a childrearing model characterized by more liberalness and emotional involvement. From "rearing children to relating to them" is the purport of this unmistakable trend, which has led to the establishment of a partner-oriented, egalitarian relation between parents and their young children who, nonetheless, still need to be reared. On the level of changed childrearing values, this trend has already been documented in relevant studies of change over time during the last 20–30 years.[1] However, in contrast to our study, this research was unable to discriminate between generation and time effects. The clear dominance of the generation effect in our findings reveals that the thrust toward this radical change in parent–child relations proceeds particularly from the younger generation.

This radical change in childrearing behavior is embedded within a general change in values that has also been apparent for many years. This takes the form of a shift from values oriented toward "duty and compliance" to a greater emphasis on "self-fulfillment."[2] This general change in mentality is also reflected on the level of personality development. For example, the epochal change revealed in our findings indicates an increasingly lower level of norm commitment over time and a higher level of independence. This reflects a transition from a "nomocentered" to an "autocentered" mentality (i.e., the development from an "externally guided" personality structure propped up by normative commitments to a more strongly "internally guided" life concept, in which personality development reveals itself to be a self-constructive process).[3]

Embedded within this general change in mentality, we find another, gender-specific developmental process, revealing—particularly in the younger generation—that women have developed more autonomy and self-assertion—that is, they have become "stronger."[4] This is complemented by a development on the personality level in young men that gives pause for thought: In comparison with their female peers, males forfeit more of their emotional spontaneity and liveliness in the transition to adulthood; at the same time, their degree of socioemotional control increases. Such findings indicate the need to pay more attention to the conditions and consequences of male socialization in the future.

Critical live events and coping with them do not just play an important role in the biography of young men. Critical life events differ clearly in terms of how the circumstances surrounding them and their consequences are perceived, and the patterns of events found show recognizable links to different forms of coping. Alongside gender-specific differences, we also find clear confirmation of a deficit in "functional" forms of coping, particularly for events that are classified as "personal problems." We consider this to be a particularly important area for applying psychological prevention directed toward strengthening relationship skills.[5]

We were surprised to see how far "relations impact on relations." Not only do parent–child relations in the distant past determine current relations with adult sons and daughters, but even the quality of the parents' marital relations is reflected in the partner relations of the younger generation. Despite all the changes in childrearing concepts and shifts in personlity development, there is clear confirmation of a cross-generational transfer of fundamental life orientations, particularly in the domain of childrearing. It would seem that continuity and change are phenomena that impact on individual development, and can also be traced from a multigenerational perspective.[6]

Even when family relations generally prove to be positive in all respondents, there are unmistakable individual differences, as well as differences between generations. We were impressed that the children's generation always has a more skeptical, less positively toned perception of family relations than the parent generation—a finding that is clearly recognizable in the quality of parent–child relations, as well as in the judgment of family climate.

Parallel to this, we find a clear trend toward a retrospective distortion of family relations 16 years before, and this also shifts toward more negatively toned perceptions. This is an important finding because it casts new light on the use of retrospective information on family relations reported so frequently in the relevant literature. This particularly concerns one clear aspect of our findings—namely, that the retrospective distortion of the perception of past phases in relationships is codetermined, to a major extent, by the quality of current relations.

A further finding that surprised us and gave us pause for thought is the extremely negative judgment on the changes in societal framing conditions. Even when the personal situation is rated much more favorably, in terms of society, we are faced with the picture of an extremely fragile collective mentality. A society in which emotional insecurity, lack of influence and orientation, and self-centeredness and coldness have increased, and one that is shaped to a major extent by external threat factors, is perceived individually as a host of precarious living conditions. Generation differences are almost imperceptible here, and thus point to an intergenerational consensus on the judgment of societal framing conditions. Unless we are prepared to dismiss this finding as a reflection of typically German "bellyaching," we have to ask what can be done to shift this strongly negative collective life feeling in a more positive direction.

We are aware that the findings of this study can make no claims to be representative, particularly because we had to accept a restriction to the socioeconomic variability of our original sample of 1976 in the follow-up. We are also aware that we refer exclusively to subjective life data that vary in their proximity to real behavior. However, we consider that this particularly reveals the strength of a genuine psychological approach, whose particular quality is given by interrelating and comparing life perspectives in different persons within the family unit.

The central topic of this study was to expose time and generation differences in the development of two generations linked together by being members of the same family, and to do this on different levels of life and experience. Although we have studied links among the individual domains in detail, we have certainly not exploited all possible variants. We also have not studied differential developmental courses in individual subgroups or systematic configurations such as certain parent–child coalitions in more detail. These are just some of the research questions that we can now answer, in principle, on the basis of the insights that mothers and fathers, sons and daughters have given us into their lives. Our future task is to tackle these and similar research questions.

END NOTES

1. In this context, see the relevant public opinion polls carried out by the EMNID Institute or the Allensbacher Institut für Demoskopie summarized in Gensicke (1994).
2. The discrimination between these two value orientations is based on Klages (1988).
3. On the differentiation between nomo- and autocentered mentalities, see Klages and Gensicke (1994).
4. Brähler and Richter (1990) also conclude that women in Germany have become "stronger."
5. Information on ways to strengthen relationship skills is provided by Nelson-Jones (1990) or Duck (1986).
6. Family therapy has paid attention to the importance of the multigenerational perspective for a long time (see e.g., Boszormenyi-Nagy, 1987; Bowen, 1978; Kramer, 1985; Toman, 1988).

REFERENCES

Adler, R. (1986). Konversion [Conversion]. In T. Uexküll (Ed.), *Psychosomatische Medizin* (3rd ed., pp. 481–488). München: Urban & Schwarzenberg.

Aldous, J. (1978). *Family careers. Developmental change in families.* New York: Wiley.

Alwin, D. F. (1988). From obedience to autonomy: Change in traits desired in children, 1924–1978. *Public Opinion Quarterly, 52,* 33–52.

Baltes, P. B. (1987). Theoretical propositions of life-span developmental psychology: On the dynamics between growth and decline. *Developmental Psychology, 23*(5), 611–626.

Baltes, P. B., Reese, H. W., & Nesselroade, J. R. (1977). *Life-span developmental psychology: Introduction to research methods.* Monterey, CA: Brooks/Cole.

Baumrind, D. (1991). Effective parenting during the early adolescent transition. In P. A. Cowan & E. M. Hetherington (Eds.), *Advances in family research* (Vol. 2, pp. 111–163). Hillsdale, NJ: Lawrence Erlbaum Associates.

Bandura, A. (1986). *Social foundation of thoughts and action: A social cognitive theory.* Englewood Cliffs, NJ: Prentice-Hall.

Bandura, A. (1992). Exercise of personal agency through the self efficacy mechanism. In R. Schwarzer (Ed.), *Self-efficacy: Thought control of action* (pp. 3–38). Washington, DC: Hemisphere.

Belsky, J., Lerner, R. M., & Spanier, G. B. (1984). *The child in the family.* Reading, MA: Addison-Wesley.

Berry, W. D., & Feldman, S. (1985). *Multiple regression in practice.* Beverly Hills: Sage.

Boszormenyi-Nagy, I. (1987). *Foundations of contextual therapy.* New York: Brunner/Mazel.

Bowen, M. (1978). *Family therapy and clinical practice.* New York: Jason Aronson.

Bowlby, J. (1969). *Attachment and Loss: Vol. I. Attachment.* New York: Basic Books.

Bradbury, T. N. (1995) Assessing the four fundamental domains of marriage. *Family Relations, 44,* 459–468.

Brähler, E., & Richter, H. E. (1990). Wie haben sich die Deutschen seit 1975 psychologisch verändert? Mehr Individualismus, mehr Ellbogen, stärkere Frauen [How have Germans psychologically changed since 1975? More individualism, more ellbows, stronger women]. In

H. E. Richter (Ed.), *Russen und Deutsche. Alte Feindbilder weichen neuen Hoffnungen* (pp. 115–134). Hamburg: Hoffmann & Campe.

Braiker, H. (1992). *Lethal lovers and poisonous people—how to protect your health from relationships that make you sick.* New York: Simon & Schuster.

Bretz, M. & coauthors (1990). Die Familie im Spiegel der Statistik [The family as mirrored in statistics]. In Statistisches Bundesamt (Ed.), *Familien heute. Strukturen, Verläufe und Einstellungen* (pp. 9–115). Stuttgart: Metzler-Poeschel.

Bronfenbrenner, U. (1979). *Ecology of human development.* Cambridge, MA: Harvard University Press.

Bronfenbrenner, U. (1986). Ecology of the family as a context of human development. *Developmental Psychology, 22,* 723–742.

Brown, G. W., & Harris, T. O. (Eds.). (1989). *Life events and illness.* London: Unwin Hyman.

Bundesminister für Jugend, Familie und Gesundheit. (1975). *Zweiter Familienbericht* [Second report on the family]. Stuttgart: Kohlhammer.

Burgess, E. (1926). The family as a unity of interacting personalities. *Family, 1,* 3–6.

Buss, D. M., & Cantor, N. (Eds.). (1989). *Personality psychology: Recent trends and emerging directions.* New York: Springer.

Carter, B., & McGoldrick, M. (Eds.). (1988). *The changing family life cycle: A framework for family therapy.* New York: Gardner Press.

Caspi, A., & Bem, D. J. (1990). Personality continuity and change across the life course. In L. A. Pervin (Ed.), *Handbook of personality—theory and research* (pp. 549–575). New York: Guilford Press.

Cattell, H. B. (1989). *The 16 PF: Personality in depth.* Champaign, IL: Institute for Personality and Ability Testing.

Cattell, R. B. (1973). Personality pinned down. *Psychology Today, 7,* 40–46.

Cattell, R. B. (1978). *The scientific use of factor analysis in behavioral and life sciences.* New York: Plenum Press.

Cattell, R. B., Eber, H. W., & Tatsuoka, M. M. (1970). *Handbook for the sixteen personality factor questionnaire (16 PF).* Champaign, IL: Institute for Personality and Ability Testing.

Clarke-Stewart, K. (1978). And Daddy makes three: The father's impact on mother and the young child. *Child Development, 44,* 466–478.

Cochrane, R., & Robertson, A. (1973). The life events inventory: A measure of the relative severity of psychological stressors. *Journal of Psychosomatic Research, 17,* 135–139.

Cohen, J., & Cohen, P. (1983). *Applied multiple regression/correlation analysis for the behavioral sciences* (2nd ed.). Hillsdale, NJ: Lawrence Erlbaum Associates.

Cohen, L. H. (Ed.). (1988). *Life events and psychological functioning. Theoretical and methodological issues.* Beverly Hills, CA: Sage.

Cohn, A. D., Silver, D. H., Cowan, C. P., Cowan, P. A., & Pearson, J. (1992). Working models of childhood attachment and couple relationships. *Journal of Family Issues, 13,* 432–449.

Conn, S. P., & Rieke, M. L. (Eds.). (1994). *The 16 PF Fifth Edition technical manual.* Champaign, IL: Institute for Personality and Ability Testing.

Cronbach, L. J. (1951). Coefficient alpha and the internal structure of tests. *Psychometrika, 16,* 297–334.

Darling, N., & Steinberg, L. (1993). Parenting style as context: An integrative model. *Psychological Bulletin, 113,* 487–496.

Delbrück, H. (1893). Die gute alte Zeit [The good old times]. *Preußische Jahrbücher, 71,* 1–28.

Demo, D. H. (1992). Parent-child relations: Assissing recent changes. *Journal of Marriage and the Family, 54,* 104–117.

Dohrenwend, B. S., & Dohrenwend, B. P. (Eds.). (1974). *Stressful live events: Their nature and effects.* New York: Wiley.

Dohrenwend, B. S., & Dohrenwend, B. P. (1978). Some issues in research on stressful life events. *Journal on Nervous and Mental Disease, 166,* 7–15.

Duck, S. (1986). *Human relationships. An introduction to social psychology.* Beverly Hills, CA: Sage.

Dunn, J. (1988). Relations among relationships. In S. Duck (Ed.), *Handbook of personal relationships. Theory, research and interventions* (pp. 193–210). Chichester: Wiley.

Duvall, E. M. (1977). *Marriage and family development.* New York: Lippincott.

Eagly, A. H. (1987). *Sex differences in social behavior: A social-role interpretation.* Hillsdale, NJ: Lawrence Erlbaum Associates.

Field, T. M., McCabe, P. M., & Schneiderman, N. (Eds.). (1988). *Stress and coping across development.* Hillsdale, NJ: Lawrence Erlbaum Associates.

Fincham, F. D., & Bradbury, T. N. (Eds.). (1990). *The psychology of marriage: Basic issues and applications.* New York: Guilford.

Freud, S. (1938). Abriß der Psychoanalyse. *Gesammelte Werke. Band 17.* Frankfurt a.M.: Fischer.

Gable, S., Belsky, J., & Crnic, K. (1992). Marriage, parenting, and child development: Progress and prospects. *Journal of Family Psychology, 5,* 276–294.

Gensicke, T. (1994). Wertewandel und Familie [Value change and family]. *Aus Politik und Zeitgeschichte. Beilage zur Wochenzeitung Das Parlament, B29-30/94,* 36–47.

Gergen, K. J. (1991). *The saturated self.* New York: Basic Books.

Glass, E., McGraw, B., & Smith, M. (1981). *Meta-analysis in social research.* Beverly Hills, CA: Sage.

Glatzer, W. (1990). Messung der Lebensqualität [Measurement of life quality]. In L. Kruse, C. F. Graumann, & E. D. Lantermann (Eds.), *Ökologische Psychologie* (pp. 240–244). München: Psychologie Verlags Union.

Glenn, N. D. (1990). Quantitative research on marital quality in the 1980s: A critical review. *Journal of Marriage and the Family, 52,* 818–831.

Glick, I. D., Clarkin, J. F., & Kessler, D. R. (1987). *Marital and family therapy* (3rd ed.). Orlando, FL: Grune & Stratton.

Goethe, J. W. (1970). *Werke in zehn Bänden* [Works in ten volumes] (bearbeitet von E. Spiekerkötter). Frankfurt a.M.: Frankenbuchhandlung.

Gorsuch, R. L. (1974). *Factor analysis.* Philadelphia: Saunders.

Groeben, N., & Scheele, B. (1977). *Argumente für eine Psychologie des reflexiven Subjekts.* Darmstadt: Steinkopff.

Grotevant, H. D., & Carlson, C. I. (1989). *Family assessment: A guide to methods and measure.* New York: Guilford.

Grotevant, H. D., & Cooper, C. R. (1986). Individuation in family relationships. *Human Development, 29,* 82–100.

Guilford, J. P. (1965). *Fundamental statistics in psychology and education* (4th ed.). New York: McGraw Hill.

Haan, N. (1982). The assessment of coping, defense and stress. In L. Goldberger & S. Breznitz (Eds.), *Handbook of stress. Theoretical and clinical aspects* (pp. 254–269). London: Free Press.

Hall, C. S., & Lindzey, G. (1978). *Theories of personality* (3rd ed.). New York: Wiley.

Hanselmann, J., Hild, H., & Lohse, E. (Eds.). (1984). *Was wird aus der Kirche? Ergebnisse der zweiten EKD-Umfrage über Kirchenmitgliedschaft* [What's about the future of the church? Findings of the second EKD poll on church membership]. Gütersloh: Selbstverlag.

Hardesty, F. P., & Priester, H. J. (1966). *Handbuch für den Hamburg-Wechsler-Intelligenztest für Kinder HAWIK* [Manual of the Hamburg-Wechsler-Intelligence Test for Children HAWIC] (3rd ed.). Bern: Huber.

Harenberg, B. (Ed.). (1993). *Harenberg Schlüsseldaten 20. Jahrhundert* [Harenberg key data of the Twentieth Century]. Dortmund: Harenberg Lexikon Verlag.

Havighurst, R. (1953). *Developmental tasks and education.* New York: McKay.

Hays, W. S. (1963). *Statistics for psychologists.* New York: Holt, Rinehart & Winston.

Heatherton, T. F., & Weinberger, J. L. (Eds.). (1994). *Can personality change?* Washington DC: American Psychological Association.

Herrmann, T. (1991). *Lehrbuch der empirischen Persönlichkeitsforschung* [Textbook of empirical personality research]. (6. Aufl.). Göttingen: Hogrefe.

Hinde, R. A., & Stevenson-Hinde, J. (Eds.). (1988). *Relationships within families*. Oxford: Clarendon Press.

Holmes, T. H., & Rahe, R. H. (1967). The social readjustment rating scale. *Journal of Psychosomatic Research, 11*, 213–218.

Hultsch, D. F., & Cornelius, S. W. (1990). Kritische Lebensereignisse und lebenslange Entwicklung: Methodologische Aspekte [Critical life events and life span development: Methodological aspects]. In S. H. Filipp (Hrsg.), *Kritische Lebensereignisse* (S. 72–90) (2. Aufl.). München: Psychologie Verlags Union.

Huston, A. C. (1983). Sextyping. In P. H. Mussen & M. E. Hetherington (Eds.), *Handbook of child psychology. Vol. 4. Socialization, personality and social development* (4th ed., pp. 387–467). New York: Wiley.

Inglehart, R. (1979). Wertwandel in den westlichen Gesellschaften: Politische Konsequenzen von materialistischen und postmaterialistischen Prioritäten [Value change in Western societes: Political consequences from materialistic and postmaterialistic priorities]. In H. Klages & P. Kmieciak (Eds.), *Wertwandel und gesellschaftlicher Wandel* (pp. 279–316). Frankfurt a.M.: Campus.

Johnson, B. M., Shulman, S., & Collins, W. A. (1991). Systemic patterns of parenting reported by adolescents: Developmental differences and implications for psycho-social outcomes. *Journal of Adolescent Research, 6*, 235–252.

Jones, E. E., & Nisbett, R. E. (1971). *The actor and observer: Divergent perceptions of the causes of behavior*. New York: General Learning Press.

Keil, S. (1988). Veränderungen im Verhältnis von Kirche und Familie seit den Anfängen der Bundesrepublik Deutschland - am Beispiel der evangelischen Kirche [Changes in the relationship between church and family since the beginnings of the Federal Republic of Germany - The sample case of Lutherian Church]. In R. Nave-Herz (Ed.), *Wandel und Kontinuität der Familie in der Bundesrepublik Deutschland* (pp. 198–221). Stuttgart: Enke.

Keupp, H. (1989). Auf der Suche nach der verlorenen Identität. [In search of lost identity]. In H. Keupp & H. Bilden (Eds.), *Verunsicherungen. Das Subjekt im gesellschaftlichen Wandel* (pp. 47–69). Göttingen: Hogrefe.

Kiecolt-Glaser, J. K., Kennedy, S., Malkolf, S., Fischer, L., Speicher, C. E., & Glaser, R. (1988). Marital discord and immunity in males. *Psychosomatic Medicine, 50*, 213–229.

Klages, H. (1988). *Wertedynamik - Über die Wandelbarkeit des Selbstverständlichen* [Dynamics of values - On the changeability of the obvious]. Zürich: Interfrom.

Klages, H., Hippler, H. J., & Herbert, W. (Eds.). (1992). *Werte und Wandel. Ergebnisse und Methoden einer Forschungstradition* [Values and change. Findings and methods of a research tradition]. Frankfurt a.M.: Campus.

Kramer, J. R. (1985). *Family interfaces: Transgenerational patterns*. New York: Brunner/Mazel.

Kruse, L., Graumann, C. F., & Lantermann, E. D. (Hrsg.). (1990). *Ökologische Psychologie - Ein Handbuch in Schlüsselbegriffen* [Ecological psychology - A handbook of concepts]. München: Psychologie Verlags Union.

Lamb, M. E. (1976). *The role of the father in child development*. Hillsdale, NJ: Lawrence Erlbaum Associates.

Lazarus, R. S. (1991). *Emotion and adaption*. New York: Oxford University Press.

Lazarus, R. S., & Folkman, S. (1984). *Stress, appraisal, and coping*. New York: Springer.

Lerner, R. M., & Busch-Rossnagel, N. A. (1981). *Individuals as producers of their development: A life-span perspective*. New York: Academic Press.

Lüscher, K., & Fisch, R. (1977). *Das Sozialisationswissen junger Eltern* [Socialization knowledge of young parents] (1. Arbeitsbericht). Konstanz: Projektgruppe Familiäre Sozialisation an der Universität Konstanz.

Lukesch, H. (1975). *Erziehungsstile: Pädagogische und psychologische Konzepte* [Parenting styles: Pedagogical and psychological concepts]. Stuttgart: Kohlhammer.

Luster, T., & Okagaki, L. (Eds.). (1993). *Parenting: An ecological perspective.* Hillsdale, NJ: Lawrence Erlbaum Associates.

Maccoby, E. (1992). The role of parents in the socialization of children: A historical overview. *Developmental Psychology, 28,* 1006–1017.

Maccoby, E., & Jacklin, C. N. (1974). *The psychology of sex differences.* Stanford: Stanford University Press.

Maccoby, E., & Martin, J. (1983). Socialization in the context of the family: Parent-child interaction. In P. H. Mussen & E. M. Hetherington (Eds.), *Handbook of child psychology: Vol. 4. Socialization, personality and social development* (4th ed., pp. 1–101). New York: Wiley.

Mahler, M., Pine, F., & Bergmann, A. (1975). *Psychological birth of human infants.* New York: Basic Books.

McAdams, D. P. (1994). *The person: An introduction to personality psychology* (2nd ed.). San Diego: Harcourt Brace Jovanovich.

McCrae, R. R., & Costa, P. T. (1990). *Personality in adulthood.* New York: Guilford Press.

McMartin, J. (1995). *Personality psychology. A student-centered approach.* Thousand Oaks, CA: Sage.

Meichenbaum, D. (1985). *Stress inoculation training.* New York: Pergamon Press.

Minuchin, S. (1974). *Families and family therapy.* Cambridge: Harvard University Press.

Minuchin, S., & Fishman, H. C. (1981). *Family therapy techniques.* Cambridge, MA: Harvard University Press.

Montada, L., Filipp, S. H., & Lerner, M. J. (Eds.). (1992). *Life crises and experiences of loss in adulthood.* Hillsdale, NJ: Lawrence Erlbaum Associates.

Moos, R. H. (1979). Messung und Wirkung sozialer Settings [Measurement and impact of social settings]. In H. Walter & R. Oerter (Eds.), *Ökologie und Entwicklung. Mensch-Umwelt-Modelle in entwicklungspsychologischer Sicht* (pp. 172–184). Donauwörth: Verlag Ludwig Auer.

Moos, R. H., & Insel, E. J. (1974). *Work environemnt scale.* Palo Alto, CA: Consulting Psychologists Press.

Moos, R. H., & Insel, P. M. (Eds.). (1974). *Issues in social ecology - human milieus.* Palo Alto, CA: National Press Books.

Moos, R. H., & Moos, B. S. (1986). *Family environment scale manual* (2nd ed.). Palo Alto, CA: Consulting Psychologists Press.

Moos, R. H., & Trickett, E. I. (1974). *Classroom environment scale manual.* Palo Alto, CA: Consulting Psychologists Press.

Moss, H. A., & Sussman, E. J. (1980). Longitudinal study of personality development. In O. G. Brim & J. Kagan (Eds.), *Constancy and change in human development* (pp. 530–595). Cambridge, MA: Harvard University Press.

Nelson-Jones, R. (1990). *Human relationship skills* (2nd ed.). London: Cassell.

Noelle-Neumann, E., & Piel, E. (Eds.). (1983). *Eine Generation später. Bundesrepublik Deutschland 1953-1979* [One generation later. Federal Republic of Germany 1953–1979]. München: Saur.

O'Leary, K. D. (Ed.). (1987). *Assessment of marital discord.* Hillsdale, NJ: Lawrence Erlbaum Associates.

Oerter, R. (1986). Developmental tasks through the life-span: A new approach to an old concept. In D. L. Featherman & R. M. Lerner (Eds.), *Life-span development and behavior* (Vol. 7, pp. 233–271). New York: Academic Press.

Olson, D. H., Stewart, K. L., & Wilson, L. R. (1989). *Health and Stress Profile (HSP).* Minneapolis: Profiles of Health Systems.

Pearlin, L. I., & Schooler, C. (1978). The structure of coping. *Journal of Health and Social Behavior, 19,* 2–21.

Perkins, D. V. (1982). The assessment of stress using life event scales. In L. Goldberger & S. Breznitz (Eds.), *Handbook of stress. Theoretical and clinical aspects* (pp. 320–331). London: Free Press.

Perrez, M., & Reicherts, M. (1992). *Stress, coping, and health.* Toronto: Hogrefe & Huber.

Pervin, L. A. (Ed.). (1990). *Handbook of personality—theory and research*. New York: Guilford Press.

Peterander, F., Bailer, J., & Henrich, G. (1987). *Familiäre Belastungen und ihre Bewältigung* [Familial strain and its coping]. (Testunterlagen). Psychologische Abteilung des Max-Planck-Instituts für Psychiatrie. München.

Peterson, C., & Bossio, L. M. (1991). *Health and optimism*. New York: The Free Press.

Phares, E. J. (1994). *Introduction to personality* (4th ed.). New York: Harper/Collins.

Rodgers, R. H., & White, J. M. (1993). Family development theory. In P. G. Boss, W. J. Doherty, R. LaRossa, W. R. Schumm, & S. K. Steinmetz (Eds.), *Sourcebook of family theories and methods. A contextual approach* (pp. 225–254). New York: Plenum Press.

Rotter, J. B. (1972). An introduction to social learning theory. In J. B. Rotter, J. E. Chance, & E. J. Phares (Eds.), *Application of a social learning theory of personality* (pp. 1–43). New York: Holt, Rinehart & Winston.

Russell, M., & Karol, D. (1994). *The 16 PF Fifth Edition administrator's manual*. Champaign, IL: Institute for Personality and Ability Testing.

Sarason, J. G., Johnson, J. H., & Siegel, J. M. (1978). Assessing the impact of life changes: Development of the life experience survey. *Journal of Consulting and Clinical Psychology, 46*, 932–946.

Schaie, K. W. (1965). A general model for the study of developmental problems. *Psychological Bulletin, 64*, 92–107.

Schmidt-Rinke, M. (1982). *Familienklassifikation in der familiären Sozialisationsforschung* [Classification of families in research on family socialization]. Unveröffentlichte Dissertation, Ludwig-Maximilians-Universität München.

Schneewind, K. A. (1980). Elterliche Erziehungsstile: Einige Anmerkungen zum Forschungsgegenstand [Parenting styles: Some remarks on the research topic]. In K. A. Schneewind & T. Herrmann (Eds.), *Erziehungsstilforschung* (pp. 19–30). Bern: Huber.

Schneewind, K. A. (1988a). Das familiendiagnostische Testsystem (FDTS): Ein Fragebogeninventar zur Erfassung familiärer Beziehungsaspekte auf unterschiedlichen Systemebenen [The Family Diagnostic Test System (FDTS): An inventory to assess family relations at different systems levels]. In M. Cierpka (Ed.), *Familiendiagnostik* (pp. 320–347). Heidelberg: Springer.

Schneewind, K. A. (1988b). Die Familienklimaskalen (FKS) [The Family Climate Scales (FCS)]. In M. Cierpka (Ed.), *Familiendiagnostik* (pp. 234–255). Berlin: Springer.

Schneewind, K. A. (1991). *Familienpsychologie* [Family psychology]. Stuttgart: Kohlhammer.

Schneewind, K. A. (1992). *Persönlichkeitstheorien* [Personality theories]. 2 Bände. (2nd ed.). Darmstadt: Wissenschaftliche Buchgesellschaft.

Schneewind, K. A. (1993). Paarklima - die "Persönlichkeit" von Partnerschaften [Couple climate—the "personality" of couple relationships]. In H. Mandl, M. Dreher, & H.-J. Kornadt (Eds.), *Entwicklung und Denken im kulturellen Kontext* (pp. 145–161). Göttingen: Hogrefe.

Schneewind, K. A. (1994). Erziehung und Sozialisation in der Familie [Education and socialization in the family]. In K. A. Schneewind (Ed.), *Psychologie der Erziehung und Sozialisation* (Enzyklopädie der Psychologie. Pädagogische Psychologie. Band 1, pp. 435–464). Göttingen: Hogrefe.

Schneewind, K. A. (1995). Familienentwicklung [Family development]. In R. Oerter & L. Montada (Eds.), *Entwicklungspsychologie* (3rd ed., pp. 128–166). München: Psychologie Verlags Union.

Schneewind, K. A., & Ruppert, S. (1992). *Eltern-Kind-Beziehungen. Nachuntersuchung* [Parent child relations. Follow-up] (Materialband). München: Universität München, Institut für Psychologie, Institutsbereich Persönlichkeitspsychologie und Psychodiagnostik.

Schneewind, K. A., Beckmann, M., & Engfer, A. (1983). *Eltern und Kinder* [Parents and children]. Stuttgart: Kohlhammer.

Schneewind, K. A., Beckmann, M., & Hecht-Jackl, A. (1985). *Familiendiagnostisches Testsystem FDTS* [Family Diagnostic Test System FDTS] (Forschungsberichte aus dem Institutsbereich Persönlichkeitspsychologie und Psychodiagnostik). München: Universität München.

Schneewind, K. A., Schröder, G., & Cattell, R. B. (1986). *Der 16 Persönlichkeits-Faktoren Test (16 PF)* [16 Personality Factors Questionnaire (16 PF)]. (2nd ed.). Bern: Huber.

Schneewind, K. A., et al. (1981). *Psychologische und sozio-ökologische Determinanten von Eltern-Kind-Beziehungen* [Psychological and socio-ecological determinants of parent child realtions]. München: Abschlußbericht an die DFG. 2 Bände.

Schütze, Y. (1988). Zur Veränderung im Eltern-Kind-Verhältnis seit der Nachkriegszeit [On changes of parent child relations in the postwar era]. In R. Nave-Herz (Ed.), *Wandel und Kontinuität der Familie in der Bundesrepublik Deutschland* (pp. 95–114). Stuttgart: Enke.

Schwarz, J. C., Barton-Henry, M. L., & Pruzinsky, T. (1985). Assessing child-rearing behaviors: A comparison of rating made by mother, father, child and sibling on the CRPBI. *Child Development, 56*, 462–479.

Schwarzer, R. (1993). *Streß, Angst und Handlungsregulation* [Stress, anxiety, and action regulation] (3rd ed.). Stuttgart: Kohlhammer.

Seitz, W., & Rausche, A. (1992). *Persönlichkeitsfragebogen für Kinder (PFK 9-14)* [Personality Questionnaire for Children (PQC)] (2nd ed.). Braunschweig: Westermann.

Seligman, M. E. P. (1992). *Learned optimism.* New York: Knopf.

Siegel, S. (1956). *Nonparametric statistics for the behavioral sciences.* New York: McGraw Hill.

Smedslund, J. (1988). *Psycho-Logic.* Berlin: Springer.

Steele, H., & Steele, M. (1994). Intergenerational patterns of attachment. In K. Bartholomew & D. Perlman (Eds.), *Attachment processes in adulthood. Advances in personal relationships* (Vol. 5, pp. 93–120). London: Jessica Kingsley.

Steiger, J. H. (1980). Tests for comparing elements of a correlation matrix. *Psychological Bulletin, 87*, 245–251.

Steinberg, L., Darling, N. E., Fletcher, A. C., Brown, B. B., & Dornbusch, S. M. (1995). Autoritative parenting and adolescent adjustment: An ecological journey. In P. Moen, G. H. Elder, & K. Lüscher (Eds.), *Examining lives in context* (pp. 424–466). Washington, DC: American Psychological Association.

Stokols, D., & Altmann, I. (Eds.). (1987). *Handbook of environmental psychology.* New York: Wiley.

Sundstrom, E., Bell, P. A., Busby, P. L., & Asmus, C. (1996). Environmental psychology 1989–1994. *Annual Review of Psychology, 47*, 485–512.

Tein, J. K., Roosa, M. W., & Michaels, M. (1994). Agreement between parent and child reports on parental behaviors. *Journal of Marriage and the Family, 56*, 341–355.

Thomas, A., & Chess, S. (1977). *Temperament and development.* New York: Brunner/Mazel.

Thomas, W. I. (1928). *The child in America.* New York: Knopf.

Toman, W. (1988). *Family therapy and sibling position.* New York: Jason Aronson.

Touliatos, J., Perlmutter, B. F., & Straus, M. A. (Eds.). (1990). *Handbook of family assessment techniques.* Newbury Park, CA: Sage.

Trautner, H. M. (1994). Geschlechtsspezifische Erziehung und Sozialisation [Gender-specific education and socialization]. In K. A. Schneewind (Hrsg.), *Psychologie der Erziehung und Sozialisation* (Enzyklopädie der Psychologie. Pädagogische Psychologie. Band 1, pp. 167–195). Göttingen: Hogrefe.

Tryon, R. L., & Bailey, D. E. (1970). *Cluster analysis.* New York: McGraw Hill.

Vaskovics, L. A. (1988). Veränderungen der Wohn- und Wohnumweltbedingungen in ihren Auswirkungen auf die Sozialisationsleistung der Familie [Changes in housing and neighborhood and their impact on socialization effects of the family]. In R. Nave-Herz (Ed.), *Wandel und Kontinuität der Familien in der Bundesrepublik Deutschland* (pp. 36–60). Stuttgart: Enke.

Wechsler, D. (1949). *The Wechsler intelligence scale for children (WISC).* New York: Psychological Corporation.

Weiß, J., Schneewind, K. A., & Olson, D. (1995). Die Bedeutung von Stressoren und Ressourcen für die psychische und physische Gesundheit - ein mulitsystemischer Ansatz [The relevance of stressors and resources for mental and physical health - a multisystemic approach]. *Zeitschrift für Gesundheitspsychologie, 3*, 165–182.

Weiner, B. (1990). Attribution in personality psychology. In L. A. Pervin (Ed.). *Handbook of personality - theory and research* (pp. 465–485). New York: Guilford Press.

Wissenschaftlicher Beirat für Familienfragen beim Bundesministerium für Jugend, Familie und Gesundheit. (1975). *Familie und Wohnen* [Family and housing]. Stuttgart: Kohlhammer.

Wohlwill, J. F. (1973). *The study of behavioral development.* New York: Academic Press.

Wynne, L. (1984). The epigenesis of relational systems. A model for understanding family development. *Family Process, 23,* 297–318.

Youniss, J., & Smollar, J. (1985). *Adolescent relations with mothers, fathers, and friends.* Chicago: University of Chicago Press.

AUTHOR INDEX

SUBJECT INDEX

www.ingramcontent.com/pod-product-compliance
Ingram Content Group UK Ltd.
Pitfield, Milton Keynes, MK11 3LW, UK
UKHW020434010325
455677UK00029B/1146